RELIGION IN 21st CENTURY

RELIGION IN 21st CENTURY

Dr Suhail Saheed

MD PUBLICATIONS PVT LTD
NEW DELHI
www.mdppl.com

Published by :

MD Publications Pvt Ltd
"MD House", 11, Darya Ganj,
New Delhi - 110 002
Phone : +91-11-41563325 (Customer Service)
+91-11-41562846 (Editorial)
E-mail (orders): order@mdppl.com
Website: www.mdppl.com

ISBN: 978-81-7533-239-3

Published and Printed by Mr. Pranav Gupta on behalf of MD Publications Pvt Ltd at Mohit Enterprises, New Delhi.

PREFACE

Throughout history differences in religious beliefs have caused a tremendous amount of social turmoil, including persecution, alienation, violence and even war. People of a religion decide that their God is the only God, so the faith of others becomes invalid. This "way of thinking" often leads to the social turmoil mentioned above. Is there a way that this can be avoided in the future?

Some people believe that we will one day see some form of "world religion", but this is unlikely and may even be unhealthy. This is true because many individuals who inhabit this earth require different ways to express their spirituality. Any attempt to force them all into the same religious mold would never succeed. Instead, where spiritual beliefs are concerned, a general philosophy of acceptance might be far more productive. Also, it should not be assumed that people need religion. Spirituality and philosophy both exist with complete independence from religion and are often healthier.

Paradoxically, regionalism and religious exclusive identity politics had appeared in the garb of democratic political power politics. Demanding economic well-being notwithstanding, struggle against backwardness, poverty and civil rights is common to all humanity irrespective of caste, creed, region or religion. Our secular social fabric had strengthened the scientific democratic structure of India which must be defended against all regional and religious politics.

I am very grateful to Mr Pranav Gupta, Director of MD Publications Pvt Ltd, New Delhi for his kind cooperation and support for this book.

Dr Suhail Saheed

Contents

1

Religion in 21st Century

An Introduction

Religion has become a major topic in the beginning of the twenty-first century. Christianity and Islam, the two largest religions in the world appear to be competing for influence across the world. These two world religions have also substantially increased their numbers. There were 376,453,000 Christians, 329,869,000 Muslims and 98,734,000 people who practiced traditional religions in Africa. In the sixteenth and seventeenth centuries the West hit upon a new way of knowing. We call it the scientific method, and it quickly replaced revelation, its predecessor, as the royal road to knowledge. Conceptually, it spawned the scientific worldview, and its technology created the modern world.

The citizens of these physical and conceptual environments constitute a new human breed whose beliefs correspond to very little in the heritage of their forebears. As a consequence, religion—the kingpin of that heritage—has been marginalized, both intellectually and politically. First, politically, Fresh continents to occupy and easier travel have introduced a new phenomenon into history: cultural pluralism. The result has been to edge religion from public life, for religion divides whereas politics seeks unity.

Concurrently, religion has been marginalized intellectually. Science has no place for revelation as a source of knowledge, and as moderns tend to think with science on matters of truth, confidence in revelation has declined. Marx considered religion "the opiate of the people," "the sob of an oppressed humanity," and Freud saw it as a symptom of immaturity. Children who cannot accept the limitations of their actual parents dream up Fathers in Heaven who are free of those limitations. Theism is wish fulfillment—a pandering to "the oldest, strongest and most urgent wishes of mankind,"—and the religious experience ("the oceanic feeling") is regression to the womb.

For religion to be marginalized socially and forced to the wall intellectually is no small event. Some see it as substantial enough to warrant the pronouncement that God has died. Sociologists compile statistics on the change, but for the intellectual historian two developments suffice. First, on the question of God's existence the burden of proof has shifted to the theist; and as proofs of the supernatural are difficult in any case, the classic proofs for God's existence have pretty much collapsed. The second sign, though, is more telling. Whereas atheists and theists used to agree that God's existence is an important issue, now even that common ground has vanished. The tension between belief and disbelief has slackened. "It leaves no mark on intellectuals now," a cultural historian has observed, adding: "we have witnessed a decline in the urgency of the debate."

The atheism of indifference or apathy simply refuses to take the question of God seriously. Such, a French psychiatrist has written, "has become the common lot of at least a considerable portion, if not the majority, of our contemporaries." Their number has given rise to a distinction between secularization and secularism. The word "secularization" is now typically used to refer to the cultural process in which the area of the sacred is progressively diminished, whereas "secularism" denotes the reasoned stand that favours that drift. It argues on grounds that are cognitive, moral, or both, that the desacralizing of reality and consequent recession of the God idea is a good thing. Whether favoured or merely accepted, though, the change itself seems undisputed. *The Chronicle of Higher Education* condensed it into a single sentence: "If anything characterizes 'modernity,' it is a loss of faith in transcendence, in a reality that encompasses but surpasses our quotidian affairs."

How, in the face of these seemingly irrefutable signs of faith's decline—"its melancholy, long, withdrawing roar" in Matthew Arnold's memorable phrase—is it possible to argue that the future of religion is promising?

The Eyes of Faith

One of the interesting recent developments in physics has been the realization that at its frontiers the observer must be included in the experiment. It's not just that we can't know where a particle is until we perform an experiment to locate it. The particle literally isn't anywhere until (by collapsing its wave packet) an experiment gives it its location. Whether or not this Copenhagen reading of the matter will prevail, it at least highlights the active component in knowing. Knowing is not a passive act. If seeing is believing, believing is also seeing, for it brings to light things that would otherwise pass unnoticed.

The Life's dim windows of the Soul

Distorts the Heavens from Pole to Pole

And leads you to Believe a Lie

When you see with, not thro' the Eye (William Blake).

How does this affect the question of religion's future? The Death-of-God prediction of religion's demise was reported through eyes that register data that is available to everyone. Religion, though, sees through the eyes of faith, and in doing so sees a different world. Or better, it sees the same world in a different light. In this new light things look different in a way that is commanding. Arguments are irrelevant here, as they are when a rope that was mistaken for a snake is recognized for the rope that it is. The sacred world is the truer, more veridical one, part of the reason being that it includes the mundane world. It also redeems that world by situating it in a context that is meaningful—completely so.

The whole (of which the visible world is part) is not only more inclusive than the visible world. It is better than the visible world—infinitely better in being able to shine its glory on everything. Because its power is ineluctable, it cannot be gainsaid, for (as William James put the point) "religion says that the best things are the more eternal things, the things in the universe that throw the last stone, so to speak, and say the final word." Backed by its ineluctable authority, religion's future (seen from this second perspective) is secure. As long as there are human beings there will be religion, for the sufficient reason that the self is a theomorphic creature—one whose *morphe* (form) has God (*theos*) built into it.

Having been created in the image of God, every human being has a God-shaped vacuum built into its heart. We know that nature abhors vacuums, so people keep trying to fill theirs. Searching for an image of the divine that will fit, they paw over images as if they were pieces of a jigsaw puzzle, matching them successively to the gaping hole at the puzzle's center. (We call the wrong images idols to underscore their inadequacy. Calvin likened the human heart to an idol factory.) They keep doing this until, the right "piece" having been found, it slips into place and life's puzzle is solved. The sight of the picture that then comes to view is so commanding that the soul finds its attention riveted to it completely; so completely that no attention remains for it to notice itself as the person who is *seeing* the picture. This sublime self-forgetfulness, this ecstatic release from ego-encasement, is salvation, or enlightenment.

It is the complete and only possible liberation from the bondage of human finitude—the cord is cut, the bird is free. Achieving this freedom amounts to graduating from the human condition, but the passage in no way threatens the human future. Other generations are always waiting in the wings, eager to have their go at life's curriculum. The gulf that separates this faith-oriented projection of religion's future from the worldly one this essay opened with is vast; but we live in the universe, so in some way we must try to bring the two together. If we are religiously "unmusical" and its account leaves us cold, the situation is simple: the worldly prognosis tells the tale. Others, though, have a problem on their hands.

The religious forecast carries weight, but so does the secular one. This is where binocular vision enters. How does the future of religion look when we take into account both what social scientists tell us—our first reading—and what the eyes of faith report? To bring the two together we need to look again at the historical developments of this century, this time with eyes that are peeled for signs of their spiritual significance.

The Ground Is Cleared. Those signs come to light when we remember the vacuum in the human heart that was mentioned a few paragraphs back, and the jigsaw pieces with which people try to fill it. None of the pieces the modern world has reached for have fit. The two most important pieces have been Marxism in the East and Progress in the West, these being the principal gods of modernity. Of course Marxism believes in progress too, but it stresses its ideological programme for affecting that progress.

We call it the scientific method, and with it, knowledge began to proliferate; for science houses the controlled experiment, the controlled experiment proves, and proven knowledge snowballs. The eighteenth century's Industrial Revolution established these points historically, for by applying the knowledge that was ballooning, it raised Europe's living standards dramatically. Together these scientific and industrial revolutions produced a third and psychological one: the Revolution-of-Rising-Expectations which have powered modernity ever since. It spawned three heady dreams which coalesced in the Enlightenment Project. Thanks to its new and reliable way of knowing, modernity would send ignorance packing. Applying its new knowledge to nature, it would send scarcity packing. And it would send superstition packing.

The superstitions the Enlightenment had in mind were principally those of the Church, and as the Church's back was being broken, it seemed that mankind was ready to step into the Age of Reason. This reason spelled Progress, the hope that has powered the modern world since it swung to view. As for Eastern Europe and subsequently China, its version of that hope has been, for the bulk of this century, Marxism. To set it in perspective we need only go back to the Revolution-of-Rising-Expectations that the scientific and industrial revolutions gave rise to. Hegel cashed in on that revolution's forward-looking stance and fashioned from it a metaphysics. From the seeming fact that things were getting better and stood a good chance of continuing to do so, Hegel extrapolated backwards to infer that they had always been improving.

Progress is the name of the game for being inscribed in the structure of the cosmos. (In Hegel's vocabulary, being is the necessary infoldment of its Idea in ever-increasing consciousness and freedom.) Support for this heady scenario was welcome from every quarter, and Darwin supplied it from science. Himself inspired by Hegel, he painted the natural history of life on earth in strokes that fitted perfectly into Hegel's version of an evolution that is cosmic in sweep, so far so good. But when we come to human history, Darwin's engine of progress—natural selection working on chance variations—chugs too slowly to explain. A principle was needed to account for progress in centuries, not eons, and Marx supplied it with his theory of class struggle. "Just as Darwin discovered the law of development of organic nature, so Marx discovered the law of development of human history," Engels intoned by Marx's grave at Highgate Cemetery.

One last step was needed, and though Marx assumed it, Engels (with Lenin's assistance) articulated it explicitly. To inspire not just hope but conviction, communism's happy ending—the classless society—needed to be assured, and that required metaphysics. For science is never enough, not even natural and social science together. To inspire conviction, hope needs to be anchored in the very nature of things. So Hegel's cosmic vision was reaffirmed, but with an important change. Its inclusive and forward-looking features were in place, but its vocabulary needed to be converted from idealism to materialism. This had the double advantage of making the theory sound scientific and at the same time directing attention to the politico-economic scene; specifically to the means of production as the place where the gears of history grind decisively.

This is the package that in this century persuaded the Eastern half of humankind—the world's largest nation (the USSR) and its most populous one (the People's Republic of China). With its "jigsaw piece" (communism) placed beside the piece the West reached for (Progress), we can proceed to the point for which they were introduced. Neither filled the spiritual hollow in the human makeup. To begin again with the West, Progress has turned into something of a nightmare. The campaign against ignorance has expanded our knowledge of nature, but science can't get its hands on values and life-giving beliefs. That's disappointing. It's discouraging to discover that not only are we no wiser (as distinct from more knowledgeable) than our forebears were; we may be less wise for having neglected value questions while bringing nature to heel. That possibility is frightening; for our vastly increased power over nature calls for more wisdom in its use, not less. The Enlightenment's second hope, of eliminating poverty, must face the fact that more people are hungry today than ever before.

As for the belief that the Age of Reason would make people sane, that now reads like a cruel joke. In the Nazi myth of a super-race (which produced the Holocaust), and the Marxist myth of a classless utopia (which produced the Stalinist Terror), our century fell for the most monstrous superstitions the human mind has ever embraced. With this last point we have already moved to the Eastern half of our twentieth century where Marxist hopes have not just declined but collapsed. The Soviet Union has disintegrated, and while Maoism remains nominally in place in China, no one believes it anymore—capitalism is advancing there faster than anywhere else on the planet. In its heyday, Marxism inspired commitment by claiming that its idealism was grounded in truth. This is indeed the winning formula, but our century has falsified both halves of its Marxist version.

All of Marx's major predictions have turned out to be wrong. (1) The European model of production has not spread throughout the world. (2) The working class has not progressively grown more miserable and radical. (3) Nationalism and religious zeal have not declined. (4) Communism does not produce goods more efficiently than free enterprise, nor distribute them more equitably. (5) And in communist countries the states show no signs whatever of withering away. Faced with this predictive shamble, apologists regularly switched their appeal from truth to idealism—are we to forget the suffering masses? But the Marxist record on compassion is no better than its record on truth. In justifying communism's (often vicious) means by the humanitarian end Marx expected them to lead to, he saddled his movement with a bloody-mindedness history has rarely seen.

Modernity's coming to see its gods for what they are—idols in their inability to deliver what was expected of them—is the most important religious event of the twentieth century. With the ground cleared of its illusions, we can now examine that ground to see if it shows signs of new life.

Renaissance

At least we can say that religion weathered its winter. On his seventy-fifth birthday, Malcolm Muggeridge looked back over his long world watch as editor of *The Manchester Guardian* and concluded that the most important single fact of the twentieth century is that the USSR, with every totalitarian means at its disposal, was unable to destroy the Russian Orthodox Church. The same can be said of the People's Republic of China respecting its religions. Confucian ethics are back in the schools, and a new church is opening in China every day. Even intellectuals who are not themselves believers now speak respectfully of religion's durability. Having discovered no society that is without religion, anthropologists (riding their "functionalist" theory that pointless institutions fall by the wayside) now agree that religion is "adaptive."

Neuroscientists trace its utility to the very structure of the human brain. Without going into details, "once the left-brain interpreter was fully in place and reflexively active in seeking consistency and understanding, religious beliefs were inevitable." Alex Comfort, a gerontologist, writes that "religious behaviours are an important integrator of man's whole self-view in relation to the world." Carl Jung reached the same conclusion as a psychologist. His conclusion "that human beings have a built-in religious need grew out of observing actual dreams of his patients." A leading authority on Freud draws all this together by likening faith to the glue that holds communities together; adding ominously that the weakening of this glue in the twentieth century has changed Dostoyevski's question, "Can civilized men believe?" to "Can unbelieving men be civilized?"

As that second question is an oblique way of affirming religion's importance, informed observers (as was noted) have returned to the pre-Enlightenment position of taking it seriously. That, though, does not touch the question of its truth. On balance, intellectuals now believe in religion. Do they believe in God? Some do and some don't, of course. What follows is an assessment of the general scene, with special attention to changes that are now occurring.

The New York Review notes that "a revival of theism seems to be taking place among intellectuals." One evidence of this is the founding (in the 1970s) of the Society of Christian Philosophers. In the middle half of our century philosophy was cool (where not hostile) toward religion, whereas in this closing quarter the just-mentioned Society—whose journal, *Faith and Philosophy,* carries Tertullian's epigraph, "Faith seeking intelligence"—boasts over a thousand members and is by far the largest subsidiary organization in the American Philosophical Association.

Things like this could not happen if the three-hundred-year tension between science and religion had not begun to ease; for science continues to be what modernity believes in, so new life for the spirit requires its imprimatur. That (unofficial, of course) endorsement is coming through the realization that science is not omni competent. Its powers respecting nature and technology are awesome, but its parade of marvels proceeds from a line of inquiry that is powerful and at the same time limited. The usual way to register its limitation is to say that science can't deal with values and existential meanings, but the more important likelihood is that there are *things* it cannot connect with—things that are as real as material objects, and that affect us as much if not more, but which scientific instruments don't register.

This withdrawal of science to its important but not omni competent domain allows religion more intellectual room than the twentieth century accorded it, for religion specializes in the invisibles that science cannot touch. The stage is being set; it seems, for the twenty-first century to accept religion (and its ally, art) as equal partners to science in discerning the full range of reality. That assessment seems secure, but another prospect is so recent that one cannot foresee its prospects. Is it possible that science, which today is still working on according religion scope and respect, will tomorrow actively endorse it?

Focally this is not possible, for as the preceding footnote indicated, controlled experiments cannot register spirit's workings. Indirectly, though, there is a way that science could eventually underwrite religion's claims. If there were not slightly more matter than anti-matter in the universe, the two would cancel each other out and the universe wouldn't exist. And if the forces of contraction and repulsion were not exactly balanced in the way they are, the universe could not support life. The list of such "coincidences" is so long that Stephen Hawking says flatly that the probability of there being a universe in which life is possible is in the order of absolute zero.

Why, then, in the face of this near-zero probability, *does* it exist? In a televised interview, the mathematical physicist Freeman Dyson answered as every theist would: "Of course there has to be a mind behind it all." It is going to be interesting if the very project that has gotten where it has by excluding final causes—explaining things via their author, or the purposes they serve—finds itself ending by proclaiming them. That would be more than a just and durable peace; it would be the final resolution to the warfare between science and religion that has troubled the modern era. It could also spell hope for the future—not just the future of religion, but the human future. For as Whitehead once observed, the future of civilization depends, more than on anything else, on the way the two most powerful forces of history, science and religion, settle into relationship with each other.

The conclusion that we have reached—that the twenty-first century will be religious; very likely more religious than our own—leaves untouched the question of the form(s) that religion will assume. Will new religions replace the traditional ones? If the great historical religions retain their vitality, will they also retain their separate identities, or will they phase into one another in the way certain Christian denominations are dropping their differences? If a world civilization emerges, will there be a single world religion? And there is the question of whether the evils that have plagued religion in the past can be mitigated—superstition, dogmatism, bigotry, oppression, neuroses, and the like. Now that Marx, Nietzsche, and Freud have brought them forcibly to our attention, can we heed the warnings of these secular prophets without ejecting the baby with its bath water? These questions are already very much with us and will continue into the next century. But they are beyond the scope of this statement.

2

Twenty-First-Century and Religion in the World

Whole generations have grown up in a United States where black-white marriage is legal, and such intermarriage is growing in frequency. While the reception for interracial couples is not unanimously welcome in all quarters, black men do not fear lynching for daring even to look at a white woman. Who could have imagined in the era of Loving that a biracial black man, Barack Obama, with an African father and a white American mother, could become President of the United States? In 1903, famous black scholar and activist W.E.B. DuBois said that the question of the twentieth century would be the colour line, and he was prophetically right within the U.S. context. The ongoing global war on terror has raised the issue of whether the question of the twenty-first century will be religious lines.

Some prominent scholars, such as Samuel Huntington, have claimed that there is a "clash of civilizations" between the Christian West and the Islamic world. While religion is clearly an important identity for many people, in my view, it would be too simplistic to state that the primary issue of the century will involve any one identity. CRF in its global dimension emphasizes the legal rights of women of colour around the world, with my own work focusing on women in the Muslim world and Africa.

This essay highlights the intersection of three identities in particular: nationality, gender, and religion, to show how a twenty-first-century Loving issue still exists in many nations. In a number of countries, interfaith marriages are still generally frowned upon due to customary and/or religious norms, and in some places, such unions are illegal or impossible. Interfaith marriages of any kind can be as problematic and as deadly as they have been for centuries. There are some jurisdictions that forbid Muslims from intermarriage altogether, such as Iran. On the other hand, there can be successful interfaith unions, as my own family demonstrates.

While there are many interesting legal aspects to interfaith relationships in this century, this essay will highlight one particular issue that draws upon my own expertise. In many Muslim countries, it is legally forbidden for Muslim women to marry non-Muslim men. Will this ancient, deeply rooted prohibition join the fate of the Virginia anti-miscegenation statute in Loving? Will such laws be legislated out of existence any time in the near future? Even if the legal prohibitions were lifted, would ongoing de facto norms still hinder Muslim women from choosing marital partners freely? Nationality, gender, and religion, in particular, are among the identities that intersect in ways that ensure most Muslim women would not and cannot consider stepping beyond interfaith boundaries, just as many American blacks and whites did not dare step beyond *de jure* racial boundaries at the time of Loving.

Subsequently, most would not violate the de facto norms. Most Muslim countries have not been inclined to reinterpret religious norms to permit such intermarriage. The essay concludes that potential legal change in this arena is unlikely in the near future. Global trends toward increased fundamentalism in all major religions may make interfaith intermarriage more difficult rather than less so. Muslim women may continue to be restricted *de jure* and de facto in their marital choices—leaving them without loving options.

Global Multiplicative Identity

The ANC reviewed the American experience with constitutional and statutory equality, and decided to take a much more comprehensive and complex approach. The South African equality clause mentions seventeen grounds, i.e., identities that are afforded protection: "race, gender, sex, pregnancy, marital status, ethnic or social origin, colour, sexual orientation, age, disability, religion, conscience, belief, culture, language and birth." The South African Constitutional Court has noted that grounds may intersect, and thus discrimination cannot be evaluated on one identity only. For example, Justice Albie Sachs noted in one case that African widows have suffered as "blacks, as Africans, as women, as African women, as widows and usually, as older people, intensified by the fact that they are frequently amongst the lowest paid workers."

Additionally, I have written about other identities not mentioned in South Africa: nationality, parental status, minority group status, geographic location (urban/rural), and one I call stature identity. This latter concept focuses on how one appears within a particular societal context. If you match the predominant standards of beauty, you will probably do better in the educational and employment spheres than if you do not. To illustrate the intersections of identities in the case of a Muslim woman, I offer the plight of a fictional character, Amira. Her story represents a composite of issues I have heard and read about in my many visits to France. She is a very dark-skinned Arab female, who is unemployed, Sudanese, and Muslim, wears a head scarf and lives as an illegal immigrant in rural France. But she does not speak French very well and is single and disabled. She is pregnant by a white Christian Frenchman, Phillippe. Amira would like to marry Phillippe, as interfaith marriages are legal in France, but such a marriage could be rejected in her home country if she ever dared return there.

She might even be subject to physical attack by family members. Phillippe is agnostic but is Catholic by descent, which is another fact that might subject them to attack if he dared accompany her to Sudan. Thus, she has asked Phillippe to convert to Islam, as required by Islamic law in most Muslim countries. He refused upon learning that conversion to Islam is irrevocable. Amira has several other reasons not to return to Sudan for the foreseeable future. While she is a devout Muslim, she is against the Islamist regime there, and escaped from an abusive marriage where she was the third polygamous wife of a Sudanese government official who visited France. She and her daughter, Jamila, vanished after a shopping trip in Paris and then fled to a rural area to avoid detection. Before she can marry Phillippe, Amira thinks that she will have to get a divorce from her husband in Sudan. Maybe French law will regard her arranged polygamous marriage, which took place when she was thirteen, as invalid? Maybe her husband has already divorced her?

If all this is too complicated to solve in a few months, the baby will be born out of wedlock. Having such a child is somewhat tolerated in France, but is against all customary and religious norms in her country; as a result, she might be subject to stoning for adultery. Amira lost her underground job in the village when she insisted on wearing a head scarf to work. She also had been unable to tolerate the fumes in the factory and is now easily winded, a condition that excludes her from many work options. Jamila has been sent home from her high school several times because she wore a head scarf, which is forbidden in French public schools. Amira and Jamila have not been getting along recently, as Amira does not like some of Jamila's new friends, who are part of the gay and lesbian community at the school. Jamila needs to finish high school so she can get a job to support Amira and the new baby, since Amira's situation with Phillippe may not work out. If Amira pressures Jamila too much, Jamila might leave her pregnant mother and/or drop out of school.

Amira is strikingly beautiful by both French and Sudanese standards and would like to seek work as a model, assuming she can relocate to an urban area and obtain asylum to correct her undocumented status. Since she is devout, however, she would not want to wear very revealing clothing. She is also afraid that any notoriety might alert her Sudanese husband to her location. While all of the various identities illustrated in Amira's story exist within each of us in some form, we usually only contemplate one or two of them at a time. Women of colour like Amira and Jamila are often discriminated against on multiple bases simultaneously, but may have no practical legal recourse in any jurisdiction. Amira's problems arising out of her religious identity are only one thread of a tapestry of issues relating to all of her identities.

It is important to note that some of the identities can also lead to privileging on one or more levels. For example, the fact that I am an African American, feminist, secular, female law professor, and a Protestant, minority-group, heterosexual mother of five, who mainly speaks English, has a bad back, and conforms to the dominant standards of beauty in the United States and the Middle East, has helped and hurt me simultaneously in my twenty-five years of work in the Muslim world. Around the world, many people perceive African Americans as an oppressed group and identify with me on that basis as well.

Muslim Family Law

This part illustrates how religious identity intertwines with the nationality and gender identities of Muslim women, who might want to intermarry with non-Muslim men. Islam is a faith for more than one billion people in the world. Its principles are supposed to guide its adherents in their everyday lives. The Islamic law known as shari'a used to govern most areas of law, including contract, criminal, trusts and estates, and family. Today, many predominantly Muslim countries only apply shari'a in the area of family law—marriage, divorce, and child custody—as well as in trusts and estates. Other areas of law may be influenced by Western civil, criminal, and constitutional law. Saudi Arabia, Sudan, and certain states in Nigeria may be among the few Muslim jurisdictions to apply shari'a in the area of criminal law, often amputating hands for theft or stoning people for adultery. These types of jurisdictions may give classical punishments for the listed hudud offences—apostasy, adultery/fornication, theft, slander, brigandage, wine drinking, and rebellion. Conversion out of Islam is the forbidden (haram) crime of apostasy in most places, and the penalty may be death. In some jurisdictions, any Muslim can carry out the penalty and will not be prosecuted.

The following are general Islamic principles that apply to family law. There may be nuanced differences in each country, and very few countries have done a thorough reconceptualization of their laws on marriage. In Islam, men and women are equal in the eyes of God, but they have different responsibilities. Women have the duty of obedience (ta'ah) to men, which many men use to justify the right to discipline their wives physically. In turn, men have the duty of guardianship (qawama) over women. Men have the right to marry four wives, whom they must treat equally. The women must be of the book (kitab), i.e., Christian, Muslim, or Jewish. Muslim women can only marry one man; no polyandry is allowed. Men must give a bride price (mahr) to women. Unlike certain cultures where payment is given to the bride's family, this amount is payable only to the bride. Since it is substantial and may depend on the educational level of the woman, it may be paid out over time and is meant to ensure that she has some resources in the event of divorce or the death of her husband. Since homosexuality is forbidden, most Muslim countries are not likely to join the growing Western trend of permitting gay marriages in the near future.

Many Muslims may agree with Iranian President Mahmoud Ahmadinejad, who recently said that there were no gay people in Iran. Some have told me that they view homosexuality as a Western disease that does not exist in the developing world. Divorce (talaq) is relatively easy for men in most countries. They only need to say "I divorce you" three times, whereas women need specific grounds. Alimony is only granted to women for three months (iddat), just long enough to ascertain if she is pregnant by her ex-husband. With respect to child custody, fathers are considered the legal guardians, even if women are granted physical custody for a few years (usually pre-puberty) or even up to the age of majority. The child's religion and nationality is determined by the fathers in most instances. Muslim women can inherit, but male relatives get a double share as compared to their sisters. As I learned in Syria, in many jurisdictions, if a non-Muslim woman marries a Muslim man, she cannot inherit from her husband.

While these rules are symbols of inequality in the modern era, they made sense historically since women were always protected. Even today, women remain under the legal jurisdiction of their father's or their husband's family. After divorce, they return to the jurisdiction of their father's family; they do not have the obligation to support their family, and they may keep any money they earn for themselves. As previously mentioned, Muslim women cannot marry non-Muslim men in most Muslim jurisdictions. Many Western liberals would not take issue if a Muslim woman chose not to marry a non-Muslim man because she views intermarriage as sinful under her religion. Koranic verse 2:221 states, "Nor marry (your girls) to unbelievers until they believe." The historic reason for the rule is that women are regarded as the weaker sex and might be tempted away from their faith by dominant men, who are the family heads of household. Men are women's legal guardians, and thus might convince women to convert out of their religion. If women remain Muslim, their husbands might disrespect their right to wear head scarves or cause them to violate Islamic norms by forcing them to cook pork or serve them alcohol.

There are notable exceptions in the Muslim world to religiously based family law. Turkey has a secular marriage law and has abolished polygamy, prohibited religious political parties, and, until recently, restricted the wearing of head scarves in schools and public buildings. In Turkey, Muslim women can marry non-Muslim men, and there are some couples, but the number is small since the country is predominantly Muslim. Families react differently to such arrangements, with some terminating communication permanently and others only warming to the situation upon the arrival of grandchildren. The husband and wife may ask each other to convert, but Turkish women are more likely to do so, which is legal. Jewish and Armenian Turkish men and their families are afraid of assimilation, and are even more likely to insist that the Muslim female spouse convert. Tunisia is another Muslim country that has followed a secular path in most respects. Using Islamic reinterpretation (ijtihad), it abolished polygamy soon after inde-pendence. It has also abolished the duty of obedience, made divorce equally accessible to both genders, and prohibited head scarves in public buildings. Interestingly, while intermarriage by Muslim women is technically permitted, an administrative ordinance prohibits it. There is also some indication that the non-Muslim man must convert and the religious authority known as the mufti must give the certificate to the city hall, with the entire process taking three months or more.

One legal solution is Islamic reinterpretation. As previously mentioned Tunisia used Islamic reinterpretation (ijtihad) to ban polygamy. In attempting to secularize the Tunisian legal system, the country's first president, Habib Bourguiba, realized that basing change on Islamic principles would be more culturally valid than would be basing it on perceived Western secular principles. On a similar note, in previous scholarship, I have argued that there is a need to support some existing progressive Islamic reinterpretation in the Palestinian women's rights context. There are some Islamic scholars, such as Azizah al Hibri, who have challenged the predominant interpretation of verse 2:221 as prohibiting intermarriage for women. She has reinterpreted the qawama guardianship principle to show that it must be understood in its historical patriarchal context of almost total female reliance on male support. Today, the options for women are much broader, and many live in societies where they receive education, marry later, have the possibility of limiting their family size, and work outside the home. Thus, there is no longer the need for the guardianship principle.

In Tunisia, women are now recognized as having equal rights to divorce. Extrapolating further, could it not then be argued that they should have equal rights to marry? As mentioned, an administrative ordinance is currently limiting their legal options. Throughout the world, it is no longer necessary to regard men as heads of households. Using the example of the Prophet Muhammed's first wife, Khadijah, who was a divorced business woman fifteen years older than he, I ask why Muslim women cannot keep their religion no matter whom they marry. Since modern studies show that mothers have the most impact on their children's religious beliefs, would not the Muslim community grow if mothers as well as fathers were considered capable of passing on their religion to the children?

Since it is extremely difficult to gather internal sectarian momentum to change religious norms, a constitutional approach may have slightly more possibility for success. On a national level, most countries today have constitutions with a gender equality clause, including those in the Muslim world. Ironically, the United States still does not, and perhaps we can learn from these countries. In the 2008 U.S. presidential campaign, we have not yet heard any of the candidates discuss the long-dormant proposed Equal Rights Amendment. Unfortunately, many of these global gender equality clauses are in the same position as the 13th, 14th, and 15th Amendments at the time of Loving—unenforced or under enforced. Most countries are still treating women far worse than men by every indicator. There is a conflict in most Muslim countries' constitutions between the gender equality clause and the clause that says that Islam is the national religion and that shari'a is a source or the source of law. Thus, this conflict perpetuates ancient patriarchal customs, resulting in the continuation of centuries-old subordination, which a twentieth- and twenty-first-century idea of gender equality cannot trump.

The international community now has a whole additional layer of law that did not really exist at the time of Loving—international human rights law. The Universal Declaration of Human Rights (UDHR) was developed in 1948 during the height of American apartheid, with former First Lady Eleanor Roosevelt driving the movement for its adoption. The UDHR mentions freedom of religion as well as equal rights in marriage, but it is a nonbinding declaration. It is a little like saying "I declare I love you"—a lovely sentiment but not one to take a country to court for violating. Some scholars do view the UDHR as customary international law, which is binding on all nations, and thus would advocate using it in a court of law. Two very important relevant international treaties were issued in 1967, which evolved during the 1950s: the International Covenant on Civil and Political Rights 16 (ICCPR) and the International Covenant on Economic, Social and Cultural Rights (ICESCR).

These documents were also inspired in part by the U.S. civil rights movement. ICCPR article 18 allows freedom of religion and conversion. This treaty binds every country that signs and ratifies it. Some countries, like the United States, consider such a treaty non-self-executing and require implementing national legislation. Some nations make reservations, understandings, and declarations that further limit their obligations. According to the Vienna Convention on the Law of Treaties, such limitations are not supposed to conflict with the "object and purpose of the treaty," and other countries can lodge objections if they see fit. Unfortunately, there is no international police force to put a violating country in jail. In 1981, the Convention on the Elimination of Discrimination against Women (CEDAW) was issued, and its article 16 discusses the right to found a family and choose a spouse freely, as well as the responsibility of both spouses to undertake equal duties with respect to marriage, divorce, and children. Many countries have gutted CEDAW by making reservations, finding that it conflicts with their customs or religion; some scholars question whether CEDAW is compatible with shari'a.

If a Muslim woman is living in a country that has accepted its obligations under the ICCPR and CEDAW and that has a gender equality clause in its constitution, she may be able to pursue a claim in several places. The national courts might hear a claim under the constitution as well as under the international treaties. Many countries are much more open to hearing claims under international law than the U.S. Supreme Court has been. In addition, there are treaty body committees. The Human Rights Committee can hear complaints regarding the ICCPR, and the Committee on the Elimination of Discrimination Against Women hears CEDAW-based claims. The treaty-based bodies are very slow, backlogged, and lack sufficient enforcement mechanisms. For example, with respect to the ICCPR, matters raised by individuals or non-governmental organizations cannot be heard unless a country has ratified the relevant Optional Protocol.

Furthermore, if a claim occurs in a country that is part of a developed regional human rights system, such as Europe or the Americas, an aggrieved party may bring a case under the relevant regional human rights treaty and may also raise international treaties and national laws.

Europe and the Americas already grant religious freedom in marriage, following the ICCPR lead. The regions that have countries that prohibit or restrict interfaith marriage, particularly for Muslim women, do not have appropriate regional options. Unfortunately, the African Court on Human and Peoples' Rights is still in its embryonic stage, and the Middle East and Asia do not have regional courts or regional treaties at this time. While there is an African Charter on Human and Peoples' Rights, there is only a draft Charter on Human Rights for the Arab world. It should be remembered that law is necessary but not sufficient to change hearts and minds on sensitive issues. There are other solutions as well. In the long term, education is an important solution, and media can be an important tool in educating children and adults. While the Internet is a growing source of information, newspapers, television, and especially radio can also make a difference even in the poorest of countries.

Sometimes we learn from our own families. Seeing harmonious relations between interracial or interfaith couples and their children during Thanksgiving or Ramadan can do more to change traditional outlooks than any outside media source. As Americans with legal training, we have privileging in many of our identities that allows us to become involved in various human rights causes in our own country as well as around the world. While each of us will no doubt gravitate to our favourite causes, perhaps others of us will decide to educate ourselves and others, and support the human rights of Muslim women wherever they may be. One aspect of that struggle may be the right to interfaith marriage for the brave few that embrace that path. The Lovings sued to overturn the Virginia antimiscegenation law, a daunting task in the context of the 1960s south, even with the ten-year-old Brown decision in place. Supporting the Loving family would not have been easy in Virginia in 1967, and it may still not be easy in many parts of the United States today. Even some forty years after Loving, the number of black-white interracial couples is still very small, with considerable family and societal stigma attaching to those who do not follow the normal trend of marrying within their race.

Muslim women desiring to marry on an interfaith basis in many Muslim countries may face even more daunting odds. The rise in fundamentalism around the world may mean it is less likely that religious norms may change in the near future. On a broader level, women are still under-represented in the executive, legislative, and judicial branches, the very places where the battles to change laws take place. Women still do most of the housework and child care globally, leaving little time for activism. The natural desire to marry within one's nationality, ethnicity, and faith make it very unlikely that much pressure will build up to change the laws. Economic problems can limit marriage options generally, especially for Muslims with respect to provision of the expensive bride price. Gender discrimination manifests itself in numerous ways, and restrictions on the right to marry across faith lines are unlikely to make it to the top of human rights priority lists. Nevertheless, surprising changes can occur. If a biracial man can become President of the United States, maybe one day a Muslim woman who marries a non-Muslim man could become leader of her Muslim country as well.

Religion in the Modern World

Religious influence is mainly at the individual level. Irrespective of one's faith or philosophy, transformation takes place within. In a way, that should give us hope. Materially, many have lost hope. However, at a deeper level, faith will sustain hope. Hope is a contributing factor for religion today. Once hope is lost, one becomes mad, commits acts of violence, participates in destructive behavior, or ultimately commits suicide. Society is made up of individuals. Because of individuals who have lost hope and behave negatively, there is more and more madness in society today. If their numbers increase, all of society will suffer. If we utilize and understand religious traditions properly, individuals benefit, and so can society as a whole.

Unfortunately, religions today place too much emphasis on ceremony and rituals. This is sometimes old-fashioned and often limiting. What is necessary now is to find the essence of what is important in our daily lives and to connect relevant religious messages, advice, or inspiration with this. I feel an important factor in religion is to be "God-fearing." Even though the individual believes he or she has individual power and faculties, a faith in God ensures there is some discipline. Many countries today face a moral crisis, and crimes are increasing. The disciplinary powers of society have conventional methods to control crime, but the individuals involved in wrongdoing are becoming more evasive and sophisticated in their methods. So without self-discipline, some acknowledgment of the spirit within one's self, and a sense of individual responsibility, it will be very diffi-cult to exercise control. Therefore, various religious traditions have an important, effective role.

All religions carry the message of love, compassion, and forgiveness. And forgiveness reflects tolerance and an understanding of the value of another's rights and views. This is the foundation for harmony. Perhaps, at a deeper level, our views are transformed because of religious traditions. Religion teaches us some obvious things, but there are some deeper meanings, deeper forces, and deeper influences that it imparts. These widen our view of life. For instance, if an individual has to face pain or suffering, a religious experience or understanding will give deeper meaning to the incident and help reduce the mental burden, anxiety, and pain that are endured.

For example, Buddhists believe in the karmic law, the law of causality, so they know that whatever is happening in their lives is because of some past action, or karma. Ultimately, they know they must take responsibility for those actions. This helps to reduce mental frustration and anxiety.

Even if all religions have the same goal, there tend to be different ideas and areas of emphasis. As someone engaged purposefully in interfaith dialogue, how would you articulate the common ground or the basis for harmony between various religions? Although all world religions carry the message of love and compassion, it would not be correct to say that all of them have the same objective or beliefs; there are substantial differences. For example, some religions believe in a Creator, and others do not—that represents a fundamental difference.

There exist fundamental differences between the philosophical approaches of the world's religions. Why did all these diverse philosophies develop? I believe there is a good purpose for these multiple views. Within humanity, there are many different dispositions; and one philosophy, one belief, simply cannot satisfy all. Therefore, the great ancient masters had to demonstrate different philosophies and traditions. For example, some like spicy food; others do not. Spirituality is food for the mind, and different religions are very necessary for different mental dispositions. For some, the philosophy that the person is nothing and the Creator is most important is suitable. If everything is in the hands of the Creator, one should do nothing against the wishes of the Creator.

If people act accordingly, it gives them a kind of mental satisfaction and moral stability. There are others who approach philosophy with logic. They have a sort of independence or some such power. If it is explained to them that everything is not in the hands of an Almighty Creator but is in their own hands, that really makes a difference. Irrespective of the different philosophies, the most important point is to have a tamed and disciplined mind and a warm heart. It is unfortunate that today there is so much conflict, division, and bloodshed in the name of religion.

When I was in Tibet, there was no contact with other religious traditions. At that time, my thinking was different. Today, as a result of the many opportunities I have had to meet people from different religious traditions, I am completely convinced that they all have the same potential to produce good human beings. My eyes were opened after speaking with such great people as the late Thomas Merton, Mother Teresa, and so many more. We exchanged deep spiritual experiences, and I realized it is important to come together and work closely with each other.

In India, there are many different traditions of thought and philosophy, including the traditions of other cultures. India is like a supermarket of many religious traditions, and I think that is one of the beautiful things about this country. And because of that reality, religious ahimsa [the doctrine of refraining from harming any living being] has become a part of the Indian tradition. In this, India has set an example for the world. People can live side by side as brothers and sisters despite following many different religious faiths. This is how the world is becoming smaller and so interdependent. In the past, nations and continents remained more or less isolated. The concept of one truth, one religion, was very relevant then. But today the situation is different. Pluralism in religious faith is necessary and relevant in today's world.

It is important for me as a Buddhist to believe that Buddhism is the true religion or one truth. It is just as important for a Christian to believe that Christianity is the true religion for him as it is for others. But how do we overcome the contradiction that there is relevance for different truths and traditions? In reality, there is no contradiction. For the individual, the concept of one truth, one religion, is very important. However, in terms of society and the masses, the concept of several truths, several traditions, is relevant. That does not mean that any one of my brothers—whether Hindu, Christian, Muslim, or Jewish—is following a religion of lesser validity. We are all involved in a religion that is appropriate for us.

Today we have the opportunity for closer contact with different traditions, which helps us develop the idea of pluralism and appreciate the values and sanctity of other customs. Conversion is one-sided when it is without alternatives and is coerced. This is wrong. Voluntary conversion is when an individual makes a choice according to his mental disposition. This seems more suitable to me. Some-times disaster and confusion follow a change of religion, so it is safer and healthier, perhaps, for people to involve them-selves in their own cultural traditions. Some Westerners who change their religion suddenly, without proper or care-ful thought, experience confusion. In case you find the Bud-dhist way or approach more effective and logical, think carefully. Time spent thinking and examining is worth-while. Finally, if you really feel it is more suitable to your mental disposition, it is okay. An individual has the right to embrace a new religion.

And to digress a bit, when one changes one's personal religion, there is a tendency to be critical of the original religion in order to justify one's decision. That's very bad. It must be avoided. Buddhism may be more suitable for many, yet that does not mean that millions of other people have no values. Those millions do benefit from their religions. Some practitioners of Buddhism have expectations that are too high, possibly because some of our teachers say that you can achieve Buddha hood within three years. Such a teaching is simply propaganda—you cannot achieve the highest spiritual realization in such a short period, except in exceptional cases. Too many expectations, in the beginning, are wrong. I myself think about the limit-less eons that have given me inner strength. One hundred years of a life period is nothing.

Some practitioners cling to one practice without understanding the whole Buddhist system. The transformation of our mind cannot be achieved through just one effort or one practice. Our mind is both very weak and very strong, and it is very sophisticated. When your emphasis is more on learning, you may develop pride. If your emphasis is less on pride, sometimes you lose self confidence. When you develop more self-confidence, pride also follows.

The mind is very sophisticated, so the antidote to it should also be sophisticated. Think about impermanence; think about eons; think about Buddha's nature, about the ultimate reality of emptiness; and also think about the mental potential. Think in various ways, and adopt different methods for different situations. That's the way to shape or change our mind. It takes time. For that reason it is very important to know the basic structure of the Buddhist practice. That's my advice or suggestion.

To give an explanation from tantra: We can infer certain experiences through the gross levels of our mind and others through the subtle mind. During sleep, in the dream state, our consciousness has reached a subtler level than during the waking state. This provides us with the opportunity to get a glimpse of certain experiences that are not possible during the waking state when the mind is active at grosser levels. Because of that, one can actually engage in certain investigations during the dream state. Therefore, one can also say that certain things exist that one can only understand through unusual experiences or experiences in dreams.

As I said earlier, all major religions have a single aim—to make good human beings. In this respect, they are the same. Beyond that, there are differences within the different spiritual traditions. One group—for example, Christians—believe that human beings ultimately reach Heaven. However, Buddhism, Jainism, and some ancient Indian traditions accept nirvana, *moksha*. Within Buddhism, there are different definitions and interpretations of *moksha*. The main point is that among the systems that agree on the existence of nirvana and *moksha*, there are differences. Even among Buddhists, there are differences in the presentation of what is meant by nirvana. Buddhists explain nirvana as the true cessation of all delusions, a mind free of delusions. However, if we were asked whether other systems existed in which such a state could be achieved, the answer would have to be no. In the same way, if we Buddhists were asked if a Buddhist practice existed by which we could achieve going to Heaven—as Christians do—the answer would again have to be no.

A complete system of methods has to be practiced in order to achieve the state of nirvana as explained in Buddhism. There are many people who are not interested in practicing that type of path. There are many people to whom faith appeals more than reason.

However, your question implies that Buddhist teaching presents the path in an exclusively logical way, but if we analyze this, it may not be immediately obvious. There are different levels of direct experience and perception of both ultimate and relative truth that can be achieved through intense meditative and yogic practices. During the early stages, we can understand such experiences only by using logic and reasoning. We cannot experience them directly. There are only a few people who have had these deep, nuanced, and direct insights of the different levels of truth, for example.

Three types of phenomena exist: some are obvious, some slightly hidden, and others are completely hidden. For example, when we ask how this book came into existence, the usual explanation is that it was produced by causes and conditions. When we ask why it came into existence through such causes and how all these conditions and causes aggregate it, and then, if we delve further, we will come to the point where we will have to say that it was possible due to the karma of the person who has contact with this book. If we investigate even further in order to explain the book's existence, we might have to go as far as the big bang theory—the beginning of the universe.

The continuity of matter, even simple matter, goes like this, back to the previous stage, then to a stage before that stage, right to the beginning of the whole cosmos. The next question is: what is the reason for the creation of such things? Either God or some different instance is the answer. If the answer were the Creator God, it might solve one problem but create others, create more questions. There is no beginning; this is endless because of sentient beings, because of the continuity of consciousness. That is the Buddhist explanation. This may not answer all the questions, but it answers some. This theory gives some satisfactory answers, which can be established through reasoning.

For example, certain facts cannot be proved, and we have to rely on the statements of a third person. We know that we are a certain number of years old, but we do not know this through our own experience, nor can we prove it through reasoning. We have to believe our mothers. We have faith in our mothers because there is no reason why they should lie. When we finally find that a person is completely reliable, we accept his or her statements. What is meant by reasoning or faith is to understand the consequences of certain actions that have accumulated over a certain period of time. If we are to rely on the direct perceptions of a Buddha, we have to be convinced that the Buddha is free of ignorance and obscuration. We realize that there is no reason for him to tell lies and that the statements are not inconsistent and have no contradictions.

When these conditions are fulfilled, we believe him and have faith in him.

New religious Movement

New religious movement (NRM) is a term used to refer to a religious faith or an ethical, spiritual, or philosophical movement of recent origin that is not part of an established denomination, church, or religious body. The term *NRM* comprises a wide range of movements ranging from loose affiliations based on novel approaches to spirituality or religion to communitarian enterprises that demand a considerable amount of group conformity and a social identity that separates its adherents from mainstream society. Its use is not universally accepted among the groups to which it is applied.

As a field of scholarly endeavour, the study of New Religions emerged in Japan in the wake of the explosion of religious innovation following the Second World War. Even the name new religions are a direct translation of *shinshukyo,* which Japanese sociologists coined to refer to this phenomenon. The term was adopted in turn by Western scholars as an alternative to the older term *cult,* which acquired a pejorative connotation during the 1970s, and was subsequently used indiscriminately by lay critics to disparage faiths whose doctrines they saw as unusual or heretical. A number of scholars, especially in the sociology of religion, use "new religious movement" to describe non-mainstream religions, while others use the term for benign alternative religions and reserve "cult" for groups - whether religious, psychotherapeutic, political or commercial - they believe to be extremely manipulative and exploitative.

Although there is no one criterion or set of criteria for describing a group as a "new religious movement," use of the term usually requires that the group be both *of recent origin* and *different from existing religions*. Debate surrounds the phrase "of recent origin": some authors use World War

II as the dividing line after which anything is "new", whereas others define as "new" everything after the advent of the Bahá'í Faith (mid-19th century) or even everything after Sikhism (17th century).

"New" in the sense of "different from existing religions" is considered straightforward in definition but not as much in categorization. Some scholars have a more restricted approach to what counts as "different". For them, "difference" applies to a faith that, though it may be seen as part of an existing religion, meets with rejection from that religion for not sharing the same basic creed or declares itself either separate from the existing religion or even "the only right" faith. Other scholars expand their measurement of difference, considering religious movements new when, taken from their traditional cultural context, they appear in new places, perhaps in modified forms. Examples of these kinds of "new movements" would be the Western importation and establishment of Hindu or Buddhist groups.

NRMs vary in terms of leadership; authority; concepts of the individual, family, and gender; teachings; organizational structures; etc. These variations have presented a challenge to social scientists in their attempts to formulate a comprehensive and clear set of criteria for classifying NRMs. Generally, Christian denominations that are an accepted part of mainstream Christianity are not seen as new religious movements. However, to some, The Church of Jesus Christ of Latter-day Saints, Jehovah's Witnesses, Christian Scientists, and Shakers have been studied as NRMs. Evangelicals usually consider these groups to be cults because of believing their theologies to be unconducive or preventive of salvation according to the teachings of the Bible. There are also examples of such groups as the Seventh-day Adventist Church and even tent revivalists being characterized as cults, generally by other evangelicals who are hostile to their proselytizing efforts. Certain other groups do not define themselves as religions but nonetheless find some scholars labelling them NRMs.

Debates among academics on the acceptability of the word *cult* continue. Similarly, no consensus has been reached in the definition of *new religious movement* among scholars. An article on the categorization of new religious move-ments in U.S. print media published by *The Association for the Sociology of Religion* (formerly the American *Catholic Sociological Society*), criticizes the print media for failing to recognize social-scientific efforts in the area of new religious movements, and its tendency to use popular or anti-cultist definitions rather than social-scientific insight, and asserts that "The failure of the print media to recognize social-scientific efforts in the area of religious movement organizations impels us to add yet another failing mark to the media report card Weiss (1985) has constructed to assess the media's reporting of the social sciences."

Examples

NRMs are diverse in their beliefs, practices, organization, and societal acceptance. Irving Hexham and Karla Poewe have consequently proposed that there are NRMs, particularly those who have gained adherents in a number of nations, which can be understood as forming global subcultures. In general, the number of people who have affiliated with NRMs worldwide is small when compared to major world religions. However, the diversity of NRMs has seen the emergence of different groups in Africa, Japan, and Melanesia. In Africa, David Barrett has documented the emergence of 6,000 new indigenous churches since the late 1960s. In Japan a number of NRMs based on revitalised Shinto belief, as well as neo-Buddhist and New Age groups, have emerged, some of which originated in the late Nineteenth century in the Meiji Era and others in the aftermath of World War Two.

Around twenty-five percent of the world's distinct cultures are found in Melanesia, spanning the island nations from Papua New Guinea, the Solomon Islands, Vanuatu and Fiji. It was here that the phenomena of Cargo Cults were first discerned by anthropologists and religious studies scholars. The Cargo Cults are interpreted as indigenous NRMs that have arisen in response to colonial and postcolonial cultural changes, including the influx of modernisation and capitalist consumerism. At the time of their foundation, the religious traditions considered "established" or "mainstream" today were seen as new religious movements. For example, Christianity was opposed by people within Judaism and within the Roman culture as sacrilege toward existing doctrines. Likewise, Protestant Christianity was originally seen—and is still considered by some today—as a new religious movement or breakaway development.

In similar fashion , some of the contemporary naturalistic religions(Naturalism (philosophy)) have evolved out of traditional Christianity and Judaism via process theology or using the term 'God' as a metaphor. Others have emerged via a dominating scientific perspective or by atheistic rebellion to the established beliefs of their culture. Still others have added a religious ingredient to their humanistic thinking. Most of these see the ritual/spiritual aspects of religious practice as necessary for broad adoption by many people. Examples are Religious Naturalism, Scientific Pantheism, Religious Humanism and some liberal Unitarians, Quakers and Jews.

Criticism

Criticism of some new religious movements, a subset of which are often described by their critics as being "cults," has been a contentious issue with both sides sometimes using epithets such as "hate group" to describe the other side. Disaffected former members, stating that they are seeking redress for perceived wrongs or looking to expose perceived wrongdoings, have, in turn, had their motives called into question. They have themselves come under attack for allegedly using methods themselves that have been characterized as polemic, hostile, and verbally or emotionally abusive. Critics, both those who are ex-members and who aren't, have had their character and credibility impeached. The Church of Scientology, in particular, makes a practice of investigating its critics and publicizing any past crimes or wrongdoings.

CESNUR's president Massimo Introvigne, writes in his article *"So many evil things: Anti-cult terrorism via the Internet"*, that fringe and extreme anti-cult activism resorts to tactics that may create a background favorable to extreme manifestations of discrimination and hate against individuals that belong to new religious movements. Critics of CESNUR, however, call Introvigne a cult apologist who defends harmful religious groups and cults. Somewhat in concurrence with Introvigne, professor Eileen Barker asserts in an interview that the controversy surrounding certain new religious movements can turn violent by a process called deviancy amplification spiral.

Aspects of the *guru-shishya* (teacher-disciple) tradition are commonly brought forward in disputes related to asserted abuse of authority by gurus and spiritual teachers of new religious movements. In a paper by Anson Shupe and Susan Darnell presented at the 2000 meeting of the Society for the Scientific Study of Religion, they affirm that although the International Cultic Studies Association (ICSA, formerly known as AFF or American Family Foundation) has presented "slanted, stereotypical images and language that has inflamed persons to perform extreme actions," the extent to which the ICSA and other anti-cultist organizations are hate groups as defined by law or racial/ ethnic criteria in sociology, is open for debate. The Foundation against Intolerance of Religious Minorities, associated with the Adidam NRM, sees the use of terms "cult" and "cult leader" to suggest that these are to be detested, avoided at whatever cost and see this as the exercise of prejudice and discrimination against them in the same manner as "nigger" and "commie" were used in the past to denigrate blacks and Communists.

Faith and Rationality

Faith and rationality are two modes of belief that exist in varying degrees of conflict or compatibility. Faith is belief in inspiration, revelation, or authority. Rationality is belief based on reason or evidence. Broadly speaking, there are three categories of views regarding the relationship between faith and rationality. Rationalism holds that truth should be determined by reason and factual analysis, rather than faith, dogma, or religious teaching. Fideism holds that faith is necessary, and that beliefs must be held without evidence or reason, or even in conflict with evidence and reason. Natural theology holds one can rationally infer that God exists, through inductive or deductive reasoning.

The Relationship between Faith and Reason

From at least the days of the Greek Philosophers, the relationship between faith and reason has been hotly debated. Plato argued that knowledge is simply memory of the eternal. Aristotle set down rules by which knowledge could be discovered by reason. Rationalists point out that many people hold irrational beliefs, for many reasons. There may be evolutionary causes for irrational beliefs — irrational beliefs may increase our ability to survive and reproduce. Or, according to Pascal's Wager, it may be to our advantage to have faith, because faith may promise infinite rewards, while the rewards of reason are necessarily finite.

Believers in faith — for example those who believe salvation is possible through faith alone — point out that everyone holds beliefs arrived at by faith, not reason. The belief that the universe is a sensible place and that our minds allow us to arrive at correct conclusions about it, is a belief we hold through faith.

Beliefs held "by faith" may be seen existing in a number of relationships to rationality:

- Faith as underlying rationality: In this view, all human knowledge and reason is seen as dependent on faith:

faith in our senses, faith in our reason, faith in our memories, and faith in the accounts of events we receive from others. Accordingly, faith is seen as essential to and inseparable from rationality.

- Faith as addressing issues beyond the scope of rationality: In this view, faith is seen as covering issues that science and rationality are inherently incapable of addressing, but that are nevertheless entirely real. Accordingly, faith is seen as complementing rationality, by providing answers to questions that would otherwise be unanswerable.
- Faith as contradicting rationality: In this view, faith is seen as those views that one holds despite evidence and reason to the contrary. Accordingly, faith is seen as pernicious with respect to rationality, as it interferes with our ability to think, and rationality is seen as the enemy of faith, since it interferes with our ability to believe.

Views of the Magisterium

Dei Filius was the dogmatic constitution of the First Vatican Council on the catholic faith. It was adopted unanimously on 24 April 1870 and was influenced by the philosophical conceptions of Johann Baptist Franzelin, who had written a great deal on the topic of faith and rationality. Fides et Ratio is an encyclical promulgated by Pope John Paul II on 14 September 1998. It deals primarily with the relationship between faith and reason.

Reformed epistemology

Faith as underlying rationality

The view that faith underlies all rationality holds that rationality is dependent on faith for its coherence. Under this view, there is no way to comprehensively *prove* that we are actually seeing what we appear to be seeing, that what we remember actually happened, or that the laws of logic and mathematics are actually real. Instead, all beliefs depend for their coherence on *faith* in our senses, memory, and reason, because the foundations of rationalism cannot be proven by evidence or reason.

Fideism

Martin Luther taught that faith and reason were antithetical, in the sense that questions of faith could not be illuminated by reason. He wrote, "All the articles of our Christian faith, which God has revealed to us in His Word, are in presence of reason sheerly impossible, absurd, and false." and "[That] Reason in no way contributes to faith. [...] For reason is the greatest enemy that faith has; it never comes to the aid of spiritual things." However, though seemingly contradictorily, he also wrote in the latter work that human reason "strives not against faith, when enlightened, but rather furthers and advances it", bringing claims he was a fideist into dispute.

The Rationalist Point of View

In this view, there are many beliefs that are held by faith alone, that rational thought would force the mind to reject. As an example, many people believe in the Biblical story of Noah's flood: that the entire Earth was covered by water for forty days. But most plants cannot survive being covered by water for that length of time, so one must choose between accepting the story on faith and rejecting reason, or rejecting the story by reason and thus rejecting faith (in the instance).

In Jewish Philosophy

The 14th Century Jewish philosopher Levi ben Gerson tried to reconcile faith and reason. He wrote, "The Torah cannot prevent us from considering to be true that which our reason urges us to believe." His contemporary Hasdai ben Abraham Crescas argued the contrary view, that reason is weak and faith strong, and that only through faith can we discover the fundamental truth that God is love, that through faith alone can we endure the suffering that is the common lot of God's chosen people.

3

Voice of 21st Century

Freedom of Religion

Freedom of religion is a principle that supports the freedom of an individual or community, in public or private, to manifest religion or belief in teaching, practice, worship, and observance. The concept is generally recognized to also include the freedom to change religion or not to follow any religion. Freedom of religion is considered by many in many nations and people to be a fundamental human right. In a country with a state religion, freedom of religion is generally considered to mean that the government permits religious practices of other sects besides the state religion, and does not persecute believers in other faiths.

Today there are concerns about the persecution of religious minorities in the Muslim world and in some communist states such as China and North Korea, as well as other forms of intolerance in other countries—for example, the banning of worn religious articles such as the Muslim veil, in certain European countries. Article 18 of the U.N. International Covenant on Civil and Political Rights shows that it is a form of injustice (spiritual injustice) when persons are denied the liberty to exercise their religious freedom. Freedom of religion as a legal concept is related to, but not identical with, religious toleration, separation of church and state, or secular state (*laïcité*). Where individuals and not governments are concerned, religious toleration is generally taken to refer to an attitude of acceptance towards other people's religions. Such toleration does not require that one view other religions as equally true; rather, the assumption is that each citizen will grant that others have the right to hold and practice their own beliefs.

Against this backdrop, proselytism can be a contentious issue, as it could be regarded as an offense against the validity of others' religious beliefs, including irreligious belief. The Universal Declaration of Human Rights adopted by fifty of the Member States of the United Nations General Assembly on December 10, 1948, with eight abstentions, at the Palais de Chaillot in Paris, France defines freedom of religion and belief as follows: "Everyone has the right to freedom of thought, conscience and religion; this right includes freedom to change his religion or belief, and freedom, either alone or in community with others and in public or private, to manifest his religion or belief in teaching, practice, worship, and observance."

Historically *freedom of religion* has been used to refer to the tolerance of different theological systems of belief, while *freedom of worship* was defined as freedom of individual action. Each of these has existed to varying degrees. While many countries have accepted some form of religious freedom, this has also often been limited in practice through punitive taxation, repressive social legislation, and political disenfranchisement. Compare examples of individual freedom in Italy or the Muslim tradition of dhimmis, literally "protected individuals" professing an officially tolerated non-Muslim religion.

Antiquity

In Antiquity a syncretic point-of-view often allowed communities of traders to operate under their own customs. When street mobs of separate quarters clashed in a Hellenistic or Roman city, the issue was generally perceived to be an infringement of community rights. The Greek-Jewish clashes at Cyrene provided one example of cosmopolitan cities as scenes of tumult. Some of the historical exceptions have been in regions where one of the revealed religions has been in a position of power: Judaism, Zoroastrianism, Christianity and Islam. Others have been where the established order has felt threatened, as shown in the trial of Socrates or where the ruler has been deified, as in Rome, and refusal to offer token sacrifice was similar to refusing to take an oath of allegiance. This was the core for resentment and the persecution of early Christian communities.

Freedom of religious worship was established in the Maurya Empire of ancient India by Ashoka the Great in the 3rd century BC, which was encapsulated in the Edicts of Ashoka. Religious freedom for Muslims, Jews and pagans was declared in the Constitution of Medina by Muhammad in the 7th century AD. The Islamic Caliphate later guaranteed religious freedom under the conditions that non Muslim communities accept *dhimmi* (protected) status and their adult males pay the *jizya* tax as a substitute for the *zakat* paid by Muslim citizens. The Norman Kingdom of Sicily under Roger II was characterised by its multi-ethnic nature and religious tolerance. Normans, Jews, Muslim Arabs, Byzantine Greeks, Longobards and "native" Sicilians lived in harmony.

Rather than exterminate the Muslims of Sicily, Roger II's grandson Emperor Frederick II of Hohenstaufen (1215—1250) allowed them to settle on the mainland and build mosques. Not least, he enlisted them in his — Christian — army and even into his personal bodyguards. The General Charter of Jewish Liberties known as the Statute of Kalisz was issued by the Duke of Greater Poland Boleslaus the Pious on September 8, 1264 in Kalisz. The statute served as the basis for the legal position of Jews in Poland and led to creation of the Yiddish-speaking autonomous Jewish nation until 1795. The statute granted exclusive jurisdiction of Jewish courts over Jewish matters and established a separate tribunal for matters involving Christians and Jews. Additionally, it guaranteed personal liberties and safety for Jews including freedom of religion, travel, and trade.

The statute was ratified by subsequent Polish Kings: Casimir III of Poland in 1334, Casimir IV of Poland in 1453 and Sigismund I of Poland in 1539. The first full religious freedom law (which wasn't just a tolerance as in other countries) what had "act rank" created by Edict of Turda in Transylvania, and accepted by hungarian székely and Saxon part of the diet. After the fall of the city of Granada Spain in 1492 the Muslim population was promised religious freedom by the Treaty of Granada, but that promise was short-lived. In 1501 Granada's Muslims were given an ultimatum to either convert to Christianity or to emigrate. The majority converted, but only superficially, continuing to dress and speak as they had before and to secretly practice Islam. The Moriscos (converts to Christianity) were ultimately expelled from Spain between 1609 (Castile) and 1614 (rest of Spain), by Philip III.

The Roman Catholic Church kept a tight rein on religious expression throughout the middle Ages. Jews were alternately tolerated and persecuted, the most notable examples of the latter being the expulsion of all Jews from Spain in 1492. Some of those who remained and converted were tried as heretics in the Inquisition for allegedly practicing Judaism in secret. Despite the persecution of Jews, they were the most tolerated non-Catholic faith in Europe. However, the latter was in part a reaction to the growing movement that became the Reformation. As early as 1380, John Wycliffe in England denied transubstantiation and began his translation of the Bible into English. He was condemned in a Papal Bull in 1410, and all his books were burned.

In 1414 Jan Hus, a Bohemian preacher of reformation was given a safe conduct by the Holy Roman Emperor to attend the Council of Constance. Not entirely trusting in his safety, he made his will before he left. His forebodings proved accurate, and he was burned at the stake on July 6, 1415. The Council also decreed that Wycliffe's remains be disinterred and cast out. This decree was not carried out until 1429. Martin Luther published his famous 95 Theses in Wittenberg on October 31, 1517. His aim was to stop the sale of indulgences and reform the Church from within, but this was not the result. In 1521 he was given the chance to recant at the Diet of Worms before Charles V, Holy Roman Emperor, and then only 19. After he refused to recant he was declared heretic. Partly for his own protection, he was sequestered on the Wartburg in the possessions of Frederick III, Elector of Saxony, where he translated the New Testament into German. He was excommunicated by Papal Bull in 1521.

The Protestant movement, however, continued to gain ground in his absence and spread to Switzerland. Huldrych Zwingli preached reform in Zürich from 1520 to 1523. He opposed the sale of indulgences, celibacy, pilgrimages, pictures, statues, relics, altars, and organs. This culminated in outright war between the Swiss cantons that accepted Protestantism and the Catholics. The Catholics were victorious, and Zwingli was killed in battle in 1531. The Catholic cantons were magnanimous in victory. In the meantime, in Germany Philip Melanchthon drafted the Augsburg Confession as a common confession for the Lutherans and the free territories. It was presented to Charles V in 1530. The defiance of Papal authority proved contagious, and in 1533, when Henry VIII of England was excommunicated for his divorce and remarriage to Anne Boleyn, he promptly established a state church with bishops appointed by the crown. This was not without internal opposition, and Thomas More, who had been his prime minister, was executed in 1535 for opposition to Henry.

In 1535 the Swiss canton of Geneva became Protestant, but the Protestants often proved as intolerant of differences of opinion as the Catholics. In 1536 the Bernese imposed the reformation on the canton of Vaud by conquest. They sacked the cathedral in Lausanne and destroyed all its art and statuary. John Calvin, who had been active in Geneva, was expelled in 1538 in a power struggle, but he was invited back in 1540. The same kind of seesaw back and forth between Protestantism and Catholicism was evident in England when Mary I of England returned that country briefly to the Catholic fold in 1553. However, her half-sister, Elizabeth I of England was to restore the Church of England in 1558, this time permanently. The King James Bible commissioned by King James I of England and published in 1611 proved a landmark for Protestant worship.

However, intolerance of dissident forms of Protestantism continued, as evidenced by the exodus of the Pilgrims who sought refuge, first in the Netherlands, and ultimately in America, founding the Plymouth Colony in Massachusetts in 1620. William Penn, the founder of Philadelphia was involved in a case which had a profound effect upon future American law and those of England. In a classic case of jury nullification the jury refused to convict William Penn of preaching a Quaker sermon, which was illegal. Even though the jury was imprisoned for their acquittal, they stood by their decision and helped establish the freedom of religion. In the Holy Roman Empire, Charles V agreed to tolerate Lutheranism in 1555 at the Peace of Augsburg. Each state was to take the religion of its prince, but within those states, there was not necessarily religious tolerance. Citizens of other faiths could relocate to a more hospitable environment.

In 1558 the Transylvanian Diet of Turda declared free practice of both the Catholic and Lutheran religions, but prohibited Calvinism. Ten years later, in 1568, the Diet extended the freedom to all religions, declaring that "It is not allowed to anybody to intimidate anybody with captivity or expelling for his religion". The Edict of Turda is considered by mostly Hungarian historians as the first legal guarantee of religious freedom in the Christian Europe. In France, although peace was made between Protestants and Catholics at the Treaty of Saint Germain in 1570, persecution continued, most notably in the Massacre of Saint Bartholomew's Day on August 24, 1572, in which many Protestants throughout France were killed. It was not until the converted Protestant prince Henry IV of France came to the throne that religious tolerance was formalized in the Edict of Nantes in 1598. It would remain in force for over 80 years until its revocation in 1685 by Louis XIV of France. Intolerance remained the norm until the French Revolution, when state religion was abolished and all Church property confiscated.

In 1573 the Warsaw Confederation formalized, in the newly formed Polish-Lithuanian Commonwealth, the freedom of religion that had a long tradition in the Kingdom of Poland. The first extensive Jewish emigration from Western Europe to Poland occurred at the time of the First Crusade in 1098. Under Boleslaus III (1102–1139), the Jews, encouraged by the tolerant régime of this ruler, settled throughout Poland, including over the border into Lithuanian territory as far as Kiev. The Tatars who settled in Lithuania, Ruthenia and modern-day eastern Poland were allowed to preserve their Islamic religion in exchange for military service.

Bohemia (present-day Czech Republic) enjoyed religious freedom between 1436 and 1620, and became one of the most liberal countries of the Christian world during that period of time. The so-called Basel Compacts of 1436 declared the freedom of religion and peace between Catholics and Utraquists. In 1609 Emperor Rudolf II granted Bohemia greater religious liberty with his Letter of Majesty. The privileged position of the Catholic Church in the Czech kingdom was firmly established after the Battle of White Mountain in 1620. Gradually freedom of religion in Bohemian lands came to an end and Protestants fled or were expelled from the country. A devout Catholic,

Emperor Ferdinand II forcibly converted Austrian and Bohemian Protestants.

Some of the early colonies, which were founded as a result of religious persecution, were not tolerant of dissident forms of worship. For example, Roger Williams found it necessary to found a new colony in Rhode Island to escape persecution in the theocratically dominated colony of Massachusetts. It was not until the 18th century that Enlightenment concepts of freedom of individual worship gained ground both in Europe and America. The modern legal concept of religious freedom as the union of *freedom of belief* and *freedom of worship* with the absence of any statesponsored religion, originated in the United States of America.

This issue was addressed by Thomas Paine in his pamphlet, *Common Sense* (1776):

> "As to religion, I hold it to be the indispensable duty of all government, to protect all conscientious professors thereof, and I know of no other business which government hath to do therewith...

The Virginia Statute for Religious Freedom, written in 1779 by Thomas Jefferson, proclaimed:

> "[N]o man shall be compelled to frequent or support any religious worship, place, or ministry whatsoever, nor shall be enforced, restrained, molested, or burthened in his body or goods, nor shall otherwise suffer, on account of his religious opinions or belief; but that all men shall be free to profess, and by argument to maintain, their opinions in matters of religion, and that the same shall in no wise diminish, enlarge, or affect their civil capacities."

Freedom of religion in India is a fundamental right guaranteed by the country's constitution. Every citizen of India has a right to practice and promote their religions peacefully. Freedom of religion in the Indian subcontinent is exemplified by the reign of King Piyadasi (304 B.C to 232

B.C) (Asoka). One of King Asoka's main concerns was to reform governmental institutes and exercise moral principles in his attempt to create a just and humane society. Later he promoted the principles of Buddhism, and the creation of a just, understanding and fair society was held as an important principle for many ancient rulers of this time in the East.

The importance of freedom of worship in India was encapsulated in an inscription of Asoka:

King Piyadasi (Ashok) dear to the Gods, honours all sects, the ascetics (hermits) or those who dwell at home, he honours them with charity and in other ways. But the King, dear to the Gods, attributes less importance to this charity and these honours than to the vow of seeing the reign of virtues, which constitutes the essential part of them. For all these virtues there is a common source, modesty of speech. That is to say, one must not exalt one's creed discrediting all others, nor must one degrade these others without legitimate reasons. One must, on the contrary, render to other creeds the honour befitting them.

Religious freedom and the right to worship freely was a practice that had been appreciated and promoted by most ancient India dynasties. As a result, people fleeing religious persecution in other parts of the world including Christians, Jews and Zoroastrians fled to India as a place of refuge where they could enjoy religious freedom. This had been the underlying attitude of most rulers of India until 1200 AD.

The initial entry of Islam into South Asia came in the first century after the death of the Prophet Muhammad. When around 1210 AD the Islamic Sultanates invaded India from the north-west, gradually the principle of freedom of religion deteriorated in this part of the world. They were subsequently replaced by another Islamic invader in the form of Babur. The Mughal Empire was founded by the Mongol leader Babur in 1526, when he defeated Ibrahim Lodi, the last of the Delhi Sultans at the First Battle of

Panipat. The word "Mughal" is the Indo-Iranian version of Mongol. On the main Asian continent, the Mongols were very tolerant of religions. People could worship as they wished freely and openly.

Contemporary Debates

The contemporary idea of religious freedom as a human right remains a contested topic. The major areas of debate are listed below.

Christianity

The Roman Catholic Church affirmed religious freedom for all in the Second Vatican Council Declaration *Dignitatis Humanae*. This was itself inspired by the work of the Jesuit theologian John Courtney Murray. Some Orthodox Christians, especially those living in democratic countries, support religious freedom for all, as evidenced by the position of the Ecumenical Patriarchate. Many Protestant Christian churches, including some Baptists, Churches of Christ, Seventh-day Adventist Church and main line churches have a commitment to religious freedoms. The Church of Jesus Christ of Latter-Day Saints (Latter-Day Saints) also affirm religious freedom.

However others, such as African scholar Makau Mutua, have argued that Christian insistence on the propagation of their faith to native cultures as an element of religious freedom has resulted in a corresponding denial of religious freedom to native traditions and led to their destruction. As he states in the book produced by the Oslo Coalition on Freedom of Religion or Belief — "Imperial religions have necessarily violated individual conscience and the communal expressions of Africans and their communities by subverting African religions."

In fact, the belief of some Christians that non-Christians need to be converted to Christianity in order to be "saved" may be regarded as an affront to the religious freedom of those who follow other faiths or identify as atheists. Because of this prevalent belief among Christians, Christianity has been said to be inherently counter to religious freedom, and many Christians have denounced this proselytizing aspect of their faith.

Islam

Some Islamic theologians quote the Quran ("There is no compulsion in religion," Sura 2:257, and "Say: O you who reject faith, I do not worship what you worship, nor do you worship what I worship...To you be your religion, and to me be mine," Sura 109:1-6, i.e. Sura Al-Kafirun) to show scriptural support for religious freedom. However, other verses and the Hadith mandate severe treatment for unbelievers, which is reflected in the high levels of intolerance shown in many past and contemporary Islamic societies, and some Muslim scholars, have disagreed with such ill-treatment. In Sura 2:190-194, refers to the bloody war against Pagans, Christians and Jews during the Battle of Badr in Medina, of which it was indicating that Muslims is only allowed to fight against those who intend to harm them (right of self-defense) and that if their enemies surrender, they must also stop because God does not like those who transgress limits.

In Bukhari: V9 N316, Jabir ibn 'Abdullah narrated that a Bedouin accepted Islam and then when he got a fever he demanded that Muhammad to cancel his pledge (allow him to renounce Islam). Muhammad refused to do so. The Bedouin man repeated his demand once, but Muhammad once again refused. Then, he (the Bedouin) left Medina. Muhammad said, "Madinah is like a pair of bellows (furnace): it expels its impurities and brightens and clears its good." In this narration, there was no evidence demonstrating that Muhammad ordered the execution of the Bedouin for wanting to renounce Islam. In addition, in Sura 5:3, which is believed to be God's final revelation to Muhammad, states that Muslims are to fear God and not those who reject Islam, and 53:39 every one is accountable only to one's own actions. Therefore, it postulates that in Islam, in the matters of practising a religion, it does not relate to a worldly punishment, but rather these actions are accountable to God in the afterlife. Thus, this supports the argument against the execution of apostates in Islam.

However, on the other hand, some Muslims support the practice of executing apostates who leave Islam, as in Bukhari: V4 B52 N260; "The Prophet said, 'If a Muslim discards his religion, kill him." In Iran, the constitution recog-nizes four religions whose status is formally protected: Zoroastrianism, Judaism, Christianity, and Islam. The constitution, however, also set the groundwork for the institutionalized persecution of Bahá'ís, who have been subjected to arrests, beatings, executions, confiscation and destruction of property, and the denial of civil rights and liberties, and the denial of access to higher education. In Egypt, a December 16, 2006 judgment of the Supreme Administrative Council created a clear demarcation between recognized religions — Islam, Christianity and Judaism — and all other religious beliefs; no other religious affiliation is officially admissible.

The ruling leaves members of other religious communities, including Bahá'ís, without the ability to obtain the necessary government documents to have rights in their country, essentially denying them of all rights of citizenship. They cannot obtain ID cards, birth certificates, death certificates, marriage or divorce certificates, and passports; they also cannot be employed, educated, treated in public hos-pitals or vote, among other things.

Changing religion

Among the most contentious areas of religious freedom is the "Right to Change" one's religion. Other debates have centered on restricting certain kinds of missionary activity by religions. Many Islamic states, and others such as China, severely restrict missionary activities of other religions. Greece, among European countries, has generally looked unfavorably on missionary activities of denominations others than the majority church and proselytizing is constitutionally prohibited. A different kind of critique of the freedom to propagate religion has come from non-Abrahamic traditions such as the African and Indian. African scholar Makau Mutua criticizes religious evangelism on the ground of cultural annihilation by what he calls "proselytizing universalist faiths."

The (human) rights regime incorrectly assumes a level playing field by requiring that African religions compete in the marketplace of ideas. The rights corpus not only forcibly imposes on African religions the obligation to compete—a task for which as non proselytising, noncom petitive creeds they are not historically fashioned—but also protects the evangelizing religions in their march towards universalisation ... it seems inconceivable that the human rights regime would have intended to protect the right of certain religions to destroy others. Some Indian scholars have similarly argued that the right to propagate religion is not culturally or religiously neutral.

In Sri Lanka there have been debates regarding a bill on religious freedom that seeks to protect indigenous religious traditions from certain kinds of missionary activities. Debates have also occurred in various states of India regarding similar laws, particularly those that restrict conversions using force, fraud or allurement. In 2008 Christian Solidarity Worldwide, a Christian human rights non-governmental organisation which specializes in religious freedom launched an in-depth report on the human rights abuses faced by individuals who leave Islam for another religion.

The report is the product of a year long research project in six different countries. It calls on Muslim nations, the international community, the UN and the international media to resolutely address the serious violations of human rights suffered by apostates.

Secular Law

Religious practice may also conflict with secular law creating debates on religious freedom. For instance, even though polygamy is permitted in Islam it is prohibited in secular law in many Western countries. Does prohibiting polygamy then curtail the religious freedom of Muslims? The USA and India have taken two different views of this. In India polygamy is permitted, but only for Muslims, under Muslim Personal Law. In the USA polygamy is prohibited for all. This was a major source of conflict between the early Mormon Church and the United States until the Church amended its position on polygamy. Similar issues have also arisen in the context of the religious use of psychedelic substances by Native American tribes in the United States as well as other Native practices.

International Law

In international law the freedom of religion and belief is protected by the International Covenant on Civil and Political Rights (ICCPR). This protection extends to specifically non-religious beliefs, such as Humanism. However, minority or disfavored religions still receive the spiritual injustice of persecution in many parts of the world.

Children's Rights

The law in Germany provides the term of "religious majority" (*Religionsmündigkeit*) with a minimum age for minors to follow their own religious beliefs even if their parents don't share those or don't approve. Children 14 and older have the unrestricted right to enter or exit any religious community. Children 12 and older cannot be compelled to change to a different belief. Children 10 and older have to be heard before their parents change their religious upbringing to a different belief. There are similar laws in Austria and in Switzerland.

US foreign relations

The United States formally considers religious freedom in its foreign relations. The International Religious Freedom Act of 1998 established the United States Commission on International Religious Freedom which investigates the records of over 200 other nations with respect to religious freedom, and makes recommendations to submit nations with egregious records to ongoing scrutiny and possible economic sanctions. Many human rights organizations have urged the United States to be still more vigorous in imposing sanctions on countries that do not permit or tolerate religious freedom. Some critics charge that the United States policy on religious freedom is largely directed towards the rights of Christians, particularly the ability for Christian missionaries to evangelize, in other countries.

New Age

The New Age (also known as the New Age Movement and New Age Spirituality) is a decentralized Western social and spiritual movement that seeks "Universal Truth" and the attainment of the highest individual human potential. It combines aspects of cosmology, astrology, esotericism, alternative medicine, music, collectivism, sustainability, and nature. New Age Spirituality is characterized by an individual approach to practices and philosophies, while rejecting religious doctrine and dogma.

The New Age Movement includes elements of older spiritual and religious traditions ranging from atheism and monotheism through classical pantheism, naturalistic pantheism, and panentheism to polytheism combined with science and Gaia philosophy: particularly archaeoastronomy, astronomy, ecology, environmentalism, the Gaia hypothesis, psychology, and physics. New Age practices and philosophies sometimes draw inspiration from major world religions: Buddhism, Chinese folk religion, Christianity, Hinduism, Judaism, and Sufism; with particularly strong influences from East Asian religions, Gnosticism, Neopaganism, New Thought, Spiritualism, Theosophy, Universalism, and Western esotericism. Addi-tional phrases which refer to the New Age Movement include *All is One* and *Mind-Body-Spirit*.

The modern New Age Movement began in the late 1960s and early 1970s, although elements can be traced back to the late 19th and early 20th centuries. It gained momentum in the 1980s and strengthened with the Harmonic Convergence event in 1987. Diverse individuals from around the World practice New Age Spirituality. Some of the New Age Movement's constituent elements appeared initially in 19th century metaphysical movements: Spiritualism, Theosophy, and New Thought; also, alternative medicine movements' chiropractic and naturopathy. These movements in turn have roots in Transcendentalism, Mesmerism, Swedenborgianism, and various earlier Western esoteric or occult traditions, such as the hermetic arts of astrology, magic, alchemy, and kabbalah. Some of the popularisation behind these ideas has roots in the work of early 20th century writers such as D. H. Lawrence and William Butler Yeats.

The first known use of the *New Age* in this context was in Madame Blavatsky's book *The Secret Doctrine,* which was published in 1888. Although, the phrase had been used earlier to refer to a belief in a spiritual and artistic "New Age" by William Blake circa 1809 in his preface to *Milton: a Poem*; it was originally coined by fellow Christian mystic Emanuel Swedenborg in the 18th century. A weekly journal of Christian liberalism and socialism titled *The New Age* was published as early as 1894; it was sold to a group of socialist writers headed by Alfred Richard Orage and Holbrook Jackson in 1907. Other historical personalities were involved: H. G. Wells, George Bernard Shaw, and William Butler Yeats; the magazine became a forum for politics, literature, and the arts. Between 1908 and 1914, it was instrumental in pioneering the British avant-garde from vorticism to imagism.

After 1914, publisher Orage met P. D. Ouspensky, a follower of G. I. Gurdjieff, and began correspondence with Harry Houdini, becoming less interested in literature and art, with an increased focus on mysticism and other spiritual topics; the magazine was sold in 1921. According to Brown University, *The New Age* "helped to shape modernism in literature and the arts from 1907 to 1922." In the early to middle 1900s, American mystic, theologian, and founder of the Association for Research and Enlightenment Edgar Cayce was a seminal influence on what later would be termed the *New Age Movement*; he was known in particular for the practice some refer to as *channeling*. The early New Age Movement in Russia during the 1910s was influenced by Nicholas Roerich and Helena Roerich, who taught in the Theosophical tradition and founded the Agni Yoga Society.

Former Theosophist Rudolf Steiner and his Anthroposophical Movement are a major influence. Neo-Theosophist Alice Bailey published the book *Discipleship in the New Age* (1944), which used the term *New Age* in reference to the transition from the Astrological Age of Pisces to Aquarius. While claims of racial bias in the writings of Rudolf Steiner and Alice Bailey were made, Steiner emphasized racial equality as a principle central to anthroposophical thought and humanity's progress. Any racial elements from these influences have not remained part of the Anthroposophical Society as contemporary adherents of the society have either not adopted or repudiated these beliefs. Another early usage of the term, was by the American artist, mystic, and philosopher Walter Russell, who spoke in an essay of "...this New Age philosophy of the spiritual re-awakening of man...", also published in 1944.

Contemporary Usage

The subculture that would later take on the descriptive term *New Age* already existed in the early 1970s, based on and continuing themes originally present in 1960s counterculture. The Findhorn Foundation – an intentional community near Findhorn, Moray, Scotland founded in 1962 – played an instrumental role during the early growth period of the New Age Movement; it continues to operate the Findhorn Ecovillage. Widespread use of the term *New Age* began in the mid 1970s (reflected in the title of monthly periodical *New Age Journal*) and probably influenced several thousand small metaphysical book and gift stores that increasingly defined themselves as "New Age bookstores". As a result of the large scale activities surrounding the Harmonic Convergence in the mid 1980s – the term was further popularised by the American mass media to describe the alternative spiritual subculture – including practices such as meditation, channeling, crystal healing, astral projection, psychic experience, holistic health, simple living, and environmentalism; or belief in phenomena such as Earth mysteries, ancient astronauts, extraterrestrial life, uniden-tified flying objects, crop circles, and reincarnation.

A range of New Age publications appeared by the late 1980s such as *Psychic Guide* (later renamed *Body, Mind & Spirit*), *Yoga Journal, New Age Voice, New Age Retailer*, and *NaPRA ReView* ("New Age Publishing and Retailers Association"). There were several key moments in raising public awareness of this subculture: the publication of Linda Goodman's best selling astrology books *Sun Signs* (1968) and *Love Signs* (1978); *Hair: The American Tribal Love-Rock Musical* (1967) with the opening song "Aquarius" and its memorable line "*This is the dawning of the Age of Aquarius*" [emphasis added]; the broadcast of Shirley MacLaine's television mini-series *Out on a Limb* (1987); and the Harmonic Convergence (1987) organized by José Argüelles in Sedona, Arizona. Also influential were the claims of channelers Jane Roberts (the Seth Material) and J. Z. Knight (Ramtha), as well as revealed writings *A Course in Miracles* (1976) by Helen Schucman, *The Celestine Prophecy* (1993) by James Redfield, and *Conversations with God* (1995) by Neale Donald Walsch.

Relevant works also include the writings of Eckhart Tolle, Barbara Marx Hubbard, Marianne Williamson, Deepak Chopra, John Holland, Gary Zukav, and Wayne Dyer; also, *The Secret* by Rhonda Byrne, which was based on the writings of Esther Hicks and Jerry Hicks. While authors J. Gordon Melton, Wouter Hanegraaff, and Paul Heelas have emphasised the mentioned personal aspects; Mark Satin, Theodore Roszak, Marilyn Ferguson, and Corinne McLaughlin have described New Age as a values based sociopolitical movement. The American author Ken Wilber posits that much New Age thought falls into what he termed the *pre/trans fallacy*. According to Wilber, human developmental psychology moves from the prepersonal, through the personal, then to the transpersonal (spiritually advanced or enlightened) level. He claims that 80% of New Age Spirituality is prerational (pre-conventional) and relies primarily on mythic-magical thinking—in contrast to post-rational (includes and transcends rational), a genuine world-centric consciousness.

Beliefs

There is no unified belief system, though many practices and philosophies are common in New Age Spirituality:

Terminology:

- Forces

It is commonly held that there exist certain forces, which are independent of spiritual beings or agencies and distinct from forces defined by science, such as gravitation and electromagnetism. These forces are elemental in nature and operate in an automatic manner as part of the natural order; they cause seeds to sprout, grow, and bloom, etc.

- Power

The forces, and everything else, are energized by a mystical power that exists in varying degrees in all things.

Power is transferable, through physical contact, sensory perception, or mere proximity. Power may be accumulated or depleted in a person or object through a variety of mechanisms, including fate and esoteric practices. This power is held to be physically observable as an aura or subtle body and psi energy; and when encountered in great concentration, may even be dangerous.

- Energy

In some belief systems, forces and power may seem to merge, e.g., in the concept of vital force that exists in many traditional belief systems, and finds its expression in New Age concepts such as the energies in Therapeutic Touch or Reiki and ideas of flowing streams of power in the Earth, like Ley lines in Britain and Europe and Earth energies addressed in the Chinese geomantic system of feng shui.

- Spirit

All beings (particularly sentient beings) are accompanied by a specific, intentional energy which corresponds to their consciousness, but is in some way independent of their corporeal existence. This energy typically is more primary than the physical entity, in the sense that it remains in some form after the physical death.

Philosophy and cosmology:

- Theism

There is a general and abstract idea of God, which can be understood in many ways; seen as a superseeding of the need to anthromorphize deity. Not to be confused with pantheism.

- Spiritual beings

Gods, Angels, Ascended Masters, elementals, ghosts, faeries, Spirit guides and Extraterrestrials can spiritually guide us, if we open ourselves to their guidance.

- Afterlife

Consciousness persists after death as life in different

forms; the afterlife exists for further learning through the form of a spirit, reincarnation and/or near-death experiences. There may be a belief in hell, but typically not in the traditional Christian sense or Islamic sense of eternal damnation. Universalist views of the afterlife are common.

- Age of Aquarius

The current time period is claimed by some astrologers to be the dawning of the Age of Aquarius correlated to various changes in the World and some claim that the early 1960s was the actual beginning of the Age of Aquarius, though this claim is highly contentious. Common claims about the developments associated with the Age of Aquarius include, but are not limited to, human rights, democracy, innovative technology, electricity, computers, and aviation. Esoteric claims are that the Age of Aquarius will see a rise in consciousness.

- Astrology

Horoscopes and the Zodiac are used in understanding, interpreting, and organizing information about personality, human affairs, and other terrestrial matters.

- Teleology

Life has a purpose; this includes a belief in synchronicity—that coincidences have spiritual meaning and lessons to teach those whom are open to them. Everything is universally connected through God and participates in the same energy. There is a cosmic goal and a belief that all entities are (knowingly or unknowingly) cooperating towards this goal.

- Indigo children

Children are being born with a more highly developed spiritual power than earlier generations.

- Interpersonal relationships

There are opportunities to learn about one's self and relationships are destined to be repeated until they are healthy.

- Intuition

An important aspect of perception, which has been offset by a somewhat strict rationalism, noted specially in the works of prominent psychologist Jung.

- Optimism

Positive thinking supported by affirmations will achieve success in anything. This is based on the concept that Thought Creates. Therefore, as one begins focusing attention and consciousness on the positive, on the "half-filled" glass of water, reality starts shifting and materializing the positive intentions and aspects of life. A certain critical mass of people with a highly spiritual consciousness will bring about a sudden change in the whole population. Humans have a responsibility to take part in positive creative activity and to work to heal ourselves, each other and the planet.

- Human potential

The human mind has much greater potential than that ascribed to it and is even capable of overriding physical reality.

- Spiritual Healing

Humans have potential healing powers, such as therapeutic touch, which can be developed to heal others through touch or at a distance.

Religion and science:

- Eclectic spirituality

Every person should follow their own individual path to spirituality instead of dogma. Different religions and philosophies from around the World offer different practices that may be adopted. Some adherents of traditional disciplines such as the Lakota people, a tribe of the indigenous peoples of the Americas, reject the term *New Age*. They see the movement it represents as not fully understanding, deliberately trivializing, or distorting their disciplines.

- Anti-Patriarchy

Feminine forms of spirituality, including feminine images of the divine, such as the female Aeon Sophia in Gnosticism, are deprecated by patriarchal religions.

- Ancient civilizations

Atlantis, Lemuria, Mu, and other lost lands existed. Relics such as the crystal skulls and monuments such as Stonehenge and the Great Pyramid of Giza were left behind.

- Psychic perception

Certain geographic locations emanate psychic energy (sometimes through ley lines) and were considered sacred in pagan religions throughout the World.

- Eastern world practices

Meditation, Yoga, Tantra, Chinese medicine, Ayurveda, martial arts, Tai chi chuan, Falun Gong, Qigong, Reflexology, Reiki, and other Eastern practices can assist in realizing one's potential.

- Diet

Food influences both the mind and body; it is generally preferable to practice vegetarianism by eating fresh organic food, which is locally grown and in season. Fasting can help achieve higher levels of consciousness.

- Mathematics

An appeal to the language of nature and mathematics, as evidenced by numerology, Kabbala, Sacred geometry, and gnosticism to discern the nature of God.

- Science

Quantum mechanics, parapsychology, and the Gaia hypothesis have been used in quantum mysticism to validate spiritual principles. Authors Deepak Chopra, Fritjof Capra, Fred Alan Wolf, and Gary Zukav have linked quantum mechanics to New Age Spirituality, which is presented in the film *What the Bleep Do We Know!?* (2004);

also, in connection with the Law of Attraction, which is related to New Thought and presented in the film *The Secret* (2006). They have interpreted the Heisenberg Uncertainty Principle, quantum entanglement, wave function collapse, or the many-worlds interpretation to mean that all objects in the Universe are one (monism), that possibility and existence are endless, and that the physical world is only what one believes it to be.

In medicine, such practices as therapeutic touch, homeopathy, chiropractic, and naturopathy involve hypotheses and treatments that have not been accepted by the conventional, science-based medical community through the normal course of empirical testing.

Lifestyle

New Age Spirituality has led to a wide array of literature on the subject and an active niche market: books, New Age music, crafts, and services in alternative medicine are available at New Age stores, fairs, and festivals. People who embrace New Age lifestyle or beliefs are included in the *Lifestyle of Health and Sustainability* (LOHAS) demographic market segment, currently in a growth phase, related to sustainable living, green ecological initiatives, and generally composed of a relatively affluent and well-educated segment. The LOHAS market segment in 2006 was estimated at $300 billion, approximately 30% of the United States consumer market. According to *The New York Times*, a study by the Natural Marketing Institute showed that in 2000, 68 million Americans were included within the LOHAS demographic. Author Paul H. Ray, who coined the term *Cultural Creatives* in his book *The Cultural Creatives: How 50 Million People Are Changing the World* (2000), states "What you're seeing is a demand for products of equal quality that are also virtuous."

Holistic Health

Practitioners of New Age Spirituality may use alternative medicine in addition to or in place of conventional medicine; while some conventional physicians have adopted aspects or the complete approach of holistic health.

Music

New Age music is peaceful music of various styles, which is intended to create inspiration, relaxation, and positive feelings while listening. Studies have determined that New Age music is an effective component of stress management. Some New Age music albums come with notes to encourage use in meditation. This style began in the 1970s with the works of free-form jazz groups recording on the ECM label; such as Oregon, the Paul Winter Group, and other pre-ambient bands; as well as ambient music performer Brian Eno and classical avant-garde musician Daniel Kobialka. In the early 1970s, it was mostly instrumental with both acoustic and electronic styles. New Age music evolved to include a wide range of styles from electronic space music and acoustic instrumentals using Western instruments to spiritual chanting from other cultures including Native American flutes and drums, synthesizers, and instrumental world music sounds.

Sustainable living

There is an emphasis on living in a simple sustainable way that attempts to reduce an individual's or society's use of the Earth's natural resources and shuns the consumer society.

Social Equality

Social equality is a social state of affairs in which all people within a specific society or isolated group have the same status in a certain respect. At the very least, social equality includes equal rights under the law, such as security, voting rights, freedom of speech and assembly, and the extent of property rights. However, it also includes access to education, health care and other social securities. It also includes equal opportunities and obligations, and so involves the whole society. Social equality requires the lack of legally enforced social class or caste boundaries and the lack of unjustified discrimination motivated by an inalienable part of a person's identity. For example, gender, age, sexual orientation, origin, caste or class, income or property, language, religion, convictions, opinions, health or disability must not result in unequal treatment under the law and should not reduce opportunities unjustifiably.

Social equality, however, does not require communism or income equality. "Equal opportunities" is interpreted as being judged by ability, which is compatible with a freemarket economy. A problem is horizontal inequality, the inequality of two persons of *same* origin and ability. Perfect social equality is an ideal situation that does, for various reasons, not exist in any society in the world today. The reasons for this are widely debated. Reasons cited for social inequality include commonly economics, immigration/emigration, foreign politics and national politics. Also, in complexity economics, it has been found that horizontal inequality arises in complex systems.

A counterexample to social equality was the social inequality of the medieval Europe, where a person's estate, which was usually inherited, determined the legal and social rights the person had. For example, clergy could claim the benefit of clergy to receive a more lenient punishment for a crime. Likewise, women have historically been and still are in some countries formally denied access to higher education—even if they could pay the tuition. In 19th century Europe, women had to apply for an "exemption from gender" to enroll in a university, insofar they could do so. In apartheid-era South Africa, both blacks and whites had formally access to healthcare and similar public services. However, the segregated healthcare arranged for blacks did not meet the same standards as those for whites. That is, there was enforced social inequality.

The colonists in New England and the other 13 colonies enjoyed more social equality than the people in England did. Although they believed that, they also believed that it was only natural to rank people higher than others, by using a social class. The idea of social equality in the minds of the founding generation of America was a belief that the government had the responsibility to protect equal rights, not to provide equal things. However, with the spread of socialism in the 1930s, Americans began to accept new definitions of social equality including right to certain goods and services.

Criticism of Socialist View of Social Equality

One concern about modern socialism is the taxpayersubsidized access to equal things such as health care or education. The problem arises when individual chooses not to use the public service or good, but have to subsidize it nonetheless, thus creating a social imbalance in distribution of goods and services. An example of this is education. The western education systems often provide free public education to all citizens, but it does not provide compensation to those who choose alternative education methods (such as home schooling or private schooling).

Spiritual Evolution

Spiritual evolution is the philosophical, theological, esoteric or spiritual idea that nature and human beings and/ or human culture evolve along a predetermined cosmological pattern or ascent, or in accordance with certain pre-determined potentials. This pre-determinism of evolution concept is also complemented by the idea of a creative im-pulse in human beings, known as epigenesis.

Within this broad definition, theories of spiritual evolution are very diverse. They may be cosmological (describing existence at large), personal (describing the development of the individual), or both. They can be holistic (holding that higher realities emerge from and are not reducible to the lower), idealist (holding that reality is primarily mental or spiritual) or nondual (holding that there is no ultimate distinction between mental and physical reality). All of them can be considered to be teleological to a greater or lesser degree.

Philosophers, scientists, and educators that have proposed theories of spiritual evolution include Nader Angha, Schelling, Hegel, Max Théon, Henri Bergson, Sri Aurobindo, Jean Gebser, Pierre Teilhard de Chardin, Arthur M. Young, Edward Haskell, E. F. Schumacher, Erich Jantsch, Clare W. Graves, Alfred North Whitehead, Terrence McKenna, P.R. Sarkar, and Ken Wilber. These theorists tend (for the most part) to be non-materialistic or non-reductionistic.

Precursors to the Idea

The cyclic cosmos

Mircea Eliade has suggested that in many pre-modern cultures one finds the concept of the Fall and a "nostalgia for paradise". However for those cultures that have a cyclic cosmology, the concept of a progressive deterioration of the universe (as in the Hesiodic, Hindu, and Lurianic cosmologies of degradation from a Golden Age to an Iron Age or Kali Yuga) might be balanced by a corresponding ascent to more spiritual stages and a return to paradisical conditions. This is what one finds in Buddhist and especially Jain cosmologies.

Emanation

Many premodern cosmologies and esoteric systems of thought are based on an emanationist view of reality. If the Cyclic view is temporal, then emanation is a non-temporal precursor to the theory of spiritual evolution. According to this paradigm, Creation proceeds as an outpouring or even a transformation in the original Absolute or Godhead. The Supreme Light or Consciousness descends through a series of stages, gradations, worlds or hypostases, becoming progressively more material and embodied, before finally turning around to return to the One, retracing its steps through spiritual knowledge, contemplation and ascent.

A supreme example of this form of thinking is the Neoplatonism of Plotinus and his successors. Other examples and interpretations might be found in Kashmir Shaivism and Tantra in general, Gnosticism, Sufism, and Kabbalah. The Hindu idea of the Chakras might also considered here as the "microcosmic" counterpart of macrocosmic involution and evolution (the Yogi raises the Kundalini or life force through and thus transcends each chakra in turn, until he reaches the crown chakra and liberation (Avalon).

Samkhya

An early example of the doctrine of spiritual evolution is found in Samkhya, a teaching that goes back more than two and a half thousand years (although its present form dates to around the 4th or 5th century CE.). Unlike classic Hinduism, the traditional Samkhyan philosophy is atheistic and dualistic. Pure spirit (called *purusha*) comes into proximity with *prakriti* (psychophysical nature), disturbing its equilibrium.

As a result the original root-prakriti (*mulaprakriti*) undergoes a series of progressive transformations or unfoldings, in the form of successive essences called *tattvas*. The most subtle tattwas emerge first, then progressively grosser ones, each in a particular order, and finally the elements and the organs of sense. The goal of evolution however is, paradoxically, the release of prurusha and the return to the unmanifest condition. Hence everything is tending towards a goal of spiritual quiescence.

The Great Chain of Being

The concept of the great chain of being developed by Plato and Aristotle were taken up and synthesised by

Plotinus. Plotinus in turn heavily influenced Augustine's theology, and from there Aquinas and the Scholastics. The Great Chain of Being was an important theme in Renaissance and Elizabethan thought, had an underacknowledged influence on the shaping of the ideas of the Enligh-tenment and played a large part in the worldview of 18th century Europe. And while essentially a static world-view, by the 18th and early 19th century it had been "tem-poralized" by the concept of the soul ascending or pro-gres-sing spiritually through the successive rungs or stages, and thus growing or evolving closer to God.

It also had at this time an impact on theories of biological evolution. E. F. Schumacher, author of *Small is Beau-tiful*, has recently proposed a sort of simplified Great Chain of Being, based on the idea of four "kingdoms" (mineral, vegetable, animal, and human). Schumacher rejects modernist and scientific themes, his approach recalling the universalist orientation of writers like Huston Smith, and quite likely contributing to (unless the latter developed his ideas completely independently) Ken Wilber's "holonomic" hierarchy or "Great Nest of Being".

German Idealism

Occult Concepts

Theories of spiritual evolution are important in many Occult and Esoteric teachings, which emphasise the progression and development of the individual either after death (spiritualism) or through successive reincarnations (Theosophy, Hermeticism).

Spiritualism

In the 19th century Anglo-American Spiritualist ideas emphasize the progression of the soul after death to higher states of existence, in contrast to the French and Brazilian Spiritualism of Allan Kardec, which admits reincarnation.

The Anglo-American position recalls (and is presumably inspired by) 18th century concepts regarding the temporalization of The Great Chain of Being. Spiritual evolution, rather than being a physical (or physico-spiritual) process is based on the idea of realms or stages through which the soul or spirit passes in a non-temporal, qualitative way. This is still an important part of some spiritualist ideas today, and is similar to some mainline (as opposed to fundamentalist) Protestant Christian beliefs, according to which after death the person goes to "a better place" or "heaven" (in English Spiritualism, Summerland).

Theosophical Conceptions

Theosophy presents a more sophisticated and complex cosmology than Spiritualism, although coming out of the same general milieu. H. P. Blavatsky developed a highly original cosmology, according to which the human race (both collectively and through the succession of individual reincarnation and spiritual evolution) passes through a number of Root Races, beginning with the huge ethereal and mindless Polarian or First Root Race, through the Lemurian (3rd), Atlantean (4th) and our present "Aryan" 5th Race. This will give rise to a future, Post-Aryan 6th Root Race of highly spiritual and enlightened beings, and an even more sublime 7th Root Race, before ascending to totally superhuman and cosmic states of existence.

Blavatsky's ideas were further developed by her successors, such as C.W. Leadbeater, Rudolf Steiner, and Alice Bailey, each of whom went into huge detail in constructing baroque cycles of rounds, races, and sub-races. Although including elements of the science of her day as well as both eastern and western esoteric thought, Blavatsky rejected the Darwinian idea that man evolved from apes, and most subsequent esotericists followed this lead. Darwinism, with its explanation of evolution through material factors like natural selection and random mutation, does not sit well with many spiritual evolutionists, for whom evolution is initiated or guided by metaphysical principles or is tending towards a final spiritual or divine state.

Despite this, Theosophists and Anthroposophists have tried to incorporate the facts of geology and paleontology into their cosmology and spiritual evolution (in Anthroposophy Hermann Poppelbaum is a particularly creative thinker in this regard). Some have attempted to equate Lemuria with Gondwanaland, for example. Today all these ideas have little influence outside their specialised followings, but for a time Theosophical concepts were immensely influential.

Theurgy

Theurgy has a clear relationship to neo-Platonism and Kabbalah and contains the concept of spiritual evolution and ultimately unification with God or the Godhead at its core. Theurgy is considered by many to be another term for high magic and is known to have influenced the members of the Hermetic Order of the Golden Dawn many of whom considered the order to be Theurgic in nature. Aleister Crowley also considered his Thelemic system of magical philosophy to be a Theurgic tradition as it emphasized the Great Work, which is essentially another form of spiritual evolution. The Great Work is believed to result in communication with one's personal angel or higher self.

Epigenesis

Epigenesis is the philosophical/theological/esoteric idea that since the mind was given to the human being, it is the original creative impulse, epigenesis, which has been the cause of all of mankind's development. According to spiritual evolution, humans build upon that which has already been created, but add new elements because of the activity of the spirit. Humans have the capacity, therefore, to become creative intelligences—creators. For a human to fulfill this promise, his training should allow for the exercise of originality, which distinguishes creation from imitation. When epigenesis becomes inactive, in the individual or even in a race, evolution ceases and degeneration commences.

This concept is based on the Rosicrucian view of the world as a training school, which posits that while mistakes are made in life, humans often learn more from mistakes than successes. Suffering is considered as merely the result of error, and the impact of suffering on the consciousness causes humans to be active along other lines which are found to be good, in harmony with nature. Humans are seen as spirits attending the school of life for the purpose of unfolding latent spiritual power, developing themselves from *impotence* to omnipotence (related also to development from innocence into virtue), reaching the stage of creative gods at the end of mankind's present evolution: *Great Day of Manifestation*.

Evolution towards Godhead

A Common Vision

Sri Aurobindo and Pierre Teilhard de Chardin both describe a progression from inanimate matter to a future state of Divine consciousness. Teilhard de Chardin refers to this as the Omega Point, and Sri Aurobindo as the Supermind.

Teilhard de Chardin

Teilhard, who was a Jesuit Paleontologist who played an important role in the discovery of Peking Man, presented a teleological view of planetary and cosmic evolution, according to which the formation of atoms, molecules and inanimate matter is followed by the development of the biosphere and organic evolution, then the appearance of man and the noosphere as the total envelope of human thought. According to Teilhard evolution does not cease here but continues on to its culmination and unification in the Omega Point, which he identifies with Christ.

Surat Shabda Yoga

Surat Shabda Yoga esoteric cosmology depicts the whole of creation (the macrocosm) as being emanated and arranged in a spiritually differentiated hierarchy, often referred to as eggs, regions, or planes. Typically, eight spiritual levels are described above the physical plane, although names and subdivisions within these levels will vary to some extent by mission and Master. (One version of the creation from a Surat Shabda Yoga perspective is depicted at the Sant Ajaib Singh Ji Memorial Site in "The Grand Scheme of All Creation".) The constitution of the individual (the microcosm) is an exact replica of the macrocosm. Consequently, the microcosm consists of a number of bodies, each one suited to interact with its corresponding plane or region in the macrocosm. These bodies developed over the yugas through involution (emanating from higher planes to lower planes) and evolution (returning from lower planes to higher planes), including by karma and reincarnation in various states of consciousness.

Dynamic Evolution through Successive Kingdoms

Arthur M. Young and Edward Haskell have each independently incorporated the findings of science into a larger theory of spiritual evolution, and extended the traditional human, animal, vegetable, and mineral categories with kingdoms representing photons, atoms and molecules. Arthur M. Young goes further in considering the human state as a subset of a larger kingdom of "Dominion", of which the sixth stage is represented for example by Christ and Buddha, and the seventh (final) stage an even higher level of Enlightenment or God-realisation.

Moreover, both Haskell and Young present profound accounts of evolution through these kingdoms in terms of cybernetic principles. A more "mainstream" scientific presentation of this same idea is provided by Erich Jantsch in his consummate account of how self-organising systems evolve and develop as a series of "symmetry breaks" through the sequence of matter, life, and mind. Although abiding strictly by the understanding of science, Jantsch arranges the various elements of cosmic, planetary, biological, psychological, and human evolution in a single overall framework of emergent evolution that may or may not be considered teleological.

New Age Ideas

New Age thought is strongly syncretic and based on a superficial but creative interpretation of previous spiritual and esoteric traditions, especially Eastern thought, Theosophy, and popular (mis)interpretations of science. A common theme is the evolution or the transcendence of the human or collective planetary consciousness in a higher state or higher "vibratory" (a metaphor taken from G. I. Gurdjieff) level. Among the better thinkings of the "New Age", David Spangler's communications speak of a "New Heaven and a new Earth", while Christopher Hills refers (perhaps influenced by Sri Aurobindo) to the divinization of man.

Jonathan Livingston Seagull narrated the idea of evolution in a fascinating fashion. James Redfield in his novel *The Celestine Prophecy* suggested that through experiencing a series of personal spiritual insights, humanity is becoming aware of the connection between our evolution and the Divine. More recently in his book *God and the Evolving Universe: The Next Step in Personal Evolution* (2002) cowritten with Michael Murphy, he claims that humanity is on the verge of undergoing a change in consciousness.

Integral Theory and Spiral Dynamics

An interpretation of social and psychological development that could also be considered a theory of spiritual evolution is spiral dynamics, based on the work of Clare W. Graves. More recently the concept of spiritual evolution has been given a sort of respectability it has not had since the early 19th century through the work of Ken Wilber, in whose writings both the cosmological and the personal dimensions are described. In this integral philosophy (inspired in part by the works of Plotinus, Hegel, Sri Aurobindo, Eric Jantsch, and many others) reality is said to consist of several realms or stages, including more than one of the following: the physical, the vital, the psychic, (after the Greek *psyche*, "soul"), the causal (referring to "that which causes, or gives rise to, the manifest world"), and the ultimate (or non-dual), through which the individual progressively evolves.

Although this schema is derived in large part from Tibetan Buddhism, Wilber argues (and uses many tables of diagrams to show) that these same levels of being are common to all wisdom teachings. Described simplistically, Wilber sees humans developing through several stages, including magic, mythic, pluralistic, and holistic mentalities. But he also sees cultures as developing through these stages. And, much like Hegel, he sees this development of individuals and cultures *as* the evolution of existence itself. Wilber has also teamed up with Don Beck to integrate Spiral Dynamics into his own Integral philosophy, and vice versa.

Sociological Classifications of Religious movements

Sociologists have proposed various classifications of religious movements. The most widely used classification in the sociology of religion is the church-sect typology. The typology states that churches, ecclesia, denominations, and sects form a continuum with decreasing influence on society. Sects are break away groups and tend to be in tension with society. Cults and new religious movements fall outside this continuum and in contrast to aforementioned groups often have a novel teaching. Cults and new religious movements have been classified on their attitude towards society and the level of involvement of their adherents.

The Church-sect Typology

This church-sect typology has its origins in the work of Max Weber. The basic idea is that there is a continuum along which religions fall, ranging from the protest-like orientation of *sects* to the equilibrium maintaining *churches*. Along this continuum are several additional types, each of which will be discussed in turn. The reader may notice that many of labels for the types of religion are commonly employed by non-sociologists to refer to religions and tend to be used interchangeably. Sociologists, when speaking technically, will not use these labels interchangeably as they are designations for religions with very specific characteristics.

Before describing these different religions, it is important for the reader to understand that these classifications are a good example of what sociologists refer to as *ideal types*. Ideal types are *pure* examples of the categories. Because there is significant variation in each religion, how closely an individual religion actually adheres to their *ideal type* classification will vary. Even so, the classification scheme is useful as it also outlines a sort of developmental process for religions.

Church and Ecclesia

The *church* classification describes religions that are all-embracing of religious expression in a society. Religions of this type are the guardians of religion for all members of the societies in which they are located and tolerate no religious competition. They also strive to provide an allencompassing worldview for their adherents and are typically enmeshed with the political and economic structures of society.

Johnstone (1997) provides the following seven characteristics of churches:

1. Claim universality, include all members of the society within their ranks, and have a strong tendency to equate "citizenship" with "membership".
2. Exercise religious monopoly and try to eliminate religious competition.
3. Are very closely allied with the state and secular powers frequently there is overlapping of responsibilities and much mutual reinforcement.
4. Are extensively organized as a hierarchical bureaucratic institution with a complex division of labor.
5. Employ professional, full-time clergy who possess the appropriate credentials of education and formal ordination.
6. Primarily gain new members through natural reproduction and the socialization of children into the ranks.
7. Allow for diversity by creating different groups within the church (e.g., orders of nuns or monks) rather than through the formation of new religions.

The classical example of a *church* is the Roman Catholic Church, especially in the past. Today, the Roman Catholic Church has been forced into the denomination category because of religious pluralism or competition among religions. This is especially true of Catholicism in the United States. The change from a *church* to a *denomination* is still under way in many Latin American countries where the majority of citizens remain Catholics. A slight modification of the *church* type is that of *ecclesia* (von Wiese 1932). Ecclesias include the above characteristics of churches with the exception that they are generally less successful at garnering absolute adherence among all of the members of the society and are not the sole religious body. The state churches of some European countries would fit this type.

Denominations

The *denomination* lies between the church and the sect on the continuum. Denominations come into existence when churches lose their religious monopoly in a society. A denomination is one religion among many. When churches and/or sects become denominations, there are also some changes in their characteristics. Johnstone provides the following eight characteristics of denominations:

1. Similar to churches, but unlike sects, in being on relatively good terms with the state and secular powers and may even attempt to influence government at times.
2. Maintain at least tolerant and usually fairly friendly relationships with other denominations in a context of religious pluralism.
3. Rely primarily on birth for membership increase, though it will also accept converts; some actively pursue evangelization.
4. Accept the principle of at least modestly changing doctrine and practice and tolerate some theological diversity and dispute.
5. Follow a fairly routinized ritual and worship service that explicitly discourages spontaneous emotional expression.
6. Train and employ professional clergy who must meet formal requirements for certification.
7. Accept less extensive involvement from members than do sects, but more involvement than churches.
8. Often draw disproportionately from the middle and upper classes of society.

Most of the major Christian bodies in the world are denominations (e.g., Baptists, Methodists, Lutherans, and Seventh-day Adventists).

Sects

Sects are newly formed religious groups that form to protest elements of their parent religion (generally a denomination). Their motivation tends to be situated in accusations of apostasy or heresy in the parent denomination; they are often decrying liberal trends in denominational development and advocating a return to *true* religion. Leaders of sectarian movements (i.e., the formation of a new sect) tend to come from a lower socio-economic class than the members of the parent denomination, a component of sect development that is not entirely understood. Most scholars believe that when sect formation does involve social class distinctions they involve an attempt to compensate for deficiencies in lower social status.

An often seen result of such factors is the incorporation into the theology of the new sect distaste for the adornments of the wealthy (e.g., jewelry or other signs of wealth). After their formation, sects can take only three paths - dissolution, institutionalization, or eventual development into a denomination. If the sect withers in membership, it will dissolve. If the membership increases, the sect is forced to adopt the characteristics of denominations in order to maintain order (e.g., bureaucracy, explicit doctrine, etc.). And even if the membership does not grow or grows slowly, norms will develop to govern group activities and behavior. The development of norms results in a decrease in spontaneity, which is often one of the primary attractions of sects.

The adoption of denomination-like characteristics can either turn the sect into a full-blown denomination or, if a conscious effort is made to maintain some of the spontaneity and protest components of sects, an *institutionalized sect* can result. Institutionalized sects are halfway between sects and denominations on the continuum of religious development. They have a mixture of sect-like and denomination like characteristics. Examples include: Hutterites, Jehovah's Witnesses, and the Amish. Most of the well-known denominations of the U.S. existing today originated as sects breaking away from denominations (or Churches, in the case of Lutheranism and Anglicanism). Examples include: Methodists, Baptists, and Seventh-day Adventists.

Cults or New Religious Movements

Cults are, like sects, new religious groups. But, unlike sects, they can form without breaking off from another religious group (though they often do). The characteristic that most distinguishes cults from sects is that they are not advocating a return to *pure* religion but rather the embracement of something new or something that has been completely lost or forgotten (e.g., lost scripture or new prophecy). Cults are also more likely to be led by *charismatic leaders* than are other religious groups and the charismatic leaders tend to be the individuals who bring forth the new or lost component that is the focal element of the cult (e.g., The Book of Mormon).

Cults, like sects, often integrate elements of existing religious theologies, but cults tend to create more esoteric theologies from many sources. Cults emphasize the individual and individual peace. Cults also tend to attract the socially disenchanted or unattached. Cults tend to be located in urban centers where they can draw upon large populations for membership. Finally, cults tend to be transitory as they often dissolve upon the death or discrediting of their founder and charismatic leader.

Cults, like sects, can develop into denominations. As cults grow, they bureaucratize and develop many of the characteristics of denominations. Some scholars are hesitant to grant cults denominational status because many cults maintain their more esoteric characteristics (e.g., Temple Attendance among Mormons). But given their closer semblance to denominations than to the *cult* type, it is more accurate to describe them as denominations. Some denominations in the U.S. that began as cults include: Mormons or The Church of Jesus Christ of Latter-day Saints, Christian Science, and The Nation of Islam.

Finally, it should be noted that there is a push in the social scientific study of religion to begin referring to *cults* as *New Religious Movements* or *NRMs*. The reasoning behind this is because *cult* has made its way into popular language as a derogatory label rather than as a specific type of religious group. Most religious people would do well to remember the social scientific meaning of the word *cult* and, in most cases, realize that three of the major world religions originated as cults in terms of Church-sect typology, including Islam, Christianity, and Buddhism.

Criticisms

The religious scholar John A. Saliba notes the many attempts to draw a classification or typology of cults and/or sects, but concludes that the divergences that exist in these groups' practices, doctrines, and goals do not lend themselves to a simple classification that has universal approval. He argues that the influx of Eastern religious systems (which do not fit within the traditional distinctions between church, sect, denomination and cult) have compounded classificatory difficulties.

Wallis' Distinction between Cults and Sects

The sociologist Roy Wallis (1945 - 1990) introduced differing definitions of sects and cults. He argued that a cult is characterized by "epistemological individualism" by which he means that "the cult has no clear locus of final authority beyond the individual member." Cults, according to Wallis, are generally described as "oriented towards the problems of individuals, loosely structured, tolerant, non-exclusive", making "few demands on members", without possessing a "clear distinction between members and non-members", having "a rapid turnover of membership", and are transient collectives with vague boundaries and fluctuating belief systems Wallis asserts that cults emerge from the "cultic milieu". Wallis contrast a cult with a sect that he asserts are characterized by "epistemological authoritarianism": sects possess some authoritative locus for the legitimate attribution of heresy. According to Wallis, "sects lay a claim to possess unique and privileged access to the truth or salvation and their committed adherents typically regard all those outside the confines of the collectivity as 'in error'".

Cult and/or New Religious Movements

Stark and Bainbridge

The sociologists Rodney Stark and William Sims Bainbridge (1985) distinguish three types of cults, classified on the basis of the levels of organizational and client (or adherent) involvement:

1. Audience cults, that have hardly any organization because participants/consumers lack significant involvement.
2. Client cults, in which the service-providers exhibit a degree of organization in contrast to their clients. Client cults link into moderate-commitment social networks through which people exchange goods and services. The relationship between clients and the leaders of cults resembles that of patients and therapists.
3. Cult movements, which seek to provide services that meet all of adherents' spiritual needs (although they differ significantly in the degree to which they use mobilize adherents' time and commitment).

The sociologist Paul Schnabel has argued that the Church of Scientology originated from an *audience cult*

(Hubbard's books) and a *client cult* (Dianetics the org) to a cult movement.

Roy Wallis

The sociologist Roy Wallis introduced a classification-system of new religious movements based on movements' views on and relationships with the world at large.

- World-rejecting movements view the prevailing social order as having departed from God's prescriptions and from the divine plan. Such movements see the world as evil, or at least as materialistic. They may show millenarian tendencies. ISKCON, the Unification Church and the Children of God exemplify world rejecting movements.
- World-accommodating movements draw clear distinctions between the spiritual and the worldly spheres. They have few or no consequences for the lives of adherents. These movements thus adapt to the world, but they do not reject or affirm it.
- World-affirming movements may have no rituals and no official ideology. They may lack most of the characteristics of religious movements. They affirm the world and merely claim that they have the means to enable people to unlock their "hidden potential". As examples of world-affirming movements, Wallis mentions Erhard Seminars Training and Transcendental Meditation.

Psychology of Religion

Psychology of religion is the psychological study of religious experiences, beliefs, and activities.

William James

U.S. psychologist and philosopher William James (1842-1910) is regarded by most psychologists of religion as the founder of the field. He served as president of the *American Psychological Association,* and wrote one of the first psychology textbooks. In the psychology of religion, James' influence endures. His *Varieties of Religious Experience* is considered to be the classic work in the field, and references to James' ideas are common at professional conferences. James distinguished between institutional religion and personal religion. Institutional religion refers to the religious group or organization, and plays an important part in a society's culture. Personal religion, in which the individual has mystical experience, can be experienced regardless of the culture. James was most interested in understanding personal religious experience. The importance of James to the psychology of religion - and to psychology more generally - is difficult to overstate. He discussed many essential issues that remain of vital concern today.

In studying personal religious experiences, James made a distinction between *healthy-minded* and *sick-souled* religiousness. Individuals predisposed to healthy mindedness tend to ignore the evil in the world and focus on the positive and the good. James used examples of Walt Whitman and the "mind-cure" religious movement to illustrate healthy-mindedness in *The Varieties of Religious Experience*. In contrast, individuals predisposed to having a sick-souled religion are unable to ignore evil and suffering, and need a unifying experience, religious or otherwise, to reconcile good and evil. James included quotations from Leo Tolstoy and John Bunyan to illustrate the sick soul. William James' hypothesis of pragmatism stems from the efficacy of religion. If an individual believes in and performs religious activities, and those actions happen to work, then that practice appears the proper choice for the individual. However, if the processes of religion have little efficacy, then there is no rationality for continuing the practice.

Sigmund Freud

Sigmund Freud (1856-1939) gave explanations of the genesis of religion in his various writings. In *Totem and Taboo,* he applied the idea of the Oedipus complex (involving unresolved sexual feelings of, for example, a son toward his mother and hostility toward his father) and postulated its emergence in the primordial stage of human development. In *Moses and Monotheism,* Freud reconstructed biblical history in accordance with his general theory. His ideas were also developed in *The Future of an Illusion*. When Freud spoke of religion as an illusion, he maintained that it *is a fantasy structure from which a man must be set free if he is to grow to maturity*. Freud views the idea of God as being a version of the father image, and religious belief as at bottom infantile and neurotic. Authoritarian religion is dysfunctional and alienates man from himself.

Carl Jung

The Swiss psychoanalyst Carl Jung (1875-1961) adopted a very different posture, one that was more sympathetic to religion and more concerned with a positive appreciation of religious symbolism. Jung considered the question of the existence of God to be unanswerable by the psychologist and adopted a kind of agnosticism. Jung postulated, in addition to the personal unconscious (roughly adopting Freud's concept), the collective unconscious, which is the repository of human experience and which contains "archetypes" (i.e. basic images that are universal in that they recur regardless of culture). The irruption of these images from the unconscious into the realm of consciousness he viewed as the basis of religious experience and often of artistic creativity. Some of Jung's writings have been devoted to elucidating some of the archetypal symbols, and include his work in comparative mythology.

Jung had a very broad view of what it means to be empirical. Suppose, for example, that I hear a voice from a deity but you do not, even though we are sitting next to each other. If only one person experiences something, for Jung it is an empirical observation. For most contemporary scientists, however, it would not be considered an empirical observation. Because of this, there has been little research in the psychology of religion from a Jungian perspective.

Alfred Adler

Austrian psychiatrist Alfred Adler (1870-1937), who parted ways with Freud, emphasised the role of goals and motivation in his *Individual Psychology*. One of Adler's most famous ideas is that we try to compensate for inferiorities that we perceive in ourselves. A lack of power often lies at the root of feelings of inferiority. One way that religion enters into this picture is through our beliefs in God, which are characteristic of our tendency to strive for perfection and superiority. For example, in many religions God is con-sidered to be perfect and omnipotent, and commands people likewise to be perfect. If we, too, achieve perfection, we become one with God. By identifying with God in this way, we compensate for our imperfections and feelings of inferiority.

Our ideas about God are important indicators of how we view the world. According to Adler, these ideas have changed over time, as our vision of the world - and our place in it - has changed. Consider this example that Adler offers: the traditional belief that people were placed deliberately on earth as God's ultimate creation is being replaced with the idea that people have evolved by natural selection. This coincides with a view of God not as a real being, but as an abstract representation of nature's forces. In this way our view of God has changed from one that was concrete and specific to one that is more general. From Adler's vantage point, this is a relatively ineffective perception of God because it is so general that it fails to convey a strong sense of direction and purpose.

An important thing for Adler is that God (or the idea of God) motivates people to act, and that those actions do have real consequences for us and for others. Our view of God is important because it embodies our goals and directs our social interactions. Compared to science, another social movement, religion is more efficient because it motivates people more effectively. According to Adler, only when science begins to capture the same religious fervour, and promotes the welfare of all segments of society, will the two be more equal in peoples' eyes.

Gordon Allport

In his classic book *The Individual and His Religion* (1950), Gordon Allport (1897-1967) illustrates how people may use religion in different ways. He makes a distinction between *mature religion* and *immature religion*. Mature religious sentiment is how Allport characterized the person whose approach to religion is dynamic, open-minded, and able to maintain links between inconsistencies. In contrast, immature religion is self-serving and generally represents the negative stereotypes that people have about religion. More recently, this distinction has been encapsulated in the terms "intrinsic religion", referring to a genuine, heartfelt devout faith, and "extrinsic religion", referring to a more utilitarian use of religion as a means to an end, such as church atten-dance to gain social status. These dimensions of religion were measured on the Religious Orientation Scale of Allport and Ross (1967).

A third form of religious orientation has been described by Daniel Batson. This refers to treatment of religion as an open-ended search. More specifically, it has been seen by Batson as comprising a willingness to view religious doubts in a positive manner, acceptance that religious orientation can change and existential complexity, the belief that one's religious beliefs should be shaped from personal crises that one has experienced in one's life. Batson refers to extrinsic, intrinsic and quest respectively as Religion-as-means, religion-as-end and religion-as-quest, and measures these constructs on the Religious Life Inventory.

Erik H. Erikson

Erik Erikson (1902-94) is best known for his theory of

psychological development, which has its roots in the psychoanalytic importance of identity in personality. His biographies of Gandhi and Martin Luther reveal Erikson's positive view of religion. He considered religions to be important influences in successful personality development because they are the primary way that cultures promote the virtues associated with each stage of life. Religious rituals facilitate this development. Erikson's theory has not benefited from systematic empirical study, but it remains an influential and well-regarded theory in the psychological study of religion.

Erich Fromm

The American scholar Erich Fromm (1900-1980) modified Freudian theory and produced a more complex account of the functions of religion. Part of the modification is viewing the Oedipus complex as based not so much on sexuality as on a "much more profound desire", namely, the childish desire to remain attached to protecting figures. The right religion, in Fromm's estimation, can, in principle, foster an individual's highest potentialities, but religion in practice tends to relapse into being neurotic.

According to Erich Fromm, humans have a need for a stable frame of reference. Religion apparently fills this need. In effect, humans crave answers to questions that no other source of knowledge has an answer to, which only religion may seem to answer. However, a sense of free will must be given in order for religion to appear healthy. An authoritarian notion of religion appears detrimental.

Rudolf Otto

Rudolf Otto (1869-1937) was a German Protestant theologian and scholar of comparative religion. Otto's most famous work, *The Idea of the Holy* (published first in 1917 as *Das Heilige*), defines the concept of the holy as that which is *numinous*. Otto explained the numinous as a "non-rational, non-sensory experience or feeling whose primary and immediate object is outside the self." It is a mystery (Latin: *mysterium tremendum*) that is both fascinating (*fascinans*) and terrifying at the same time; A mystery that causes trembling and fascination, attempting to explain that inexpressible and perhaps supernatural emotional reaction of wonder drawing us to seemingly ordinary and/or religious experiences of grace.

This sense of emotional wonder appears evident at the root of all religious experiences. Through this emotional wonder, we suspend our rational mind for non-rational possibilities. It also sets a paradigm for the study of religion that focuses on the need to realise the religious as a nonreducible, original category in its own right. This paradigm was under much attack between approximately 1950 and 1990 but has made a strong comeback since then.

Psychometric Approaches to Religion

Since the 1960s psychologists of religion have used the methodology of psychometrics to assess different ways in which a person may be religious. An example is the Religious Orientation Scale of Allport and Ross, which measures how respondents stand on intrinsic and extrinsic religion as described by Allport. More recent questionnaires include the Religious Life Inventory of Batson, Schoenrade and Ventis, and the Age-Universal I-E Scale of Gorsuch and Venable. The former assesses where people stand on three distinct forms of religious orientation - religion as means, religion as end, and religion as quest. The latter assesses Spiritual Support and Spiritual Openness.

Religious Orientations and Religious Dimensions

Some questionnaires, such as the Religious Orientation Scale, relate to different religious orientations, such as intrinsic and extrinsic religiousness, referring to different motivations for religious allegiance. A rather different approach, taken, for example, by Glock and Stark (1965), has been to list different dimensions of religion rather than different religious orientations, which relates to how an individual may manifest different forms of being religious. Glock and Stark's famous typology described five dimensions of religion - the doctrinal, the intellectual, the ethicalconsequential, the ritual, and the experiential.

In later work these authors subdivided the ritual dimension into devotional and public ritual, and also clarified that their distinction of religion along multiple dimensions was not identical to distinguishing religious orientations. Al-though some psychologists of religion have found it helpful to take a multidimensional approach to religion for the purpose of psychometric scale design, there has been, as Wulff (1997) explains, considerable controversy about whether religion should really be seen as multi-dimensional.

Questionnaires to assess religious experience

What we call religious experiences can differ greatly. Some reports exist of supernatural happenings that it would be difficult to explain from a rational, scientific point of view. On the other hand, there also exist the sort of testimonies that simply seem to convey a feeling of peace or oneness - something which most of us, religious or not, may possibly relate to. In categorizing religious experiences it is perhaps helpful to look at them as explicable through one of two theories: the Objectivist thesis or the Subjectivist thesis.

An objectivist would argue that the religious experience is a proof of God's existence. However, others have criticised the reliability of religious experiences. The English philosopher Thomas Hobbes asked how it was possible to tell the difference between talking to God in a dream, and drea-ming about talking to God. The Subjectivist view argues that it is not necessary to think of religious experiences as evidence for the existence of an actual being that we call God. From this point of view, the important thing is the experience itself and the effect that it has on the individual.

4

The Developmental Approaches to Religion and Science

Developmental Approaches to Religion

Attempts have been made to apply stage models, such as that of Jean Piaget and Lawrence Kohlberg, to how children develop ideas about God and about religion in general. By far the most well-known stage model of spiritual or religious development is that of James W. Fowler, a developmental psychologist at the Candler School of Theology, in his *Stages of Faith*. He follows Piaget and Kohlberg and has proposed a staged development of faith (or spiritual development) across the lifespan in terms of a holistic orientation, and is concerned with the individual's relatedness to the universal.

The book-length study contains a framework and ideas considered by many to be insightful and which have generated a good deal of response from those interested in religion, so it appears to have at least a reasonable degree of face validity. James Fowler proposes six stages of faith development as follows:

1. Intuitive-projective
2. Symbolic Literal

3. Synthetic Conventional
4. Individuating
5. Paradoxical (conjunctive)
6. Universalising

Although there is evidence that children up to the age of twelve years do tend to be in the first two of these stages, there is evidence that adults over the age of sixty-one do show considerable variation in displays of qualities of Stages 3 and beyond. Fowler's model has generated some empirical studies, and fuller descriptions of this research (and of these six stages) can be found in Wulff (1991). However, this model has been attacked from a standpoint of scientific research due to methodological weaknesses. Of Fowler's six stages, only the first two found empirical support, and these were heavily based upon Piaget's stages of cognitive development.

The tables and graphs in the book were presented in such a way that the last four stages appeared to be validated, but the requirements of statistical verification of the stages did not come close to having been met. The study was not published in a journal, so was not peer-reviewed, and never drew much attention from psychologists. Other critics of Fowler have questioned whether his ordering of the stages really reflects his own commitment to a rather liberal Chris-tian Protestant outlook, as if to say that people who adopt a similar viewpoint to Fowler are at higher stages of faith development. Nevertheless, the concepts Fowler introduced seemed to hit home with those in the circles of academic religion, and have been an important starting point for various theories and subsequent studies. A recent contributor here has put forward a stage model, Vicky Genia.

Religion and Coping with Stress

Psychologists of religion have looked at how individuals may use religion as a resource in coping with stress. A major contributor to this theory is Kenneth Pargament, whose work shows the influence of attribution theory. Pargament has distinguished styles of coping into the *deferring*, in which people leave God to see to their problems; the *non-religious*, in which they do not appeal to God; and the *collaborative*, in which people believe that a co-operation of God and their own efforts are necessary to help them to cope with stress. Some of Pargament's papers have been published in the *Journal for the Scientific Study of Religion*.

Religion and Health

There is considerable literature on the relationship between religion and health. Psychologists consider that there are various ways in which religion may benefit both physical and mental health, including encouraging healthy lifestyles such as abstinence from tobacco, providing social support networks and encouraging an optimistic outlook on life; prayer and meditation may also help to benefit physiological functioning. The journal "American Psychologist" published important papers on this topic in 2003. Haber, Jacob and Spangler have considered how different dimensions of religiosity may relate to health benefits in different ways.

Evolutionary Psychology of Religion

Evolutionary psychology is based on the hypothesis that, just like hearts, lungs, livers, kidneys, and immune systems, cognition has functional structure that has a genetic basis, and therefore evolved by natural selection. Like other organs and tissues, this functional structure should be universally shared amongst humans and should solve important problems of survival and reproduction. Evolutionary psychologists seek to understand cognitive processes by understanding the survival and reproductive functions they might serve.

Pascal Boyer is one of the leading figures in the cognitive psychology of religion, a new field of inquiry that is less than fifteen years old, which accounts for the psycho-logical processes that underlie religious thought and practice. In his book *Religion Explained*, Boyer shows that there is no simple explanation for religious consciousness. Boyer is mainly concerned with explaining the various psychological processes involved in the acquisition and transmission of ideas concerning the gods. Boyer builds on the ideas of cognitive anthropologists Dan Sperber and Scott Atran, who first argued that religious cognition represents a by product of various evolutionary adaptations, including folk psychology, and purposeful violations of innate expectations about how the world is constructed (for example, bodiless beings with thoughts and emotions) that make religious cognitions striking and memorable.

Religious persons acquire religious ideas and practices through social exposure. The child of a Zen Buddhist will not become an evangelical Christian or a Zulu warrior without the relevant cultural experience. While mere exposure does not cause a particular religious outlook (a person may have been raised a Roman Catholic but leave the church), nevertheless some exposure seems required - this person will never invent Roman Catholicism out of thin air. Boyer says cognitive science can help us to understand the psychological mechanisms that account for these manifest correlations and in so doing enable us to better understand the nature of religious belief and practice. To the extent that the mechanisms controlling the acquisitions and transmission of religious concepts rely on human brains, the mechanisms are open to computational analysis. All thought is computationally structured, including religious thought. So presumably, computational approaches can shed light on the nature and scope of religious cognition.

Boyer moves outside the leading currents in mainstream cognitive psychology and suggests that we can use evolutionary biology to unravel the relevant mental architecture. Our brains are, after all, biological objects, and the best naturalistic account of design in nature is Darwin's theory of evolution. To the extent that mental architecture exhibits intricate design, it is plausible to think that the design is the result of evolutionary processes working over vast periods of time. Like all biological systems, the mind is optimised to promote survival and reproduction in the evolutionary environment. On this view all specialised cognitive functions broadly serve those reproductive ends. For Steven Pinker the universal propensity toward religious belief is a genuine scientific puzzle. He thinks that adaptationist explanations for religion do not meet the criteria for adaptations. An alternative explanation is that religious psychology is a by-product of many parts of the mind that evolved for other purposes.

Religion and Drugs

The American psychologist James H. Leuba (1868-1946), in *A Psychological Study of Religion*, accounts for mystical experience psychologically and physiologically, pointing to analogies with certain drug-induced experiences. Leuba argued forcibly for a naturalistic treatment of religion, which he considered to be necessary if religious psychology were to be looked at scientifically. Shamans all over the world and in different cultures have traditionally used drugs, especially psychedelics, for their religious experiences. In these communities the absorption of drugs leads to dreams (visions) through sensory distortion.

William James was also interested in mystical experiences from a drug-induced perspective, leading him to make some experiments with nitrous oxide and even peyote. He concludes that while the revelations of the mystic hold true, they hold true only for the mystic; for others they are certainly ideas to be considered, but hold no claim to truth without personal experience of such.

Drug-induced Religious Experiences

The drugs used by religious communities for their hallucinogenic effects were adopted for explicit and implicit religious functions and purposes. The drugs were and are reported to enhance religious experience through visions and a distortion of the sensory perception (like in dreams in a state of sleep).

- *Cannabis*, which grows all over the world except in very cold climates, is used in religious practices in Indian and African communities.
- Certain psychedelic mushrooms are used by Indians in Latin America, especially in the state of Oaxaca in southern Mexico. The chief species is *Psilocybe mexicana*, of which the active principles are psilocin and its derivative psilocybin, in their chemical composition and activity not unlike LSD (D-lysergic acid diethylamide); the latter is synthesized from the alkaloids (principally ergotamine and ergonovine) that are constituents of ergot, a growth present in grasses affected by the disease also called ergot. *Amanita muscaria* (fly agaric) is another mushroom having hallucinogenic properties that has not been thoroughly studied. It may be extremely important, since it may have been the natural source of the ritual soma drink of the ancient Hindus and the comparable haoma used by the Zoroastrians (although other sources point toward ephedra as the main ingredient of Soma). Fly agaric is mildly toxic at high dosages and is said to have, in addition to its hallucinogenic properties, the ability to increase strength and endurance. It is said also to be a soporific.
- *Peyote* used by some Indian communities of Mexico. The chief active principle of peyote is an alkaloid called mescaline. Like psilocin and psilocybin, mescaline is reputed to produce visions and other evidences of a mystical nature. Despite claims of missionaries and some government agents that peyote - from the Nahuatl word *peyotl* ("divine messenger") - is a degenerative and dangerous drug, there appears to be

no evidence of this among the members of the Native American Church, a North American Indian cult that uses peyote in its chief religious ceremony. Peyote, like most other hallucinogenic drugs, is not considered to be addictive and, far from being a destructive influence, is reputed by cultists and some observers to promote morality and ethical behaviour among the Indians who use it ritually.

- *Ayahuasca, caapi,* or *yajé,* is produced from the stem bark of the vines *Banisteriopsis caapi* and *B. inebrians.* Indians who use it claim that its virtues include healing powers and the power to induce clairvoyance, among others. This drink has been certified by investigators to produce remarkable effects, often involving the sensation of flying. The effects are thought to be attributable to the action of harmine, a very stable indole that is the active principle in the plant. While the Indians themselves attribute the properties of the drink Ayahuasca to *B. caapi,* this is not the common scientific view; the MAOIs present in the *B. caapi* instead allow the extremely psychedelic ingredients in other plants added to the brew, noticeably plants containing DMT, to be activated and produce an intense experience.
- *Kava* drink, prepared from the roots of *Piper methysticum,* a species of pepper, and seemingly more of a hypnotic-narcotic than a hallucinogen, is used both socially and ritually in the South Pacific, especially in Polynesia.
- *Iboga,* a stimulant and hallucinogen derived from the root bark of the African shrub Tabernanthe iboga is used within the Bwiti religion in Central Africa. The active ingredient in T. iboga is ibogaine, a drug that has been studied for its use in treating addiction.
- *Coca,* source of cocaine, has had both ritual and social use chiefly in Peru.

- *Datura*, one species of which is the jimsonweed, is used by native peoples in North and South America; the active principle, however, is highly toxic and dangerous. A drink prepared from the shrub *Mimosa hostilis*, which is said to produce glorious visions in warriors before battle, is used ritually in the ajuca ceremony of the Jurema cult in eastern Brazil.
- *Salvia divinorum*, a member of the sage family of plants, is a hallucinogen used by Mazatec shamans for "spiritual journeys" during healing.

The Effects of Meditation

The large variety of meditation techniques shares the common goal of shifting attention away from habitual or customary modes of thinking and perception, in order to permit experiencing in a different way. Many religious and spiritual traditions that employ meditation assert that the world most of us know is an illusion. This illusion is said to be created by our habitual mode of separating, classifying and labelling our perceptual experiences. Meditation is *empirical* in that it involves direct experience. Though, it is also *subjective* in that the meditative state can be directly known only by the experiencer and may be difficult or impossible to fully describe in words. Concentrative meditation can induce an altered state of consciousness characterised by a loss of awareness of extraneous stimuli, one-pointed attention to the meditation object to the exclusion of all other thoughts, and feelings of bliss.

Relationship between Religion and Science

The relationship between religion and science has been a focus of the Demarcation problem. Statements about the world made by science and religion rely on different methodologies. Religions rely on revelation while science relies on observable, repeatable experiences. Some scholars say the two are separate, as in John William Draper's conflict thesis and Stephen Jay Gould's non-overlapping magisteria, while others (Thomas Berry, Brian Swimme, Ken Wilber, et al.) propose an interconnection. The Pew Forum has published data on attitudes to religion and science.

Perspectives on the Relationship

The kinds of interactions that might arise between science and religion have been classified using the following typology:

1. Conflict when either discipline threatens to take over the legitimate concerns of the other.
   - For example, John William Draper and Andrew Dickson White's conflict thesis
2. Independence treating each as quite separate realms of enquiry.
   - For example, Steven Jay Gould's NOMA
3. Dialogue suggesting that each field has things to say to each other about phenomena in which their interests overlap.
   - For example, William G. Pollard's studies in *Physicist and Christian: A dialogue between the communities.*
4. Integration aiming to unify both fields into a single discourse.
   - For example, Pierre Teilhard de Chardin's Omega point and Ian Barbour's sympathy towards process philosophy/process theology.

This typology is similar to ones found in Ian Barbour and John Haught. More typologies that categorize this relationship can be found among the works of other science and religion scholars such as Arthur Peacocke.

Conflict

Conflict Thesis

The conflict thesis view was popularized in the 19th century by John William Draper and Andrew Dickson White. Most contemporary historians of science now reject it, considering that the conflict thesis has been superseded by subsequent historical research:

Although popular images of controversy continue to exemplify the supposed hostility of Christianity to new scientific theories, studies have shown that Christianity has often nurtured and encouraged scientific endeavour, while at other times the two have co-existed without either tension or attempts at harmonization. If Galileo and the Scopes trial come to mind as examples of conflict, they were the exceptions rather than the rule. Today, much of the scholarship in which the conflict thesis was based is considered to be inaccurate. For instance, the claim that people of the Middle Ages widely believed that the Earth was flat was first propagated in the same period that originated the conflict thesis and is still very common in popular culture.

This claim is mistaken, as the contemporary historians of science David C. Lindberg and Ronald L. Numbers write: "there was scarcely a Christian scholar of the Middle Ages who did not acknowledge [Earth's] sphericity and even know its approximate circumference." Other misconceptions such as: "the Church prohibited autopsies and dissections during the Middle Ages", "the rise of Christianity killed off ancient science", and "the medieval Christian church suppressed the growth of the natural sciences", are all reported by Numbers as examples of widely popular myths that still pass as historical truth, even though they are not supported by current historical research. They help maintain the popular image of "the warfare of science and religion".

While H. Floris Cohen states that most scholars reject crude articulations of the conflict thesis, such as Andrew D. White's, he also states that milder versions of this thesis still hold some sway. This is because "it remains an incontrovertible fact of history that, to say the least, the new science was accorded a less than enthusiastic acclaim by many religious authorities at the time." Cohen therefore considers it paradoxical "that the rise of early modern science was due at least in part to developments in Christian thought — in particular, to certain aspects of Protestantism" (a thesis first developed as what is now known as the Merton thesis).

A tight review of alternatives to the White/Draper conflict thesis has been composed by Ian G. Barbour, "Ways of relating science and theology" in *Physics, philosophy, and theology: a common quest for understanding*.

Independence

A modern view, described by Stephen Jay Gould as "non-overlapping magisteria" (NOMA), is that science and religion deal with fundamentally separate aspects of human experience and so, when each stays within its own domain, they co-exist peacefully. Gould's view can also be seen as an attitude of neglect towards religion. It has been compared with a similar attitude of neglect towards evolutionary science, which has been seen in the works of theologians Karl Barth (who fails to mention evolution in his major work *Church Dogmatics*), Emil Brunner, and Hans Kung (whose *Theology for the Third Millennium* (1988) has a chapter on the relationship between religion and science yet never mentions evolution).

Two Takes on Experience

Both science and religion represent distinct ways of approaching experience and these differences are sources of debate. Science is closely tied to mathematics—a very abstract experience, while religion is more closely tied to the ordinary experience of life. As interpretations of experience, science is descriptive and religion is prescriptive. For science and mathematics to concentrate on what the world *ought to be* like in the way that religion does can be inappropriate and may lead to improperly ascribing properties to the natural world as happened among the followers of Pythagoras in the sixth century B.C.

The reverse situation where religion attempts to be descriptive can also lead to inappropriately assigning properties to the natural world. A notable example is the now defunct belief in the Ptolemy planetary model that held sway until changes in scientific and religious thinking were brought about by Galileo and proponents of his views.

Parallels in Method

Many language philosophers (e.g., Ludwig Wittgenstein) and religious existentialists (e.g., those who ascribe to neo-orthodoxy) accepted Ian Barbour and John Polkinghorne's type II categorization of Independence. On the other hand, many philosophers of science have thought otherwise. Thomas S. Kuhn asserted that science is made up of paradigms that arise from cultural traditions, which is similar to the secular perspective on religion. Michael Polanyi asserted that it is merely a commitment to universality that protects against subjectivity and has nothing at all to do with personal detachment as found in many conceptions of the scientific method. Polayni further asserted that all knowledge is personal and therefore the scientist must be performing a very personal if not necessarily subjective role when doing science.

Polanyi added that the scientist often merely follows intuitions of "intellectual beauty, symmetry, and 'empirical agreement'". Polayni held that science requires moral commitments similar to those found in religion. Two physicists Charles A. Coulson and Harold K. Schilling both claimed that *"the methods of science and religion have much in common."* Schilling asserted that both fields—science and religion—have "a threefold structure—of experience, theoretical interpretation, and practical application." Coulson asserted that science like religion "advances by creative imagination" and not by "mere collecting of facts," while stating that religion should and does "involve critical reflection on experience not unlike that which goes on in science." Religious language and scientific language also show parallels (cf. Rhetoric of science).

Dialogue

A degree of concord between science and religion can be seen in religious belief and empirical science. The belief that God created the world and therefore humans, can lead to the view that he arranged for humans to know the world. This is underwritten by the doctrine of imago dei. In the words of Thomas Aquinas, "Since human beings are said to be in the image of God in virtue of their having a nature that includes an intellect, such a nature is most in the image of God in virtue of being most able to imitate God". Many well-known historical figures who influenced Western science considered themselves Christian such as Copernicus, Galileo, Kepler, and Boyle.

Concerns over the Nature of Reality

Science in the Enlightenment and Colonial eras was conceived as ontological investigation which uncovered 'facts' about physical nature. This was often explicitly opposed to Christian Theology and the latter's assertions of truth based on doctrine. This particular perspective on science faded in the early 20th century with the decline of Logical Empiricism and the rise of linguistic and sociological understandings of science. Modern scientists are less concerned with establishing universal or ontological truth (which is seen, and dismissed, as the pursuit of philosophy), and more inclined towards the creation of pragmatic, functional models of physical systems.

Christian Theology - excluding those fundamentalist churches whose aim is to reassert doctrinal truths - has likewise softened many of its ontological claims, due to increased exposure to both scientific insights and the contrasting theological claims of other faiths. Scientific and theological perspectives often coexist peacefully. Non-Christian faiths have historically integrated well with scientific ideas, as in the ancient Egyptian technological mastery applied to monotheistic ends, the flourishing of logic and mathematics under Hinduism and Buddhism, and the scientific advances made by Muslim scholars during the Ottoman Empire. Even many 19th century Christian communities welcomed scientists who claimed that science was not at all concerned with discovering the ultimate nature of reality.

Integration

Christianity and Science

The reconciliation of Christianity with science has had at least three attempted solutions that have proven themselves quite problematic. These three problematic solutions are biblical literalism, religious experience, and the evolving consensus of scientific truth. Each of these methods of reconciliation has various historical and present day examples. Respective examples include creationism, liberal christianity, and scientific imperialism. Earlier attempts at reconciliation of Christianity with Newtonian mechanics appear quite different from later attempts at reconciliation with the newer scientific ideas of evolution or relativity. Many early interpretations of evolution polarized themselves around a *struggle for existence.*

These ideas were significantly countered by later findings of universal patterns of biological cooperation. According to John Habgood, all man really knows here is that the universe seems to be a mix of good and evil, beauty and pain, and that suffering may somehow be part of the process of creation.

Habgood holds that Christians should not be surprised that suffering may be used creatively by God, given their faith in the symbol of the Cross. Habgood states that Christians have for two millennia believed in the love of God because he revealed "Himself as Love in Jesus Christ," not because the physical universe does or does not point to the value of love.

Reconciliation in Britain in the early 20th Century

In *Reconciling Science and Religion: The Debate in Early twentieth-century Britain*, historian of biology Peter J. Bowler argues that in contrast to the conflicts between science and religion in the U.S. in the 1920s (most famously the Scopes Trial), during this period Great Britain experienced a concerted effort at reconciliation, championed by intellectually conservative scientists, supported by liberal theologians but opposed by younger scientists and secularists and conservative Christians. These attempts at reconciliation fell apart in the 1930s due to increased social tensions, moves towards Neo-orthodox Theology and the acceptance of the modern evolutionary synthesis.

Buddhism

In Buddhism, the Kalama Sutta precludes the use of numerous non-systematic methods and sources, including authority, common sense, opinions, tradition, and scripture.

Bahá'í View

A fundamental principle of the Bahá'í Faith is the harmony of religion and science. Bahá'í scripture asserts that true science and true religion can never be in conflict. 'Abdu'l-Bahá, the son of the founder of the religion, stated that religion without science is superstition and that science without religion is materialism. He also admonished that true religion must conform to the conclusions of science.

Current Scholarship

The modern dialogue between religion and science is rooted in Ian Barbour's 1966 book *Issues in Science and Religion*. Since that time it has grown in to a serious academic field, with academic chairs in the subject area, and two dedicated academic journals, *Zygon: Journal of Religion & Science* and Theology and Science. Articles are also sometimes found in mainstream science journals such as American Journal of Physics and Science.

Biblical World View on Early Modern Science

In *The Scientific Revolution: A Historiographical Inquiry* historian of science H. Floris Cohen presents scholarship arguing for a Biblical influence on the early development of modern science. Cohen presents Dutch historian R. Hooykaas' argument that a Biblical world-view holds all the necessary antidotes for the hubris of Greek rationalism: a respect for manual labour, leading to experimentation and a greater level of empiricism and a supreme God that left nature "de-deified" and open to emulation and manipulation. This argument gives support to the idea that the rise of early modern science was due to a unique combination of Greek and biblical thought.

Cohen summarises Hooykaas' conclusion as attributing the rise of modern science to the combination of the "Greek powers of abstract reasoning and of thinking up idealized constructions" in combination with "the biblical humility toward accepting the facts of nature as they are, combined with a view of man as fitted out by God with the power to take nature on".

Cohen also notes that Richard S. Westfall "brought out the ultimate paradox" in stating:

Despite the natural piety of the virtuosi [English 17th-century scientists], the skepticism of the Enlightenment was already present in embryo among them. To be sure, their piety kept it in check, but they were unable to banish it. ... They wrote to refute atheism, but where were the atheists? The virtuosi nourished the atheists within their own minds.

Historian and professor of religion Eugene M Klaaren hold that "a belief in divine creation" was central to an emergence of science in seventeenth-century England. The philosopher Michael Foster has published influential analytical philosophy connecting Christian doctrines of creation with empiricism. Historian William B. Ashworth has argued against the historical notion of distinctive mindsets and the idea of Catholic and Protestant sciences in "Catholicism and early modern science." Historians James R. Jacob and Margaret C. Jacob have published the paper "The Anglican Origins of Modern Science," which endeavors to show a linkage between seventeenth century Anglican intellectual transformations and influential English scientists (e.g., Robert Boyle and Isaac Newton).

Two well-respected theological surveys, which also cover additional interactions occurring in the 18th, 19th, and 20th centuries, are John Dillenberger's *Protestant Thought and Natural Science* (Doubleday, 1960) and Christopher B. Kaiser's *Creation and the History of Science* (Eerdmans, 1991).

When natural philosophers referred to *laws* of nature, they were not glibly choosing that metaphor. Laws were the result of legislation by an intelligent deity. Thus the philosopher Rene Descartes (1596-1650) insisted that he was discovering the "laws that God has put into nature." Later Newton would declare that the regulation of the solar system presupposed the "counsel and dominion of an intelligent and powerful Being.

Historian Ronald L. Numbers has stated that this thesis "received a boost" from mathematician and philosopher Alfred North Whitehead's *Science and the Modern World* (1925). Numbers has also claimed "Despite the manifest shortcomings of the claim that Christianity gave birth to science—most glaringly, it ignores or minimizes the contributions of ancient Greeks and medieval Muslims—it too, refuses to succumb to the death it deserves. The sociologist Rodney Stark at Baylor University, a Southern Baptist institution, is only the latest in a long line of Christian apologists to insist that 'Christian theology was essential for the rise of science.'"

Religious Community's Perspective

Historical Judeo-Christian-Islamic view

In the Medieval era, some leading thinkers in Judaism, Christianity and Islam, undertook a project of synthesis between religion, philosophy, and natural sciences. For example, the Islamic philosopher Averroes, the Jewish philosopher Maimonides, and the Christian philosopher Augustine of Hippo, held that if religious teachings were found to contradict certain direct observations about the natural world, then it would be obligatory to re-evaluate either the interpretation of the scientific facts or the understanding of the scriptures. The best knowledge of the cosmos was seen as an important part of arriving at a better understanding of the Bible, but not yet equal with the authority of the Bible.

This approach has continued down to the present day; Henry Drummond, for example, was a 19th century Scot who wrote many articles, some of which drew on scientific knowledge to tease out and illustrate Christian ideas. From the 11th century, however, scientific methods were being applied by both Muslim scientists and Christian scientists to domains such as optics and planetary orbits, with results which threatened some of the Church's doctrines. Christianity asserted religious certainty at the expense of scientific knowledge, by giving more explicit sanction to officially correct views of nature and scripture.

Similar developments occurred in other religions. This approach, while it tended to temporarily stabilize doctrine, was also inclined toward making philosophical and scientific orthodoxy less open to correction, as accepted philosophy became the religiously sanctioned science. Observation and theory became subordinate to dogma. In Europe, scientists and scholars of the Enlightenment responded to such restrictions with increasing skepticism.

Non-fundamentalist Religious Views

A great many Christians and Jews still accept some or many traditional religious beliefs taught in their respective faith communities, but they no longer accept their tradition's teachings as unquestionable and infallible (indeed this is a basic tenet of mainstream Protestant Christian thought and of other faith perspectives open to dialogue with science). Liberal religious believers do believe in god, and believe that in some way their god revealed their will to humanity. They differ from religious fundamentalists in that they accept that even if their religious texts were divinely inspired, they are also human documents which reflect the cultural and historic limitations and biases of their authors.

Many support allegorical interpretations of Genesis. Such believers are often comfortable with the findings of archaeological and linguistic research and historical-critical study. They will often make use of literary and historical analysis of religious texts to understand how they developed, and to see how they might be applied in our own day. This approach developed among Protestant scholars in the 18th and 19th centuries, and is now found among other Christians, Liberal Jewish communities and others.

Some religious approaches acknowledge the historical relationship between modern science and ancient doctrines. For example, John Paul II, leader of the Roman Catholic Church, in 1981 spoke of the relationship this way: "The Bible itself speaks to us of the origin of the universe and its make-up, not in order to provide us with a scientific treatise, but in order to state the correct relationships of man with God and with the universe. Sacred Scripture wishes simply to declare that the world was created by God, and in order to teach this truth it expresses itself in the terms of the cosmology in use at the time of the writer". This statement would reflect the views of many non-Catholic Christians as well. An example of this kind of thinking is Theistic evolution. This understanding of the role of scripture in relation to science is captured by the phrase: "The intention of the Holy Spirit is to teach us how to go to heaven, not how the heavens go." Thomas Jay Oord said: "The Bible tells us how to find abundant life, not the details of how life became abundant."

The Scientific Community's Perspective

The Attitudes of Scientists towards Religion

In the 17th century, founders of the Royal Society largely held conventional and orthodox religious views, and a number of them were prominent Churchmen. While theological issues that had the potential to be divisive were typically excluded from formal discussions of the early Society, many of its fellows nonetheless believed that their scientific activities provided support for traditional religious belief. Clerical involvement in the Royal Society remained high until the mid-nineteenth century, when science became more professionalised.

Among contemporary scientists—physicists and biologists—about 40% hold strong religious beliefs, which closely matched those of a similar 1916 poll. Prominent scientists advocating disbelief in religion include evolutionary biologist Richard Dawkins and Nobel Prize winning physicist Stephen Weinberg. Prominent scientists advocating belief include Nobel Prize winning physicist Charles Townes and climatologist John T. Houghton.

According to a 1996 survey, belief in a god that is "in intellectual and affective communication with humankind" and belief in "personal immortality" are most popular among mathematicians and least popular among biologists. In total, about 60% of scientists in the United States expressed disbelief or doubt in such a god. This compared with 58% in 1914 and 67% in 1933. Among leading scientists defined as members of the National Academy of Sciences, 72.2% expressed disbelief and 93% expressed disbelief or doubt in the existence of a personal god in 1998.

A survey conducted between 2005 and 2007 by Elaine Ecklund of University at Buffalo, The State University of New York and funded by the Templeton Foundation found that over 60% of natural and social science professors are atheists or agnostics. When asked whether they believed in God, nearly 34% answered "I do not believe in God" and about 30% answering "I do not know if there is a God and there is no way to find out," According to the same survey, "[m]any scientists see themselves as having a spirituality not attached to a particular religious tradition." In further analysis, published in 2007, Ecklund and Christopher Scheitle conclude that "the assumption that becoming a scientist necessarily leads to loss of religion is untenable" and that "it appears that those from non-religious backgrounds disproportionately self-select into scientific professions. This may reflect the fact that there is tension between the religious tenets of some groups and the theories and methods of particular sciences and it contributes to the large number of non-religious scientists."

A explanation has been offered by Farr Curlin, a University of Chicago Instructor in Medicine and a member of the MacLean Center for Clinical Medical Ethics, that science-minded religious people instead elect to study medicine. He helped author a study that "found that 76 percent of doctors believe in God and 59 percent believe in some sort of afterlife." and "90 percent of doctors in the United States attend religious services at least occasionally, compared to 81 percent of all adults." He reasoned, "The responsibility to care for those who are suffering and the rewards of helping those in need resonate throughout most religious traditions."

Prominent scientist Albert Einstein supported the compatibility of religion and science. In an article originally appearing in the New York Times Magazine in 1930, he wrote:

Accordingly, a religious person is devout in the sense that he has no doubt of the significance and loftiness of those super personal objects and goals which neither require nor are capable of rational foundation. They exist with the same necessity and matter-of-factness as he himself. In this sense religion is the age-old endeavor of mankind to become clearly and completely conscious of these values and goals and constantly to strengthen and extend their effect. If one conceives of religion and science according to these definitions then a conflict between them appears impossible. For science can only ascertain what is, but not what should be, and outside of its domain value judgments of all kinds remain necessary. Religion, on the other hand, deals only with evaluations of human thought and action: it cannot justifiably speak of facts and relationships between facts. According to this interpretation the well-known conflicts between religion and science in the past must all be ascribed to a misapprehension of the situation which has been described.

Scientific Study of Religion

Scientific studies have been done on religiosity as a social or psychological phenomenon. These include studies on the correlation between religiosity and intelligence (often IQ, but also other factors). A recent study on serotonin receptors and religiosity suggests a correlation between low density of serotonin receptors and intense religious experiences. Also of popular interest are the studies regarding prayer and medicine, in particular whether there is any causal or correlative link between spiritual supplication and improvement of health. Surveys by Gallup, the National Opinion Research Centre and the Pew Organisation conclude that spiritually committed people are twice as likely to report being "very happy" than the least religiously committed people.

An analysis of over 200 social studies that "high religiousness predicts a rather lower risk of depression and drug abuse and fewer suicide attempts, and more reports of satisfaction with life and a sense of well-being" and a review of 498 studies published in peer-reviewed journals concluded that a large majority of these studies showed a positive correlation between religious commitment and higher levels of perceived well-being and self-esteem, and lower levels of hypertension, depression and clinical delinquency, Surveys suggest a strong link between faith and altruism. Studies by Keith Ward show that overall religion is a positive contributor to mental health. Michael Argyle and others claim that there is little or no evidence that religion ever causes mental disorders.

Other studies have showed that certain mental disorders, such as schizophrenia and obsessive-compulsive disorder, are also associated with high levels of religiosity. In addition, anti-psychotic medication, which is mainly aimed to block dopamine receptors, typically reduces religious behaviour and religious delusions. Some historians, philosophers and scientists hope that the theory of memetics, reminiscent of the theory of genetics, will allow the modeling of the evolution of human culture, including the evolutionary origin of religions. Daniel Dennett's book *Breaking the Spell* (2006) attempts to begin such an analysis of modern religions. The idea that evolutionary processes are involved in the development of human culture and religion is not particularly controversial among natural scientists, however other approaches based on social sciences such as anthropology, psychology, sociology and economics are more prevalent in academic use.

Religion and Science Community

The *religion and science community* consists of those scholars who involve themselves with what has been called the "religion-and-science dialogue" or the "religion-and science field." The community belongs to neither the scientific nor the religious community, but is said to be a third overlapping community of interested and involved scientists, priests, clergymen, and theologians. Institutions interested in the intersection between science and religion include the Center for Theology and the Natural Sciences, the Institute on Religion in an Age of Science, and the Faraday Institute. Journals addressing the relationship between science and religion include Theology and Science and Zygon: Journal of Religion & Science.

Institute on Religion in an Age of Science

The Institute on Religion in an Age of Science (IRAS) is a non-denominational society that promotes and facilitates the ongoing dialectic between religion and science. Both members of IRAS and non-members congregate at the IRAS conference held annually at Star Island in New Hampshire. IRAS evolved from the ideas of two pioneer groups. The first was a group of scientists from the Committee on Science and Values of the American Academy of Arts and Sciences. The second group was an interfaith, religious coalition which hoped to revitalize religion for today's needs. Members of both groups saw the, at times, battlefield of conflicting ideologies of religion and science as a place of opportunity for a constructive relationship to emerge.

In 1954 the scientists accepted an invitation to present their views to the religious group at a seven-day conference on Religion in an Age of Science on Star Island. The 1 October issue of Science reported on the conference:

> *Ten scientists explained how they thought scientific and religious knowledge could be integrated... While there were a number of both scientists and clergy who held that religious truth was hardly susceptible of being approached by scientific beliefs, there was a strong recognition that today we can increase the scope and validity of our understanding of our destiny and*

our relationship to that "in which we live and move and have our being," not only by reading ancient texts, but also by building up the science of theology in harmony with other science.

On November 9, 1954, members of the two groups established the Institute on Religion in an Age of Science to work toward these goals.

5

Religion and Monarchy
Study of the Relationship

The Constitution of Nepal 1990, on the basis of which the country is currently governed, defines the kingdom as a multiethnic, multilingual, democratic, independent, indivisible, sovereign, Hindu and Constitutional Monarchial Kingdom. According to the current constitutional provision, 'Hindu' is a core attribute of the kingdom. This provision, however, has not been accepted by all sections of society and remains controversial. There are some who argue for retaining the relationship between the state and Hinduism, while there are others who argue against it and demand that the state be declared secular.

While proponents of the former argue for retaining the relationship to safeguard the identity of Nepal as the 'only Hindu kingdom in the world' and to stem the tide of conversion to other religions, the proponents of the latter argue that by associating the state with Hinduism, all other religions are discriminated by the state. In the debate between secularism versus Hinduism in Nepal, the experiences of countries such as France, United States, Turkey and India have often served as points of reference while other countries with monarchial forms of government, and ones with which Nepal shares some commonality as far as state structures are concerned, have not (Sharma, forthcoming). For instance, the relationship between the state and religion in the United Kingdom, which recognizes the Anglican Church as the official church and where the monarch is both the head of the state as well as the head of the church, but where the state at large is secular, does not inform the current debate in Nepal.

In the debate on Hinduism and secularism and the question of the monarchy's relationship with organized religion, the experiences of Thailand would be of even greater relevance than those of countries like the United Kingdom. Thailand, like Nepal, is an Asian country that has a monarchial form of government. More importantly, it has not succumbed to colonial rule. This in turn means that there has been no rupture between polity and religion as has been evinced in many other Asian countries which have experienced colonial rule. Moreover, it also means that there has been continuity in tradition, though traditions, in turn, have been adapted and improvised to suit modern times. There is still another similarity: the dynasty that rules modern Thailand and one that rules modern Nepal began roughly from the same period which is the late eighteenth century. Lastly, both polities existed up to the present times through skillful negotiations first with colonial powers and subsequently with popular forces.

Aside from questions of secularism and religious tolerance, additional information on the role of the Thai monarchy in modernizing Thai society, ensures the consolidation of democratic rule in the country, while simultaneously maintaining stability would be of relevance for the Nepali public. The present Thai monarch, though not actively engaged in politics, enjoys wide popularity among the Thai public, while the beleaguered monarch in Nepal does not. Thus additional explorations on the Thai monarchy, aside from the question of the relationship between the polity and religion, would be interesting to a country that would like to see the consolidation of constitutional monarchy and parliamentary democracy.

The broad objective is to examine the relationship between kingship and religion in contemporary Buddhist and Hindu societies with particular reference to Thailand and Nepal. The specific objectives of the research project are as follows:

1. To describe how Buddhist and Hindu religious texts envisage kingship.
2. To examine the historical relationship between kingship, on the one hand, and Buddhist and Hindu denominations on the other, with particular reference to Thailand and Nepal.
3. To examine how traditional kingship in Buddhist and Hindu societies has been transformed through engagement with colonialism and then through negotiations with popular forces in either democratic or socialist forms.
4. To assess the role of the monarchy in the ongoing transition from tradition to modernity in Buddhist and Hindu societies with particular reference to Thailand and Nepal.

At one end are those who insist that Nepal continue to remain a Hindu state while at the other are those who argue for a secular country. Adding complexity to the problem are the royalists and the Maoists. The royalists eulogize kingship blindly, often turning to religious scriptures to endorse absolute monarchy while for the Maoists, the institution is the epitome of feudalism and backwardness. These extreme views tend to surface in the media, though the major political parties and large sections of the public do not subscribe to them, abiding by the present constitution of Nepal which envisages constitutional monarchy. The problem in Nepal has been the lack of resources in the form of books, journals and network with other research organizations through which a more balanced and well-informed view on the concerned topic – i.e., the role of monarchy in contemporary Nepali society, particularly its relationship with the dominant religion - could arise and inform public debate. At stake is the possibility of a religiously tolerant society and a largely secular state.

In terms of methodology, this research is descriptive-comparative, analytical and normative. It is descriptive-comparative in that it describes and compares the historical relationship prevailing between the polity and religion in different periods of Nepali and Thai history. In this context a note about historiography as practiced in Nepal and Thailand may be relevant. In Nepal, the various epochs are reckoned in terms of the dynasties that ruled the Kathmandu valley, the capital of contemporary Nepal and the seat of civilization in the central Himalayas for over two millennia. (Not so long ago, the word 'Nepal' meant the Kathmandu valley and it is only from the nineteenth century onwards that the word has come to mean the entire kingdom.) In Nepal, the major dynasties that ruled and continue to rule the country constitute of the Licchavis, the Mallas and the Shahs.

In Thailand, the different epochs are reckoned on the basis of the main kingdoms: the Sukothai, the Ayutthya and the Bangkok era. While in Nepal, the seat of power has always been the Kathmandu valley, in Thailand it shifted with the location of the center of the kingdoms. Sukhothai was located in the northern part of Thailand, while Ayutthya, and was located south of Sukhothai along the Chao Phraya River. The Ayutthya kingdom continued for four centuries until it was sacked by the Burmese in 1767. The capital of Thailand then moved further south of the Chao Phraya River to Thornburi for a short period and then permanently shifted to the present-day location at Bangkok.

In Nepal there has been continuity in the dynasties that ruled the valley and thus three distinct dynasties can be identified: the Licchavis, the Mallas and the Shahs. In Thailand, there has been a dynastic continuity in the Bangkok era, where the ruling dynasty has been the

Chakkri dynasty, whereas during the Ayutthya era, dynasties frequently changed. The paper is analytical in the sense that it tries to unravel an underlying pattern or configuration between kingship and religion. The paper also takes a normative position in the sense that value judgments are made and recommendations forwarded. It argues that there are certain features regarding the relationship between monarchy and religion, between the state and religion and regarding monarchy itself that the Nepali state could learn from the Thai experience. This is discussed towards the end.

Sukothai Period (1238-1438)

The first kingdom to arise in Thailand was the Sukhothai (from Sanskrit "Sukhodaya" or the dawn of happiness), which was centered in the Lopburi region in northern Thailand. Before the emergence of this kingdom, the Tai people who had begun migration a few centuries ago from southern China were organized around a social institution known as muang. This was the primary unit of social and political organization above the simple village level (Wyatt, D. 1982). When northern Thailand was still under Ankhorian domination during the twelfth and thirteenth centuries, more and more Tai people had migrated into the region. Gradually the Tai people under the leadership of Mangrai consolidated their hold in upland Southeast Asia. Mangrai was later given the title Sri Indraditya by the Ankhorian monarch. Tai unification took place around the thirteenth century. From this period onwards, a distinctive Thai culture is said to have begun. Chiang Mai which literally means "new city," was established in 1292.

Mangrai was succeeded by his three sons. The first two died early but the third, Rama (meaning bold) Kamhaeng, was crowned in 1279. A well-known Thai scholar, Prince Dhani Nivat, has written about kingship during the Sukhothai period in his article "The Old Siamese Conception of the Monarchy." The monarch at that time, according to Dhani Nivet, was the people's leader in battle, and in peacetime, a father whose advice was sought and whose judgment was accepted by all. Moreover, he was accessible to his people. The kingly style was that of a Lord Father. The king's paternal benevolence was emphasized, rigid social hierarchy was avoided and so was arbitrary administration of justice and heavy taxation. An inscription that was found in the region had this to say about the reign of King Rama Kamhaeng:

During the lifetime of king Rama Kamhaeng, the city of Sukhodaya has prospered. There are fish in its waters and rice in its rice-fields. The lord of the country does not tax his subjects who throng the roads leading cattle to market and ride horses on their way to sell them...; if any one in the kingdom has some grievance or some matter that is ulcerating his entrails and troubling his mind, and wishes to lay it before the king, the way is easy: he has only to strike the bell hung there. Every time King Rama Kamhaeng hears this appeal, he interrogates the plaintiff about the matter and gives an entirely impartial decision.

Kingship seems to have been based on personal kinlike relations rather than on impersonal formal relations. The realm was more like a super-muang than a kingdom in a conventional sense. The unit is held together by pyramidical personal loyalties. The inscription also indicates that Siamese Thai was used as the language of administration (Wyatt, D. 1982). During the reign of Rama Kamhaeng, we find Brahmans in the court. We also find the Devalaya-mahaksetra – a complex that houses the monks. Though influence of Hinduism – both Saivism and Vaishnavism – and Mahayana Buddhism have been found in the Dvaravati kingdom and in early Sukhodaya, these were to decline with the penetration of a reinvigorated Theravada Buddhism from Sri Lanka. The gradual consolidation of Tai rule in northern Thailand and their Buddhization went hand in hand. Though subsequently some Hindu and Mahayana

Buddhist influences made their way during the Ayutthya period, Theravada Buddhism was definitely the variant of religion the state supported, though kingship rituals remained largely Hindu.

Rama Kamhaeng was succeeded by his son King Loetai, who was, in turn, succeeded by his son King Lithai. King Lithai was a scholar and patron of Buddhism. He is said to have studied the Tripitakas thoroughly. He enjoyed the title of Mahadhammaraja ("Mahadharmaraja"), the Great Righteous Monarch. King Lithai wrote the famous epic of Tribhumikatha – the story of the three planes of existence, a text that is still popular among the monks and lay believers in Thailand. The emergence of a distinctive type of a relationship between kingship and the Buddhist sangha could be evidenced as early as the time of Rama Khamhaeng. Records show that he invited a monk from Nakhon Si Thammarat ("Nagara Sri Dharmaraja"), called Mahathera Sangkharat, asked this monk to sit on his throne called Manansilapatra, and then listened to the monk's sermon. Why does a king ask a monk to sit on his throne and listen to his sermon? What does this symbolize? Is he following a precedent? To answer this question, one will have to explore some of the canonical texts of Buddhism and unravel its archetypical king, Emperor Ashok.

Ashok as an Archetype

The Agganna Suttanta gives the Buddhist version of the origins of the world, society and kingship. The text is composed of two parts. The first is a dialogue between the Buddha and two Brahmin disciples – Vasettha ("Vashistha") and Bharadvaja – in which the Buddha disputes the social and moral claims of the Brahmins. The second part tells how the world came to be (Tambiah, S. 1976). When disorder prevails in human society, human beings come together and select a king. He is described as one "who should be wrathful when indignation is right, who should censure that which should be censured, and should banish him who deserves to be banished." The king is given a portion of the people's rice. The above description of the king underlines an elective and contractual theory of kingship.

The one chosen should be the best among men—the most handsome in physical form and the most perfect in conduct. He is "Mahasammata" or the great elect because has been nominated through the consensus of all; he is also called "raja" because he charms others by his norms and he is khattiya ("kshetriya") because he is the lord of the fields. The interesting feature about this story of societal creation is that the four strata are described as forming after the founding of kingship itself, i.e., society and its gradations develop under the umbrella of kingship. The king Mahasammata – himself orders society to prevent disorder. In society, the khattiya comes first, followed by brahmana, vessa ("vaishya") and sudda ("sudra"). Contrary to the Brahminical theory of emergence, it is the nobles who come before the Brahmins. The brahmanas are of two types the jhayaka (meditators) and ajjhayaka (non-meditators) the former being of a higher status than the latter.

Brahmins of both kinds live by the gift of food in contrast to the khattiya rulers and nobles who, as lords of the field, receive a tax or tribute of rice. Other beings adopted the married state, engaged in various trades – these are the vessa. Those who remained unmarried took to hunting and other such pursuits became the sudda. Referring back to the supposed superiority of the Brahmins, according to the Agganna Suttanta, if there is at all anyone who is superior in this scheme of things, it is the bikkhu, an arhat - a recluse who can be drawn from all four strata irrespective of rank. "This bhikkhu, who breaks through the bond of society, is chief among them all…by virtue of the norms he follows…." Thus according to the Buddhist scheme of things relating to the world, there are two foremost or superior beings the bhikkhu and the king. While the king is the mediator between social order and disorder, the bhikkhu is the mediator between a world of fetters and a free state of deliverance and is therefore even superior to the king.

There are other ideas that can be gleaned from early Buddhist literature. These relate to the cakkavatti ("Chakravarti"), the virtuous wheel-rolling world ruler. Again, according to Anguttara Nikaya which contains stories recounted by the Buddha about his previous lives, in a previous life the Buddha is said to be a wheel-turning rajah, implying that this form of existence was inferior to Buddhahood. It extols the Buddha as a mahapurusha (great being) par excellence – though his real role in the cosmological process is to reveal it; the second Mahapurusha is the cakkavatti, the virtuous wheel-rolling world ruler. It further states that the king who rolls the wheel of the state is a dhamma raja, a righteous monarch.

We do not know as much about Ashok as we do about the Buddha. What we do know about Ashok is that he was one of the sons of Bindusara (who in turn was the son of Chandra Gupta Maurya, the founder of the Maurya dynasty) and that he probably struggled for the throne with other prince-claimants. This in turn means that he probably had to eliminate his brothers before emerging victorious.

Thus a Buddhist root dilemma for those who have aspired to become like him is the need to kill before becoming a great king who can rule righteously. Scholars have tried to reconstruct what the dharma of Ashoka was by looking at the inscriptions he has left behind. Reading the rock edicts, scholars have argued that what emerges is that Ashoka's policy of dharma is not strictly Buddhist, though it is informed by Buddhism. Stanley Tambiah in his book, *World Conqueror World Renouncer* (1976), rightly points out that "...it would be surprising indeed if the king preached the Buddha vacana.

As a king he would have seen it as his rightly duty – not to preach how ordinary mortals can attain enlightenment – but to act in such a way as to lead to a prosperous and virtuous society in which the sangha and its dharma may flourish…." Concludes Tambiah, "The welfare measures – as evidenced in the Edicts – can be read as making it easier for Ashoka's subjects to observe the moral law and provide opportunities for meditation for the monks towards the pursuit of nirvana." When Ashoka renounced violence after the Kalinga war and aspired to become a righteous ruler, he already had an archetype in the early Buddhist literature – that of a cakkavatti – who after conquering a country ruled righteously, "not needing rod or sword." These wheel-turning emperors allowed the conquered kings to keep their possessions, simply ensuring that in their kingdom the lay population follows the five precepts the panchasheela.

Another feature we find in Ashok, and something those who have aspired to become righteous Buddhist monarchs have emulated, is his stern disapproval of schism in the sangha. Thus with Ashok as an archetype, we have periodic "purifications" of the sangha by powerful monarchs as well as the perennial tendency of the political authority to regulate the sangha by devising an eccleastical hierarchy. Ashoka, had once invited Nigrodha, the saintly samenera, to sit on his throne and had listened to his doctrines. By this gesture – asking a monk to sit on his throne – and listening to his sermons, Ashoka had made the samanera, the lord of his palace. This gesture has been interpreted to mean a symbolic acknowledgement of the higher authority of the sangha by the polity and the followers' willingness to be subservient to it. This is another of Ashoka's gestures repeated by South East Asian Buddhist monarchs.

When king Rama Kamheang of Sukhodaya had asked Mahathera Sangkharat to sit on his throne, Manansilapatra, Rama Kamheang was emulating the behaviour of Ashoka, and through this logic projecting himself as a righteous

Buddhist ruler. Moving from the earliest kingdoms in Thailand to Nepal, we find an interesting process at work. In Thailand, Buddhism was consolidated as the "backbone" of society, while Hindu elements were incorporated in state structures and Hindu-animistic elements prevailing among the population at large. In Nepal, by contrast, Hinduism was consolidated as the "backbone" of state structures and of society, while Buddhist practices prevailed among large sections of the population. While Theravada Buddhism gained in salience in Thailand, it was Mahayana and then subsequently Vajrayana that became the dominant type of Buddhism that prevailed in the valley.

Pre-Licchavi Era

It is only from the Licchavi era (from the fifth century A.D. onwards) that Nepali historiography is set on a more firm footing because of the existence of inscriptions. Historical reconstructions prior to the Licchavi era have had to rely on royal chronicles and occasional artifacts that have been unearthed. One well-known royal chronicle is the *Gopalarajavamshavali* – the chronicle of the Gopala dynasty. Certain conjectures can be made on the basis of *Gopalarajavamshavali*. It appears that the Gopalas i.e., cow herders were the first royal dynasty in Nepal. They were soon displaced by the Mahisapala i.e., buffalo-herders. In all probability, the Mahisapalas were the Kiratas because buffalo herding was a central part of life of both groups. Some scholars are of the opinion that while the cow herders were an Indo-Aryan people, the buffalo herders were a Tibeto-Burman people.

The earliest religion in the Kathmandu valley seems to have been the non-Aryan cult of the Pasupata or the 'Lord of the Animals.' This deity was later to become identified with the Hindu god Shiva. This cult later on coalesced around the temple of Pashupati, which in subsequent centuries achieved salience as the patron deity of Nepal. The Kathmandu valley, from ancient times, had been a place of refuge for people living in the surrounding regions. Once their confederacies were annexed by the expanding Magadhan State during the fifth century B.C., the Shakyas of Kapilvastu, the Lichavis of Vaishali, the Mallas of Koligrama and the Vrijjis took refuge in the valley. Among these different immigrant groups, it was the Licchavis who were to consolidate their position and emerge as the rulers of the valley within the next few centuries.

The Lichavi Era (5th Century A.D. to 9th Century A.D.)

The Licchavis, who claimed descent from the solar dynasty, defeated the lunar dynasty and began ruling around 400 A.D. There have been many illustrious rulers in the nearly 500 years of Licchavi rule in Nepal. Some of the names that stand out are Vrsadeva (around 400) Manadeva (464-505) and Amshuvarman (606-621) and Narendradeva (643-649) (Shah, 1996). During the Licchavi era, kings called themselves *Bhattaraka Maharajadhiraj*, which means the Revered King of Kings. Another more elaborate title was *Giriraja Chakra Chudamani Paramabattaraka*.

During the time of the Licchavis and their successors, Shaivism, Vaishnavism and Buddhism were known in the valley. Religious antagonism was not evident among the adherents of the different religious sects. This can be deduced from the fact that not only fathers and sons of the same ruling line worshipped deities of the different sects, but their wives were themselves free to worship any deity they chose.

In fact, among the king's titles we find designations such as *parama-sugata, parama-bhagavata or parama-maheswara* (supreme worshiper of Buddha, Vishnu and Shiva respectively) which indicates that the kings did not see themselves as the protector of Hinduism or Buddhism per se, but were devoted to special deities (ista-devata). Though the kings had personal inclinations towards one sect or denomination, their personal proclivities to one, however, did not prevent them from providing patronage to others. Among the Licchavi rulers, Vrsadeva was a devotee of Buddha, while Manadeva and Amshu Varman were devotees of Vishnu and Shiva respectively. Nevertheless, Manadeva built monasteries for Buddhists and Amshu Varman married the princess Bhrikuti to the king of Tibet and helped to propagate Buddhism there (Singh, 1999).

Post-Licchavi and Pre-Malla (880-1200)

The post-Licchavi and pre-Malla era was largely a transition period in Nepali history. A clear picture of this period has yet to emerge. From the various sources available, one is able to deduce the existence of dual rulership (*dvairajya*) during many reigns. It was during this period, towards the end of the eleventh century, that a strong kingdom emerged in Tirhut, located in the southern part of present Nepal. Returning to Thailand we find interesting processes occurring. No longer was it interacting only with the Indic, Sinic and peninsular Southeast Asian worlds, it had also begun interacting with the European world. Europeans traders and merchants had arrived on the shores of the Chao Phraya and through their mediation; Siam began interacting with the European states.

Ayutthya (1340-1767)

Soon south of the Sukhothai, the kingdom of Ayutthya would emerge, so powerful it would even defeat the formidable Ankhorian Empire. The kingdom was founded when a leader called U Tong moved people to this new location to escape from an epidemic. U Thong came from a Chinese merchant family. He was able to forge a working relationship between the Chinese commercial interests, the Tai people (i.e., mainly the military) and Khmer-oriented bureaucratic families from Lopburi. All these elements were to go into the making of the kingdom of Ayutthya ("Ayodhya" the ideal city ruled by Lord Rama). The very fact that the capital of the kingdom was named Ayutthya speaks of the permeation of Hindu-Brahminical ideology in statecraft.

During coronation, the title Ramathibodhi (1350-1369) was given to him. King Ramathibodhi recruited specialized personnel from the Khmerized urban elite of Lopburi, who in turn developed a special court language based on Khmer and Sanskrit. Later on Ramathibodhi fought against the Khmers and amalgamated the western parts of the Khmer empire into the kingdom of Ayutthya. Once the new kingdom was stabilized, Ramathibodhi formulated the Thammasat, the civil code (Wyatt, D. 1976). If Sukhothai, being a fledgling kingdom, tried to show its distinctiveness vis-à-vis the Khmer, this was no longer necessary for the mature Ayutthya. In Ayutthya, there was a massive influence of Khmer culture and religion.

A very different type of kingship (compared to the Sukhodaya era) emerged during the Ayutthya era due to the Khmer influence. State rituals became more anchored in Hindu-Brahmanic rituals. During the coronation rites, the Hindu deities were invoked to pervade the anointed monarch and the monarch was given the regalia of Vishnu and Shiva. (For example the present Chakkri dynasty has as its symbol Vishnu's chakkra and Shiva's trishul). The devaraja concept of the Khmers, which believed that the king had portions of divinity in him, overshadowed the paternalistic ruling style of the Sukhothai and the dharmaraja concept.

During the Ayutthya era, the realm was transformed from a super-muang into a kingdom with its own division of labour and hierarchy. Likewise, the king became more distant from the ordinary people. The state rituals, ceremonies and courts further enhanced their status as divine beings. The king was the lord of the land and the kingdom represented a microcosm of the universe. As at Ankhor, the capitals and palaces of the king were laid out in cosmological fashion so as to match the universal order as described in Hindu-Buddhist cosmology.

Some scholars have deplored the fact that the importation of the devaraja concept from the Khmers, with its focus on the special coronation ritual, made kings into divine beings and simultaneously made them inaccessible to his subjects. Others have argued that the Hindu coronation ritual confers divinity on the office of kingship and not on the king personally. From the statements pronounced by the monarch during the ritual, it appears that divinity was empowered upon him for the purpose of protecting his subjects and facilitating their happy livelihood (Puengpraser 2000).

The major rulers of Ayutthya are Paramaraja, Borommatrailokanot (1448-1488), Naresuan (1590-1605) and Narai (1656-1688). By the end of the Ayuthya era, the king was referred to by certain terminologies each having a specific meaning of its own. The king's title can be grouped into five types:

1. "Phra Chao Yoo Hua": the word is derived from the words "Phra Chao" meaning Supreme Being and "Yoo Hua" meaning Leader. Thus Phra Chao Yoo Hua signifies that the king is the leader and the head of the state and the subjects.
2. "Phra Chao Phaen Din" means that the king possesses the entire territorial land of the country. It is the duty of the king to maintain the prosperity and fertility of the land.
3. "Chao Cheewit" means that the lives of the subjects belong to the king. The king is empowered to execute or grant full pardons. This signifies that the king is obliged to protect the lives of his subjects while maintaining the stability of the country.
4. "Dhamma Raja" means that the king upholds the rule of Buddhist righteousness and follows the teachings of

the Lord Buddha. This signifies that the king exercises everything in accordance with Buddhist righteousness.

5. "Phra Maha Kasat" means Great Warrior. During wartime, the king is the supreme commander of the armed forces. This signifies that the king is responsible for the protection of the country and the people.

These five terms have been clearly integrated into the Thai concept that defines the monarchical institution. The kingdom of Ayutthya, particularly from the seventeenth century onwards, began engaging with European countries and with Safavid Persia. Portuguese, then Dutch, and then French traders made their way to Ayutthya. A diplomatic mission was sent by Ayutthya to Europe as early as 1608. Another major diplomatic mission was sent to France – to the court of Leo IV - in 1688.

By the 1750s, however, changes began to manifest themselves in the Ayutthya kingdom; that did not brood well for its future. There was increasing tension between the royal and noble power, and the centralized kingdom was less and less able to have access to manpower. Ayutthya was in this vulnerable situation when it was attacked, plundered and devastated by the Burmese in 1767. The attack by the Burmese was so ferocious and thorough that it led to the demise of the Ayutthya kingdom. It would take several years before Siam, with a new capital, would emerge again (Wyatt, D. 1982).

The Malla Era (1200-1769)

The Mallas, like Licchavis, appear and reappear on the scene of Indian history. The Mallas of the Kathmandu valley, in all probability, were the Mallas of Koligrama that prevailed during Buddha's time. This linkage, however, is as yet tentative. The first Malla ruler of the Kathmandu valley was Ari Malla (1200-1216). It is not known how he acquired the throne – whether by conquest, marriage alliance, election or dynastic link. While the earlier documents of his reign refer to him merely as *rajah* or *nripa*, only in 1211 A.D. is he given the full royal title *rajadhiraja paramesvara paramabhattaraka*.

It was during the early part of the fourteenth century (1324) that Tirhut, with its capital at Simraungarh, was attacked and annexed by Ghiyas ud-din Tughlaq, the sultan of Delhi. The ruler of Tirhut, Harisimhadeva, and his court then fled to the hills and settled in a place near Kathmandu valley. Later, his wife, son and relatives entered Nepal as refugees.

Shumshud-din Iliyas, formerly a vassal of Mahummad Tughlaq, declared himself independent of his overlord and in 1345-46 conquered Tirhut. From Tirhut, Iliyas invaded the Kathmandu valley in 1349. The Muslim invasion despoiled the temples of their ancient treasures accumulated from time immemorial, and also destroyed images of gods and goddesses. The Muslim invasion left its mark on the valley in the shape of damaged and broken images. During the earlier medieval period, among the other kingdoms of the country, mention must be made of the Khasa Malla dynasty of the Karnali basin in western Nepal. The Khasa Malla kingdom was probably as large as present day Nepal. Although the Khasa kingdom of the Mallas in the west did not attain the same level of artistic and cultural development as the Kathmandu valley, its achievements are not insignificant.

Following the successive waves of the invasion by Mohammad of Ghazni (around 999 A.D.) in northern and western India, immigrant Hindu chiefs from Rajasthan are said to have made their way into the hill areas of western Nepal. The Khasa Malla Empire subsequently broke down into twenty-four principalities ruled by these immigrant chiefs. Among the twenty-four principalities, Gorkha was to play an important role later in unifying the various petty kingdoms into the present state of Nepal. The kings of Gorkha (along with the kings of Bhirkot, Nuwsakot, Kaski and Lamjung) trace their ancestry to the lunar dynasty ruling the house of Chittor in Rajputtana in western India.

Coming back to the case of the valley, it was divided into three kingdoms after the reign of Yakhsya Malla: Kathmandu (also known as Kantipur), Lalitpur (Patan) and Bhaktapur (Bhadgaon). After the valley was divided into the three kingdoms, there was much infighting among them. Though Kathmandu has generally been the most affluent among the three, it was not able to subdue the other two kingdoms permanently. Nepal's cultural process was marked by synthesis, flexibility and eclecticism. Nepali religious culture came to be influenced by streams of Hinduism, Buddhism, Tantricism and animism.

With the devastation of Ayutthya by the Burmese, the Thais were about to embark on a new phase. This period coincided with the consolidation of European powers in South and Southeast Asia and much of the effort of the nascent Thai state was to be spent on safeguarding their independence from these ascending powers. Ironically the Thai state was to emerge much stronger than it had previously been in history.

King Taksin (1767 - 1782)

In the wake of the devastation brought about by the Burmese assault on Ayutthya, the person who was able to restore law and order and begin life anew for the Siamese people was Taksin. King Taksin was instrumental in shifting the new capital of Siam to Thonburi, further south of the Chao Phraya River from Ayutthya. Later on in life - after law and order had been maintained and rival centers of power crushed - Taksin took to religious excesses. French envoys residing in Siam at that time considered Taksin to have been mentally deranged. Taksin began to think of himself as a bodhisattva, an enlightened being and began forcibly disrobing monks who questioned his ideas. There was a rebellion against him and Taksin was unceremoniously removed and executed in 1784 (Wyatt, D. K. 1984). Some say he was given clemency with the understanding that he would be a recluse and retire away at an isolated monastery for the rest of his life (Shakya, 1994).

The Early Bangkok Era

Those opposed to the excesses of Taksin declared Thong Duang, a general in the army, as king. Following the deposition of King Taksin, Thong Duang was crowned king in 1782 and given the title Ramathibodhi. He is also known as Rama I since the present dynasty has the title 'Rama.' Rama I thus became the founder and first ruler of the present Chakri dynasty, a dynasty that continues up to the present time. Rama I stand out to be someone familiar with the ideology of a Buddhist king – a dharmaraja. This becomes evident, for instance, in the process he followed in expelling lax monks; this was not done randomly, but as in the case of Ashok who deputed Mahataras for questioning monks, Rama I deputed his officers to question monks on a number of matters. Monks that were found ignorant were de-robed. Rama I issued a series of ecclesiastical laws to restore discipline in the monk hood, sponsored the convening of an ecclesiastical council and convened a grand council to establish the definitive text of the Pali-language Tipitaka. Thus Rama I's reign reveals the classical paradigm of purification and revival of sasana, a pattern that is found in other Buddhist monarch archetypes (Tambiah, 1976).

Rama II sought to consolidate the gains made by the previous reign. The king himself was an artist who loved all kinds of art. During his reign, handicrafts, art, literature, dancing, music, etc. were encouraged. There was some controversy surrounding the accession of Rama III. He was the son of King Rama II by a concubine and it was usually the norm to choose a king only from those borne by queens. He was given the title Chetsadakodin.

Rama III encouraged trade, especially trade with China. During his reign, the country's income increased enormously. The nobility itself engaged in trade and received profits. One of the reasons for the clash of interests with the British was precisely because the Siamese nobility was not willing to recognize British interests in regional trade. Ultimately however, concessions had to be made to the British through the Burney Treaty signed in 1826.

One of the major events that shaped Thai society during this period was the emergence and growth of the Dhammyutika movement initiated by Prince Mongkut. Mongkut was the eldest son of Rama II to be born from a queen and so he should logically have been the king. However, at the young age of 20, while Rama II was in his final days, Prince Mongkut was sent off to a monastery – some say to protect him from the political maelstrom, but it could have been a strategy of eliminating him politically. He remained a monk and subsequently became the abbot of Wat Bovonnives, the royal monastery, for another 27 years. In retrospect his entry into the monastery may have been a blessing in disguise because this enabled Prince Mongkut to study and read on a wide array of subjects and to travel throughout the country, in the process speaking to the people with whom princes only rarely interacted during those times. It eventually led to the placement of an enlightened individual as the monarch of Siam.

From early childhood, Prince Mongkut had a restless and inquisitive mind and once he joined the monastery, he was soon disquieted by the Buddhism he found there. He first became associated with forest monks that focused on meditation, but he was discouraged by what he considered to be the pedantic attitude of the teachers and returned to the scholarly city monastery. There, he began a study of original Buddhist texts in the Pali language, covering the core Buddhist teachings. Comparing the original practices of religion with what then prevailed in contemporary Siam, he was appalled. He found that monks and lay people alike were blindly following the Buddhism of their fathers and grandfathers without any understanding of the teachings and the doctrines. Wat Bowonniwet, the monastery of which he was subsequently promoted as abbot, eventually grew into a separate order within Siamese Buddhism with the name *Thammayutika*, the "Order Adhering to the Dhamma," while the older was called *Mahanikai*.

Its distinctive feature was a stricter interpretation of the Vinaya rules, such as not hoarding food or money, a different ordination ritual, a different style of wearing the robes and a critical study of original Pali scriptures. From the early 1830s, Mongkut also developed relations with the western missionaries in Siam. This included both the American Protestants and the French Catholic missionaries. While the Catholic missionaries focused on the religious domain calling themselves "Phra" which means venerable monk in Thai, the American missionaries called themselves "Khru" or teacher and focused on practical aspects like medicine, science, technology, etc. Prince Mongkut perceived the Protestants as the greater threat and so engaged with them more than with the Catholics.

He sought to isolate the claims of missionaries from western science and technology, accepting western science and technology while rejecting Christianity (However, he was influenced by Protestantism in a round about way in the sense that his method, like that of Protestantism, emphasized rationalism and scripturalism.

Some scholars, however, claim that these traits could be discerned even before he began engaging with the missionaries.) With the missionaries, Mongkut learned Latin and English, science and mathematics and astronomy. Mongkut also studied the Bible. He used some of his newly acquired sensibilities in seeking to purge Buddhism of what he considered to be later accretions.

During the 1840s, he began corresponding with the Buddhist monks of Ceylon regarding what constituted authentic Buddhism. Soon Wat Bowonniwet became a center of western learning besides ushering in reform within the Buddhist sangha. Prince Mongkut, as the abbot of Wat Bowonniwet, led this Buddhist revival in Thailand. Thailand had to be constantly on its guard vis-à-vis France and Britain. Similarly, the East India Company was consolidating its position in the Indian subcontinent and the nascent Nepali state had to be vigilant against the East India Company and just as the territory of modern Thailand was demarcated by its engagements with the colonial powers so too the territory of modern day Nepal.

The Shah Era and its Eclipse by the Rana (1769-1950)

The origins of present-day state of Nepal may be traced to the conquest of the Kathmandu valley in 1769 by a king from Gorkha, a small hill principality. Prior to the unification of the country, the area that is now Nepal was divided into numerous petty states. By the end of the eighteenth century, the Shah dynasty of Gorkha, through conquest, marriage and diplomacy succeeded in annexing the small principalities and forming the country that is today known as Nepal. Towards the end of the unification campaign in the early nineteenth century, the King's power waned and state reign went effectively into the hands of military families. During the same period, the young state's interests collided with that of the British East India Company regarding the ownership of the recently acquired territory in the central Tarai, which resulted in the 1814-1816 war. The expansion of the young Nepali state was halted with its defeat by the forces of the British East India Company and its size was reduced by one third.

Competition for the control of the state led to bloody struggles between different military families. From the middle of the nineteenth century onwards, state machinery went effectively into the hands of one family – the Ranas. The power of this family was consolidated through the institution of hereditary Prime Ministership. The King during this period was the *de jure* figurehead, the *de facto* rulers being the hereditary Rana Prime Ministers. While the Shah monarchs were referred to as *Maharajadhiraj*, the Rana Prime Minister was referred to as *Maharaja*. While the peculiar relationship that Nepal had with British India inhibited modernization, Thailand, with its strong monarchy, was able to usher in modernization in the country.

The Modernization Thrust

After 27 years in the monastery, Prince Mongkut became king at the age of 47. Surprisingly, King Mongkut did not undertake major reforms after he became the monarch. This was probably because he was afraid that such a move would alienate the people; his experience of ordinary people objecting to his reform of the sangha was not far behind. He did undertake some simple reforms, though. For instance, he began the publication of the government gazette, employed a handful of foreign advisers, including a British nanny to educate his children in English. He allowed his subjects to refer to the reigning monarch by his personal name and abolished the prohibition against watching a royal procession. He tried to ameliorate the conditions of the slaves and allow women some choice in marriage. It was left to his son, Chulalongkorn or Rama V, to initiate major reforms in the country.

King Mongkut saw his role as a defender of Buddhism. A Christian attack on Buddhism was construed as a political as well as a religious challenge. However, the strategy adopted in meeting this challenge was not by outlawing religious conversion but by reforming Buddhism so that it could resist the onslaught of western missionary religions. While simultaneously reforming Buddhism so that it would be able to meet the challenge posed by missionary religions, he extended freedom of religion to the missionaries and to the people. Ironically some of the values specific to Protestantism were internalized by the reformist Buddhist movement in Thailand symbolized by the Thammayut movement, and these are: assigning importance to the fundamental texts or the original scriptures, emphasizing rationalism and rejected popular forms of religion. Rama V whose name was Chulalongkorn was the king who ushered in modernization in Thailand and helped transform the 'mediaeval' kingdom of Siam into a modern day nation-state.

From the 1890s onwards, the kingdom of Siam could be said to be moving towards a new nation state. What assisted in the transition was the long reign of Chulalongkorn – he ruled for 42 years. Just as a common theme with King Mongkut had been the need to separate western science and technology from Christianity, for King Chulalongkorn, acquiring European modern science and institutions, while safe-guarding Siam's independence and individuality, was a constant theme. The growing Thammayutika movement with its new orientation helped instil a new civic sense that drew inspiration from religion but was modern in its outlook. There were rapid reforms in the Buddhist sangha, a consequence of which was the emergence of a pan-Thai Buddhist order and this variant of Buddhism reached the countryside. Since it was the traditional rulers themselves who undertook the religious reforms, there was no resistance from the monks unlike in other colonized Theravada countries where there was much resistance against the state.

By the end of Chulalongkorn's rule in 1910, the Siamese state had reached a power and centralization never before seen in its history. Siam, at the turn of the twentieth century, became a "patrimonial bureaucracy" headed by an "absolute (enlightened) monarch." What made the bureaucratic transition so effective was the degree of control over the government that was established by the king; it was like a revolution from above.

Rama VI (1910-1925)

Modernity was a persistent theme during the sixth reign, an idea that was reflected in the numerous plays composed by Rama VI himself. Similarly there was focus on the idea of the Thai nation, with nationalism being conceived as a triumvirate of "nation-religion-monarch" (chat-satsana-phramahakasat). To show disrespect towards one was to show disrespect towards the others. Though Rama VI helped develop the idea of the nation, ironically one of the casualties of nationalism in the next decade was absolute monarchy itself.

Beginning of Constitutional Monarchy

Since King Vajirabudh had no male descendants when he passed away in 1925, the crown went to his youngest brother Prince Prajadhipok who upon enthronement was given the title Rama VII. In June 1932, there was a swift coup de etat by a group of 123 middle level officials – both civil and military – that forced King Prajadhipok to relinquish his power thereby ending absolute monarchial rule in Thailand. King Prajadhipok agreed to the conditions set by this small group, who styled themselves as the "promoters," and accepted his new role as a constitutional head.

Royalty was suddenly physically absent from Siam; it was to be absent for the next 25 years. Kingship was there but the reigning monarch resided outside the country most of the time during this period. Rama VII fell out with the military and abdicated in 1935. Rama VIII (1935-1946) was just a boy when crowned King. Except for a brief homecoming in 1938, he was abroad most of the time. He returned home in 1945 only to be murdered the following year. Rama IX (1946-) began to have a visible role in society only from 1957 onwards. During these 25 years, Thailand was to be dominated by the handful of "promoters" of the 1932 coup.

Active Constitutional Monarchy

In June 9 1946, King Ananda Mahidol was found dead in a palace bedroom and subsequently, his younger brother Bhumibol Adulyadej was declared king. King Bhumibol along with his family went back to Switzerland to continue his studies. The king came back to Thailand permanently in 1951. Some have characterized 1932 to 1957 as a period of "passive" constitutional monarchy and after 1957 as a period of "active" constitutional monarchy. The king's role in the crisis of 1973, 1976 and 1992 stands out as important landmarks in the evolution of active constitutional monarchy. These crises have led to the categorization of King Bhumibol as an active constitutional monarch. Had he been a literal constitutional monarch, he would perhaps not have intervened in those situations, preferring to abide by the constitutional strictures that limit his role. But King Bhumibol has intervened at specific junctures in Thai history. In playing out his role, he has evolved a new style of constitutional monarchy – an active one, in contrast to the passive Westminster model.

Bhumibol sought to embody not just the ethnic Thai and the Buddhist, but minority ethnic and religious communities as well. From the mid-1950s onwards, he had begun visiting remote parts of the country and had begun interacting with marginal ethnic and religious communities. He visited the Lao people of the northeast, the Muslim Malays of the south and the hill people such as the Karens, Meos, Akhas and Yaos of the north and northwest. For the benefit of these people, he launched projects on rural development, agriculture and public health and raised funds for the purpose from private endowments as well as through government support.

In regions and among peoples where there was very little government presence, and which continued to remain outside the ambit of development, this gesture by the Thai King helped the marginal peoples gradually identify with the Thai nation-state and participate in its development. The visit by the king in these areas was to be a significant factor in turning the tide against the communist insurgency. During the mid-1960s and early 1970s, there was an insurgency movement launched by the Communist Party of Thailand, which sought to broaden its base in the northeast and among the northern hill people. The presence of the monarch and the rapport that the local people had with the Thai monarch was one of the reasons why the insurgency movement could not make much headway in those regions.

Through his engagements with ethnic and religious minorities over the decades, the Thai monarch has indeed sought to embody all the people who compose Thailand and not just the dominant ethnic and religious community. Over the period of 57 years that Bhumibol Adulyadej has been the monarch of Thailand, he has intervened in Thai politics only a few times. Had he intervened more frequently, he would perhaps not have remained a constitutional monarch. His interventions in politics have been aimed at diffusing crisis, restoring stability and consolidating democracy and as soon as things are back on track, he withdraws from the scene. Not having to look after the day to day affairs of the state has meant that he could concentrate his energies elsewhere – in those spheres that are more important for the well-being of the nation in the longer term. It has been mainly due to his efforts that the cultural and religious minorities of Thailand have come to identify themselves with the Thai nation and participate in its development. It is this distinctive style that has made King Bhumibol Adulyadej of Thailand an active constitutional monarch.

In general, the Thai monarchy has played a more imaginative and creative role in Thai society than Nepali monarchy has in the Nepali context. It was monarchy that ushered in modernization in Thailand from the late nineteenth to the early twentieth century. With the end of absolute monarchy in 1932, monarchy in Thailand has reinvented its role. And though monarchy remains a symbol of tradition in Thailand, tradition has been re-invented time and again. Over the past fifty years, King Rama IX has brought the institution, which had almost been marginalized by history, to the center-stage in Thai life once more. What is especially noteworthy is that he has been able to do so without any control whatsoever over the army or the civil bureaucracy.

What is the way out of the current impasse between Hinduism versus secularism? How can the Thai case illuminate us in our choice? In the case of Nepal, to what extent would it be possible to dissociate Hinduism from the kingdom? What are the possibilities of declaring Nepal secular? The answer to these questions is that it is extremely difficult to dissociate the kingdom from Hinduism given the symbiotic relationship that Hindu kingship has had with Hinduism historically. 'Secular' as an attribute of the kingdom (which presumes a king) is as unworkable as 'Hindu' as an attribute of a republic (no matter how hard political parties, for instance, in India with the Hindutva agenda may like to try).

In the debate between Hinduism versus secularism, the opinion of this researcher is that the specific conditions leading to the emergence of the nascent Nepali state during the late eighteenth century in which kingship had a symbiotic relationship with Hinduism, and the continuity of that nation-state up to modern times, preclude the possibility of dissociating Hinduism from kingship. But inserting secularism in its place will not do either. The solution lies in opting for a middle ground that gives continuity to past traditions while simultaneously dissociating the state from aligning with Hinduism. This could be done by deleting the word 'Hindu' from the clause that defines the kingdom, though not necessarily replacing it with the word 'secular.'

Inserting the word 'secular' in place of the word 'Hindu' as mentioned earlier is not the solution. To say the least, a 'secular kingdom' is a contradiction in terms because a kingdom implies the existence of a king and by implicit logic the king's religion. There is a clause in the constitution that safeguards the position of the king and his alignment with Hinduism when it outlines that the latter should be "an adherent of Aryan culture and a follower of Hindu religion." This clause in the constitution has already identified Hinduism as the religion of the monarch, identifying the kingdom as Hindu. That modern laws are not derived from Hindu religious sources becomes a vacuous statement. It is also unnecessarily provocative and dysfunctional.

This is the solution that comes to mind if one also examines the Thai case more carefully. Some 94 per cent of the population in Thailand is Buddhist. But nowhere does the Thai constitution declare Buddhism to be the state religion. It does, however, declare Buddhism to be the king's religion, though he is also seen as the protector of all religions. Chapter II Section 9 of the constitution of Thailand states: "The king is a Buddhist and an upholder of religions." These are the core ideas present in the Thai constitution which may be useful to Nepal.

To be more explicit, the Thai constitution does the following: (1) Leaves the religious status of the kingdom deliberately undefined. The Thai constitution does not say that Buddhism is the official religion of Thailand, nor does it say that Thailand is a secular state. (2) Specifies the religious adherence of the monarch. The Thai constitution states that the king is a Buddhist. Another idea it articulates is that the king is an upholder of religions. The implication of the two statements once they are seen in conjunction is that the kingdom cannot literally be declared secular when the reigning king is Buddhist – 'kingdom' is after all an extension of 'kingship' – but that it can be secular for all practical purposes. By perceiving the king to be Buddhist while simultaneously a protector of various religions – an idea that can be traced back to Emperor Ashoka, the archetype of the righteous monarch or *dhammaraja* - space is allowed for adherents of minority faiths to identify with the monarchy. Moreover it does not portray the monarchy as a zealot institution, which may have been the case had it said that the king is a protector of Buddhism. As mentioned previously, this imaginative reinterpretation of the Thai king being an "upholder of religions" has made the Thai monarch the chief patron of Islam and other religions in Thailand.

In seeing to it that Nepal evolves into a largely secular kingdom, certain amendments in the constitution, and ones that entail certain rephrasing, are necessary, while others need to address specific laws. The recommendations below are directed toward the role of the monarchy and its relationship with religion. (Others that deal with the policies pursued in running the statecraft have been mentioned elsewhere).

- The clause that defines the kingdom needs to be modified. At present, the clause which defines the kingdom says, "Nepal is a multiethnic, multilingual, democratic, independent, indivisible, sovereign, Hindu and Constitutional Monarchial Kingdom." The word 'Hindu' should be deleted from the clause.
- The clause that defines the monarchy needs to be modified. The said clause defines the king as "an adherent of Aryan culture and a follower of Hindu religion." It should be modified into "the king is a Hindu and a protector of religions." The earlier clause read together with the present clause will mean that

the king is Hindu, not the Kingdom. As such it will bring about some amount of differentiation between the person of the king and the kingdom. It will also give continuity to past traditions while simultaneously evolving the polity in a secular direction.

- Re-inventing the role of the monarchy. As in the case of the Thai king who has sought to embody all the people who compose Thailand and not just the dominant Buddhist-Tai, so too in the case of the Nepali king: he should embody not just the Hindu-Parbatiya. That the Nepali king is a Hindu by religion and a Parbatiya by ethnicity is a fact of history. However, he need not embody the dominant religion and ethnicity. As in the case of the Thai monarch, the Nepali king, through symbolic gestures and commitments for their well-being, should embody all of Nepal's religious and ethnic communities. He should be a king not just of the Hindus and the Parbatiyas, but also of Buddhists, Muslims, Christians and followers of indigenous religions. He should aspire to be a king of Gurungs, Magars, Tamangs Rais, Limbus, Newars, Dalits, Sherpas, Tharus, Yadavs, and all the various communities living in the Himalayas, the hills and the Tarai of Nepal. The first two clauses that differentiate the king from the kingdom and ensure that the king is a protector of religions would facilitate this new role for the king. It will also help boost the flagging legitimacy of the monarchy in a culturally and religiously plural society.
- Constitutional monarchy. As long as the monarch becomes directly involved in politics and in the day to day running the state, he will not have the energy or the time to devote to these issues which are of greater importance for the well-being of the nation in the longer term. Only a constitutional monarchy that does not involve itself in politics, or does so only in diffusing a serious national crisis (and withdraws from the scene

once the task is accomplished) will have the time and energy to embody the different ethnic and religious communities that make up Nepal.

- Uniform civil law. The little remaining Hindu elements in the uniform civil law need to be repealed so that religious and ethnic minorities are not discriminated.

What cannot be overlooked is that in spite of the constitution not advocating secularism, secularization as a process has continued unabated in our society. Functions taken up by Hinduism in past are undertaken by specialized nonreligious institutions in contemporary Nepali society. Lastly, given that secularism is a part of the larger package consisting of a set of standardized ideological products and social processes and given that the constitution essentially participates in the modernist discourse on democracy, freedom and equality, secularism is inescapable in the longer run.

6

The Relationship between Religion, Ethics, Morals and Spirituality

Religion has been defined as a system of Faith & Worship. Judaism is believed to be a revealed religion. Ethics/Morality (these words are interchangeable) is the attempt to arrive at a view of the nature of human values, of how we ought to live and of what constitutes right conduct, by force of reason alone and not by revelation. In order to arrive at a view, it sets goals and assesses actions by the extent to which they further these goals, e.g. if happiness is a goal then the action which produces most happiness to all affected is the right one. Revelation too, through the written and oral law, directs people to an understanding of the nature of human values, of how they ought to live and of what constitutes right conduct; such teachings and examples are scattered amongst various verses and sources. Examples of such moral teachings are:-

- You shall do right and good (beyond the call of duty)
- Love your neighbor
- Correct behaviour between man and man
- Discipline or training of character under the law
- Piety beyond the law

The need to be respectful, earn a living, and engage in learning and culture and so forth. It can be seen that whilst both the secular person who wishes to behave ethically and the religious person who wishes to behave in accordance with the revealed code may do similar good deeds in order to achieve similar good and worthwhile objectives, their motivation is quite different. Indeed, there is some debate as to whether the religious person is behaving ethically in the strict sense of the word. Ethics is a branch of philosophy that deals with ideas such as Right, Good and Duty and these concepts were discussed in ancient Greece by Plato and Aristotle in the 3rd & 4th Century BCE.

The role of philosophers is to accurately try to define and promote these concepts based upon logic and reason. A religious person on the other hand, follows his code of conduct because he believes that it is proper behaviour and reaction to the varying challenges and circumstances which arise during the course of life. The word "ethics" does not appear in the Jewish language, nor did it appear in Judaism until the beginning of the 19th Century. Immanuel Kant, himself a religious person stated that moral acts depend upon the motives. An Act which is moral is done for its own sake; an act which is done in self-interest is non-moral. Since a religious person does his good deed not necessarily for own sake, but because he has been instructed to do so by God, then, by Kant's definition, his act is non-moral. Kant's definition is a challenge to religion for it suggests that one can be both irreligious and moral. Acting autonomously, doing right for its own sake, suggests that a person has the right to choose what is right.

A challenge by Plato to religion is posed by the dilemma:-

a. X is right because God has commanded it, or
b. Does God command X because it is right?

If we accept (a) we have the arbitrary morality of "might is right". If we accept (b) it indicates that God too is bound by morality and, therefore, in one sense, morality preceded God. This poses the stronger challenge to religion for it indicates that secular morality pre-dates and is independent of, religion and is a basic necessity of the "good" life. There are modern Jewish religious philosophers who would also agree that ethics have no part in religious behaviour. Professor Leibowitz is a leading exponent of this view. He says that Jews agree on nothing except the revealed code of conduct. (Hallachah) Judaism is about ordinary life and Torah has no utilitarian value. We need to know only why we have been given the Torah in order to know what to aim for in life. He maintains that:-

1. We must choose either religion or ethics and
2. We must receive no benefits from religion, e.g. if one gives to charity and at the same time prays for the renewed health of a loved one, the gift ceases to be a Mitzvah and the prayer an expression of one's selfishness and not a service to God. Professor Leibowitz's view appears to be a minority one.

Other modern Religious Jewish philosophers put an opposing view and do combine revelation with ethics. One such exponent is Rabbi Louis Jacobs. He says that one needs to know the underlying value of the revealed code of conduct so as to help set priorities where conflicting demands each have underlying ethical reasons. Another reason for knowing the underlying values is to help create legal fictions to circumvent the law for ethical reasons. Another modern Religious Jewish philosopher who opposes Professor Leibowitz is Rabbi Dr. David Hartman.

In his book, "A Living Covenant", he uses a chapter analysing and criticising Leibowitz's point of view, relying heavily on the writings of Maimonides. He concludes the chapter by saying that revelation "constitutes a God-given challenge that must be met in every generation by a covenantal community that trusts its own autonomous rational and moral judgement in applying the Torah to life."

Whilst there is friction in the relationship between religion and ethics at the theoretical level, it is more acute at the practical level. An example is to be found in the cause of animal welfare. Peter Singer, a modern philosopher, expounds a fundamental principle of equality based only upon his reasoning and logic, namely "the principle of equal consideration of interests," and states that this principle cannot be limited only to Human Beings. In practice, this means that if both an animal and a Human Being are suffering, we try to evaluate the degree of suffering of each before deciding whether to help the animal or the human on the basis of such equal consideration of interest, although he does concede that facts other than just suffering must be taken into consideration. This contrasts to religious teachings which state that whilst one must show every care, kindness and consideration to animals, the welfare of man takes priority. Here the decision is reached in accordance with the perceived revelation and reason is only a marginal factor.

Other situations which highlight the friction between religion and ethics are those concerned with suicide and euthanasia. A leading exponent against suicide was Thomas Aquinas who said that it offends against:-

1. The duty to oneself because it is contrary to natural law. Everything loves itself.
2. Duty to the community because it injures the community.
3. Duty to God. Life is God's gift to man and suicide offends against God.

Aquinas believed in God and Duty.

The philosopher Hume, in opposing Aquinas's view, replies to the three points as follows:-

1. If one may not offend against natural law then man should do nothing to protect himself from the adverse effects of any natural causes.

2. A person's duty to the community is reciprocal therefore, man should unilaterally be able to withdraw from the community. But even if man does have a duty to the community, then there must be a limit to such a duty.
3. If one believes in God and one should believe that everything is in the hands of God. If, therefore, someone commits suicide, it is God's will.

Hume believed in autonomy and maximising consequences. Mainstream modern Jewish philosophy teaches that in man's behaviour he must assume full freewill and must be responsible for his actions. The religion teaches that suicide is wrong. These teachings are generally implied from the scriptural texts "surely your blood of your lives wills I require" and "you must guard your body and not injure it." Its meaning is not immediately clear. Rashi implies from it a prohibition of suicide but Ibn Ezra believes it to be a prohibition of taking human life and has no reference to suicide. If Ibn Ezra's view is correct, whilst one can understand the revulsion which prompts the religious teachings against suicide, it nevertheless puts a questionmark on whether such teachings are soundly based. One would have thought that for such an important principle, the Torah would have expressed the prohibition more explicitly.

Events in history too, prompt one to question whether the absolute prohibition of suicide is as strict as it is stated to be. Jewish theology teaches that one should give one's life, and presumably also take one's life, in preference only to committing murder, incest or idol worship. However, King Saul was believed to have committed suicide for reasons which are not absolutely clear and his action is generally condoned. We are told of some 400 young boys and girls who committed suicide because they feared that they might become the victims of sexual assault and again their behaviour is condoned. Throughout Jewish history, whole communities have committed suicide as acts of martyrdom in order to prevent themselves being tortured, murdered or sold into slavery. Very often these communities were led by their Rabbis. Some question whether such acts of martyrdom can be justified by the Halachah but presumably the Rabbis who led the mass suicide, were aware of the Halachah and acted as they did.

Since such acts of suicide have happened all too frequently over thousands of years, then these acts in themselves must surely establish the Halachah. Although Rambam says "Pain is better than no life", the martyrs who foresaw torture and slavery obviously thought otherwise and we say that they sanctified God's name. It has been said that these communal acts of martyrdom were an Ashkanazi syndrome and whilst Halachicly correct, could be understood in the context of the Crusades. This is not so. In Andre Chouraqui's book, "Between East & West", he describes similar acts of martyrdom under similar circumstances in the North African communities which also occurred during the middle Ages. When comparing the relationship between religion and ethics on the subject of suicide, we arrive at an unexpected result. Judaism teaches suicide to be absolutely wrong but finds it difficult to find strong support for this teaching from the Sources, whilst history has produced Martyrs who have committed suicide for many reasons apart from the three permitted reasons mentioned above, i.e. murder, incest and idol worship.

The ethical secularist justifies suicide on the grounds of autonomy. Ethics however teaches that an act is ethical only if it is autonomous but it does not teach that every autonomous act is ethical. Suicide may well be an autonomous act, but it is not necessarily an ethical act. Does it for example, measure up to "the principle of equal consideration of interest"? Is it an act which "produces most happiness to all affected" The suicide may well have family, business acquaintances and community who may all be adversely affected to a greater extent than the benefit to the Suicide and, therefore, by the standard set by ethical secularists, unless the act of suicide measures up to the standards which they set for themselves, the act is not ethical.

In the matter of euthanasia, the difference between Ethics and Religion, whilst not absolutely clear cut, is much clearer. For Ethics, so long as the "victim" is subject to voluntary euthanasia or non-voluntary euthanasia, the presumption is that the "victim" wants or would have wanted his death; this death has utilitarian value and it is an autonomous decision. Ethics would not approve of involuntary suicide. Religion, on the other hand, forbids killing absolutely. It does not distinguish between killing healthy people or sick people, and, in any event, would find it difficult to draw the line between them. It also forbids both active and passive euthanasia.

There are, however, two grey areas. The first is highlighted by the stories of Rabbi Chanina and Yehuda Hanassi. Rabbi Chanina, in an act of martyrdom, was being put to death by fire. Nevertheless, he refused to do anything which would hasten his own death, namely suicide, but allowed his executioner to speed up his death, namely voluntary euthanasia. The story of Yehuda Hanassi relates how his handmaiden disturbed a group of Rabbis, causing them to cease praying for Yehuda Hanassi's continuing life and during the cessation of the prayer, the soul of the Rabbi departed; involuntary euthanasia. Both Rabbi Chanina and the handmaiden are commended for their behaviour. The second grey area relates to the life of a Goses - a person who is considered likely to die within the following 72 hours. In such cases, no action should be taken to speed up the death but nothing need be done to prevent it. For a Goses, Judaism does distinguish between active and passive behaviour.

In Rabbi Jacobs' book "A Jewish Theology", in the chapter dealing with Jewish ethics. Rabbi Jacobs writes "there is no escaping the conclusion that a thing is not good because it is in the Torah. It is in the Torah because it is good. But in that case, what is gained by having it in the Torah; the record of Revelation? The believer may reply that, although Revelation does not function in order to define good conduct, it does serve as its guarantee." In Peter Singer's book "Practical Ethics" in the chapter headed, "Why Act Morally?" he states "Why act morally?" cannot be given an answer that will provide everyone with overwhelming reasons for acting morally. Ethically indefensible behaviour is not always irrational. We will probably always need the sanctions of the law and social pressure to provide additional reasons against serious violations of ethical standards."

Affects of Structural Rigidity in School Systems

Seeking ways to wake up the spirits of students and teach them about morality and religion in ways that do not violate family beliefs or constitutional principles is a major challenge for public school educators. Acknowledging that awareness that morals, religion and spirituality are all associated with the goodness and badness of human character and principals of right and wrong does not give them freedom to share this holistic viewpoint with students or co-workers. Educational leaders' reluctance to speak of morals or values associated with religion and spirituality "has amputated . . . public discourse at the knee . . . ." Although most educators have a moral sense they "have tried to talk themselves out of it". Despite the fact the original intent of the Canadian Charter of Rights and Freedoms introduced in 1982 was to protect the country from establishing any specific religion or dogma, the results of such legislation has been a "structural rigidity of education" that does not leave room for flexibility in approaches to teaching.

This structural rigidity of education has led to "spiritual vacuum" and "moral erosion" along with "religious illiteracy" within the public school system. Under the guise of the reasoning behind the rules of charter, the system fails to demonstrate any connection between morals, religion and spirituality, which creates confusion for both educators and students on how they affect one's values. "But it is the spiritual dimension of children's lives more than any other that has been excluded from school life", despite the charter's intent to "guarantee and protect . . . the enjoyment of the rights and freedoms it enshrines". All individuals have spirituality, whether they are religious or not; it is a byproduct of evolution, located on the "third neural system in the brain". A person's spirituality can be viewed as "Spirit-in-action, God in the making . . . the entire process of unfolding itself . . . which becomes conscious of itself" when evoked and recovered by teachings about religious and moral stand points. Although spirituality transcends morals and religion, they are part of the process of Spiritinaction and God in the making. For the sake of this chapter, morals are based on people's sense and beliefs of what is right and wrong in their conduct; religion is a particular system of faith, belief and worship that can bind people together as community. And although spirituality contains common elements of all religions, such as love and compassion, it is a higher state of consciousness which gives a sense of the sacred and inner peace.

Dysfunctional Orderliness

Some educators' reluctance to acknowledge the connection between spirituality, religion and morals may be one factor impeding healthy systemic growth within the public education system and conserving a dysfunctional orderliness, resulting in many social problems. Headlines about violence in schools, such as: "First-grader opens fire in school: Boy, 6 Kills Classmate", and "Stabbed teen's plea to life-save: don't let me die" on the front pages of some newspapers demonstrate how schools across North America are plagued by a multitude of moral and spiritual issues ranging from violence, to crime, to alcohol and drug abuse. Although school boards implement programs to combat these issues, they often lack a spiritual component and are met with failure. Like sticks anchored in a river, the programs may slightly obstruct the progression of such moral problems but never appear to bring them to a halt. To turn the systemic river upside down and alter its direction, some changes of visions in public education that recognize the relationship between spirituality, religion and morals could be required.

"A one-size-fits all standardized system of education may have been useful during the industrial age, but will not be adequate to prepare our children for living together in the new millennium". Perhaps adopting the ideology that we are spiritual beings having human experiences, rather than human beings in search of spirituality, could challenge some common views on educational leadership and curriculum development. Currently, the "liberal economic" model allegedly ruling the public school system seems to reflect the main goal of a genetic researcher who strives to produce apples from an orange tree. Like an apple, attempting to grow on a foreign orange tree, a student can lose sight of his/her spiritual roots and true identity while adapting to a dysfunctional school system. As stated by Watkinson (1999), "schools in Canada . . . are . . . governed by a traditional authoritarian model that expects children to adapt or fit within the school environment". Some consequences of such an educational system appear to be alcohol and drug abuse, along with violence and crime within the student population.

By not nurturing students' spirituality, public schools run the risk of raising a generation of youth who lack the wisdom and connective ness they require to live a healthy moralistic, spiritual life. We waited for young people to really get in trouble, even kill each other, before we responded with programs to create safe schools. I hope we have learned from that past not to wait for more and more young people to lose their sense of meaning and purpose before we invite (spirit), soul into education. The tragedies of fatal shootings involving students at Columbine High School and a Taber school have led some educators and spiritual leaders to address their concerns about removing religion from the public school system. These "horrific" examples of violence in schools demonstrate the moral consequences of taking God out of the educational system. Before the Charter of Rights, and other government legislation, school days commenced with Bible reading and the Lord's Prayer. At that time, the Ten Commandments were part of the moral code. Fenn (2000) suggests:

> Spiritual influences were present within our educational system in the early days. But God and prayer have been taken out of the classroom and evil has flooded in. We think we can solve the problem with legislation. No. Our problem is spiritual and we must return to God and the Bible. . . . Will we wait for tragedy to strike or will we return to God.

During the tragedy April 20, 1999 at Columbine High School, students turned to God and prayer was brought back to the school where previously it had been outlawed. "As students took refuge, under tables, as Erick and Dylan sprayed the room with bullets- prayer was offered-and no legislator or politician could stop it". This could be viewed as an example of students' spirituality being awakened, when they sensed that it was more important to pray than to follow school policies. During this tragedy they may have learned about the relationship between religion spirituality and morals, and gained insight about the downfalls of certain school laws.

After the tragedy at Columbine High School, a parent of one of the victims forwarded a poem to some government leaders stating:

> Your laws ignore our deepest needs. Your words are empty air. You've stripped away our heritage. You've outlawed simple prayer. Now gunshots fill our classrooms.

And precious children die. You seek for answers everywhere. And ask the nation, 'why?' You regulate restrictive laws through legislative creed and yet you fail to understand that God is what we need.

In response to this poem, Fenn states "no amount of legislation can change our hearts or our nation. Only God can do that. The nation is changed one heart at a time". His statement suggests that a relationship between religion, spirituality and morals exists.

The Relationship between Christianity, Spirituality and Morals

Henry (2000) states that educators need to acknowledge "the profound relationship between the moral, the religious, and the spiritual". Religious and spiritual insights provided some of the earliest roots of moral leadership. In the new millennium, educators must continue to acknowledge that law is central to morality. "Even though there will always be new situations not envisioned by the law, there are certain unchangeable principles of right action which are almost universally held. They form the bedrock of moral action". These principles include: "do good and avoid evil; do to others as you would have them do to you; live not by lies; love and do what you will". Aside from associating morals with religion, Henry (2000) suggested that moral principles do not depend solely on a particular religious belief.

There are laws written in the hearts of individuals, which is their spirituality, and to enable these ordinances to become personal principles of action, leaders need to help educate a student's conscience. "The education of conscience is essential to growth to maturity and is lifelong. It takes place through the influence of, and personal reflection on experience". Children are pilgrims on a journey towards finding peace and a sense of connection with God. They are innately spiritual beings, who are in need of guidance while on a pilgrimage. Educators can teach a moral way of life by informing the conscience through proclamation, instruction, public debate, and "particularly by example".

Thom (2001) suggests conscience can be informed a spiritual framework that assists educators to deal with family, gender, visible minorities, violence and alcohol and drug abuse issues. To establish morals, one's conscience needs to be educated with "Godly concepts such as grace, faith, compassion and forgiveness. . . .". Christ modelled a healthy sense of "personal conscience" while in a leadership role; his "stories were an invitation to every listener to feel free to develop a private moral integrity . . . " As an ideal interpreter of life, conscience is an inner voice informing individuals what is right and wrong, and therefore setting a moral base. Henry's (2000) and Thom's (2001) viewpoints of the relationships between religion, spirituality and morals is ideal, if their educational leadership models focus on Jesus, as a spiritual leader, modelling morals and spirituality. "Jesus Christ manifested a particular style of leadership, today commonly referred to as servant leadership. He did not come as . . . a great political strategist . . . . . He came as a humble servant".

Jesus demonstrated by his own example how "moral purity may be attained". Although he sought to create an immediate link between God and humankind, "the love of one's neighbour and tolerance he taught have been replaced by self-righteous fanaticism" and church bureaucracies. Churches are filled with people who can win Bible trivia contests, but who do not understand what Jesus truly stood for. When Jesus became "managed, monopolized and codified" by churches, his voice became replaced by "narrow minded and rigidly dogmatic beliefs". Church leaders forgot that in his spiritual approach to leadership, Jesus "focussed more on connection than correction. He knew that when the connections (between people) grow strong, so would the desire the do the right thing". However, after Jesus became bureaucratised by churches, the public edu-cation system gradually weeded Him out of the curriculum, which may have resulted in a loss of clarity on some moral issues and a loss of connection between spirituality and religion.

Learning about Religion and Indoctrination

Canada's Native population could identify with how Jesus became bureaucratized by Christian churches. Historically, the education system has been noted for the institutionalized suppression of equal opportunities for Natives, under the ruling of Christian values. For example, the Native principle of protocol focussed on the value of ceremonies and prescribed rules about how to behave. However, non-Native school administrators did not consider the value of Native ceremonies and until 1952; it was illegal to practice Native spirituality in the schools. Discriminatory attitudes toward Natives led to the oppression of the children who attended residential schools. The residential schools insulated Native children from the influences of their own people and subjected them to a program designed to lead them away from who they were while adopting the ways and values of their teachers.

Children were known to scrub themselves for hours to remove their brown colour, in an attempt to become "de-Indianized." This was a form of acculturation, where as a culturally diverse group, they were being forced to acquire the behaviours of another cultural group to gain access to and function as part of the Christian group. Forcing Christianity on the native culture was an example of church bureaucracies and schools indoctrinating students, which could be perceived as an immoral and antispiritual approach to educational leadership. Perhaps, if the Native students would have been taught about Jesus, as a model of love, kindness and forgiveness, instead of being indoctrinated with Christianity, they may have gained important insights on moral and spiritual values.

Regulations Resulting in Moral, Spiritual, and Religious Illiteracy

Having no context which educators or students in the public school system can acknowledge theirs or other's religious views has led to spiritual, religious and moral illiteracy in the public school system. Giving young people an awareness of the different religious beliefs of others could encourage them to discover their own. Opposers of religion in the classroom have difficulty understanding that education about God is not value-less; although religious education can indoctrinate, education about religion can illuminate. As stated by Watkinson (1999) "schools need to be places that neither inculcate nor inhibit religion. Religious conviction should be treated with respect".

As stated by Sweet (1997): we've gone from times when the religious were often intolerant of the non-religious. . . . to a day, when it is those who hold religious convictions who are subjected to societal intolerance. It's often implied that anyone holding a religious belief system must be either brainwashed, intellectually challenged, or in direct need of a psychological crutch. The Latin root word of "religion" means "that which binds us together as people or community". As Sweet (1997) states, educational leaders attempting to free children from religious indoctrination, by excluding the topic in the public school system, may have resulted in "throwing out the baby with the bath water". Keeping religion out of the public system may be why "hundreds of thousands of parents reject public education in favour of schools that ghettoise their children on the basis of religion". Because educators are responsible for "teaching habits of the mind and habits of the heart", these parents may want their children to learn about morality, within a religious and spiritual framework found in the schools.

Examining Moral Frameworks in Education

Gilligan (1982) compares two moral orientations that

affect how educators perceive moral issues. When individuals endorse a "justice perspective", the focus is on autonomy, individualism and competing rights and rules; whereas, if people operate within a "care perspective", their concerns are on cooperative relationships, connectiveness, caring and empathy.

Thus, even if an educator followed the justice perspective and violated no rights, he/she could maltreat a student. While a justice perspective is based on the premise that everyone should be treated equal, the care perspective is built on the belief that hurting others should be avoided.

On the other hand, Strike, Haller and Soltis (1988) suggest there are three basic frameworks that influence an educator's approach to moral problems. While a "consequentialist" position leans totally on an estimation of the consequences or results of an act to measure its goodness, a "non consequentialist" position assumes judgements of goodness from loyalty to certain principles or a person's intent. Alternatively, a "social welfare" perspective relies on the belief that good consequences are the ones that add to the well-being of society. Sergiovanni's (1992) and Kidder's (1994) proposed standards to guide actions reflect a spiritual and religious context to morals.

Comparable to the values introduced by Jesus and taught in the Christian faith, Sergiovanni (1992) suggests morals should be guided by "tolerance, compassion, loyalty, forgiveness, peace, brotherhood, justice, and fairness" and Kiddler (1994) identifies eight universal ethics: "love, truthfulness, fairness, freedom, unity, tolerance, responsibility and respect for life". Since values have to do with modes of conduct, it is important that students understand and internalize them. By demonstrating a connection between morals, religion and spirituality educators could give students a standard of criterion for guiding their thoughts and actions.

Examining Spirituality, Religion and Morals in Education Models

Different from an "economic liberal" approach to learning that focuses on ranking, competition and class selection, a "student-centred" approach may find room for pedagogy that demonstrates the relationships between spirituality, religion and morals. An economic liberal educational model reflects priorities of "productivity, efficiency and uniformity" rather than on "flexibility, diversity, rights and freedom" which is encouraged in a democratic student centred model. A democratic approach to education would enable students to feel more like apples connected to an apple tree, rather than apples attempting to adapt to the foreign system of an orange tree. As a student centred model, it could lead to a community of students, teachers and administrators working as a team to nurture creative educational thinking, spirituality and a happy school life. However, the challenge of such a change is that some educational leaders may fear violation of the Charter of Rights, and thus preserve their comfort zones within a secular system that continues to sustain an orange tree.

Yob (1994) suggests that to remain true to mandates of public school learning, curriculum addressing spirituality or religion or morals cannot be filtered into the public schools without finding answers to some of the questions being proposed by educators working towards to conserving the current system. Because a clear meaning of spirituality has not been established, educators are compelled to equate it solely with religiosity and view it as esoteric. However, "peace, enlightenment, and holistic truth-these are not solely the property of religions. While religious institutions may be committed to nurturing spirituality understood in these terms, public education institutions may elaborate these terms and pursue them as goals just as enthusiastically". Creighton (1999) suggests that to promote spiritual growth and healthy morals, educational leaders must be willing to let go of certain outdated paradigms of leadership and misunderstandings of spirituality.

Although spirituality is a part of human experience, "traditional views of spirituality have been shaped by the patriarchy to make the spiritual become separate, beyond natural and arranged in hierarchical relationships". Spirituality embraces religious and mystical implications which need to be challenged and demystified by educators until spirituality becomes part of one's daily experiences, language that aims to describe it appears abstract. Therefore, educators may find it challenging to intellectually connect spirituality with morality or view it as separate from religion.

Ideological Factors Influencing Legislation and Policies in Education

A number of major ideological factors have influenced the evolution of educational policies which currently affect how educators view the relationship between spirituality, religion and morals. According to a liberal perspective, people are naturally good and can be perfected by reason alone, without any assistance from a God; however, according to a conservative view, people are flawed and capable of being good or evil; thus to discover the good, they need the wisdom of the ages to be found in religion and moral standards. Because the notions of spirituality outlined by Cooper (1997), Creighton (1999) and Yob (1994) appear to be connected with religion and morals, then examining the history of educational policies and ideologies could assist in coming to an understanding of what educational leadership models have influenced the separation of religion, morals and spirituality.

In the early 1800s, schools commonly had a religious base and were run by individual denominations. In addition to reading, writing and arithmetic courses, "good morals were the backbone of the majority of schools", that offered a "good dose of the scriptures as well". Education, in that era, was composed of a patchwork of formal and informal teachings; children learned either at home, church, in private schools or through a job apprenticeship. "The Legislature spoke in 1820 of the need for the improvement of the moral and religious habits of the rising generation". By the mid 1800s, Canadian schools had been established as public institutions to mainly provide religious instruction. Some Roman Catholic and Anglican conservatives fought to preserve denominational education in the schools, which was opposed by the political liberals. While the liberals advocated non-denominational Christian common schools, ruled by the state, the conservatives were committed to retaining church control of education.

However, the role of schools soon shifted from an agency serving private purposes to a state-controlled bureaucratic organization where "diversity was replaced by uniformity". Ryerson's School Act passed in 1846 recommended that boards of trustees decide the extent and manner of religious study in their own areas. Although a school could now offer sectarian instruction, no child was to be coerced to attend. Additionally, the government was to keep out of religious matters in schools. After this act was passed, many educators and parents voiced their concerns about schools becoming "godless" and they suggested the Bible should be a compulsory part of education. In 1849, Cameron introduced a school bill which prohibited from the schools all books containing "controversial theo-logical dogmas or doctrines". His bill was later defeated and replaced by the School Act of 1850, which appeared to encourage spirituality and help build morals within the school system. It stated: in each school the teacher should exert his best endeavours, both by example and precept, to impress upon the minds of all children and youth committed to his care and instruction, the principals of piety, justice and a sacred regard to truth, love to their country, humanity and universal benevolence, sobriety, industry frugality, chastity, moderation and temperance and those other virtues which are ornament of society and on which a free constitution of government is founded. Excluding religion from a curriculum could have made it challenging for educators to follow the School Act of 1850. However, this Act may have led to the development of Ontario's School Act of 1855 that brought religion back into the system. Ontario's School Act of 1855 stated that each school day should commence and end with prayer and Bible reading, the Lord's Prayer was to be part of the morning exercises and the Ten Commandments were to be taught to all students.

Students, however, could be excused from religious instruction, if their parents requested it. Some of the ideology surrounding the Act of 1855 could have influenced the British North American Act (B.N.A.) passed 12 years later. The B.N.A. Act, introduced in 1867, provided for the coexistence of Church and State in the education of children, where both agencies were seen as having a role to play in education. Section 43 (6) of the Act gave control of education to the provincial legislatures. "The provisions of Section 93 clearly recognized Protestants and Roman Catholics, the two groups which included (at least nominally) nearly every person in Canada in 1867". Out of certain court cases, the following definitions of these two groups arose: "a Protestant is anyone who denies the authority of the Pope in Rome; a Roman Catholic is a Christian who accepts the authority of the Pope in Rome" (p. 38). In Ontario, Catholic "schools acquired constitutional protection. . . through section 93 of the British North American Act", which gave them permission to teach Christianity.

The Common Schools Acts of 1871 and the Public School Acts of 1890 terminated Christian practices in public schools by demanding that all schools under the provisions of the Act shall be non-sectarian. These acts demonstrate why public school educators have been reluctant to acknowledge relationships between religion, spirituality and morals. New ideologies leading to changes in school policies were associated with what was taking place historically, such as the Second World War. During the Second World War, there was a sense of "instilling a moral purpose in the young as the only way to ensure a future". Thus, in 1944, a regulation was altered to enforce that religious instruction be part of the regular curriculum. "Classroom teachers were given the responsibility of teaching a Bible-based course for two half-hour periods a week". This regulation suggests that policy makers in that era acknowledged a strong relationship between religion and morals.

The three-decade period from the mid-forties to the mid-seventies was the era during which the current Canadian educational system was being formulated. School administrators were developing the "hegemonic ideology of Canadian educational policy" which swung from an "ethical liberal" perspective to an "economic liberal" view. Post-war educational policies and policy-making were controlled mainly by the "ideology of economic liberalism" which emphasizes the "equality of opportunity for individual economic achievement". Educational facilities became the main agencies for preparing a student to enter the job market, rather than for teaching morals or religion or spirituality. Schools were becoming organized like factories, and the educational process became comparable to commodity production. What happened in schools was ruled either by technological demands of society or by the economic requirements of the capitalist elite.

This "empty box view of education" suggested that schools had not been embracing a life of their own, but were acting as "passive transmitters" for external influences. To address this empty box view, the Ontario Minister of Education established an investigative group. In 1966, the Ontario Minister of Education appointed a Committee on Religious Education in Public Schools in Ontario to examine and evaluate the system in the province. By 1969, the committee had completed a report with some major observations and recommendations. Although committee members were advised to remain true to the principle that there was to be no denominational teaching of religion in the public school system of Ontario, they recognized a need for schools to instill knowledge about religion. Religion was viewed as playing a major role in developing values and attitudes obtained from one's heritage.

"The scriptures are the world's great literary treasure. History, literature, art and music cannot be understood or appreciated without an adequate background of religious knowledge. Equally important are the ethical values inherited from religion." The committee's observations reflect a relationship between spirituality, morals and religion. The Committee believed that is was possible to build a balanced program which would provide youth with sufficient knowledge of world religions. With such a program, students could be made aware that most people in society believe in a religious interpretation of life which involves acknowledging the existence of God as the creator. Despite the "pluralistic character and conflicting attitudes of our society, no student should be denied the educational advantage of a knowledge of Biblical literature, which . . . is enshrined in noble poetry, adorned with wise maxims and crowned with such a scheme of lofty morality as might insure the general happiness of mankind."

Based in this insight, the committee recommended the inclusion of some passages from the Bible in literature courses. It also suggested that courses in religion count as history courses under the English and History speciality. Despite the committee's recommendations, however, the economic liberalism ideology of that era was preserved by educators and therefore, religion, spirituality and morals were viewed as secondary to the economic requirements of the capitalist elite. Since the late 1900s, Canadian public schools have demonstrated a lack of a ruling by an ideology of ethical liberalism which is a form of "person-regarding" education that promotes self development in a humanistic sense. Thus, while merely mirroring the demands of a wider society, the educational system has been known to have spiritually and mentally burdened many students, leaving them feeling oppressed and morally confused. Their value, as individuals has been rated according to whether or not they can develop an identity that will fit into a capitalist market institution and make them employable. While being mainly ruled by an ideology of economic liberalism, students may be facing deprivation of the opportunity for self development in a humanistic sense, which is usually guided by a combination of religious, spiritual and moral principles.

The Canadian Charter of Rights and Freedoms, which became a base for some major court challenges dealing with religious matters in the schools in the late 1900s, appears to have provided a crucial turning point for how religion in the schools is viewed. "It can override provincial powers to regulate the role of religion in schooling . . . . It provides first for freedom of conscience and religion, and second, that everyone is equal before and under the law . . . (p. 44). An Alberta pastor and an Ontario Jewish parent used the provisions of the Charter to find support for religious schooling of their own faith. Also, parents form Hindu, Christian reformed, and Muslim, Mennonite and Sikh religious backgrounds "collectively petitioned the Ontario courts in search of support for religious schools for their children." These legal challenges have created some unconventional alliances among very different religious groups who all appear to see the connection between religion and morals.

The argument that religious education from the Christian perspective is used to teach morals and values is not sufficient in law to continue the practice . . . . Unless there has been initial constitutional support for denominational education, a province has no obligation to support religious education from the public purse. In Ontario, only the Roman Catholic minority denomination may legally be publicly funded. These sections of the charter demonstrate policy makers' reluctance to acknowledge the relationship between religion, morals and spirituality, despite the fact that Section 2 of the Charter "guarantees to all Canadians freedom of religion, belief, assembly and association". Therefore, many educators have raised concerns about how the Charter has limited their "professional autonomy and judgement", made discipline too lax and given too many rights to minority groups and suffocated their spirituality. In the future, the Charter will continue to be a major instrument of alteration in the area of religion in schools. "The charter is not actively antireligion or . . . anti-Christian . . . . It guarantees generally freedom of religion".

However, within a multicultural society and the current constitutional framework, it is challenging for educators to acknowledge and teach anything about relationships between religion, spirituality and morals. As employees of a school district, governed by provincial regulations and curriculum requirements, teachers are not granted freedom to teach whatever content they please. They are "required by law to teach the curriculum as established by the province or other legitimate authorities and to obey the legitimate instruction given to them by administrators and school boards".

Integrating Religion, Spirituality and Morals in Education

Subscribers of Calgary's Change Agency (2000) have been chatting on line about spirituality, religion and morals in the school system. After having attended a Schools and Spirituality Seminar, several subscribers introduced postings that acknowledged the value of awakening the spiritual essence of students and breathing life into them. Others wrote about the importance of breaking away from a dysfunctional educational vision and establishing a new one that recognizes the connection between spirituality, religion and morals. One subscriber, Kevin Cameron (2000), wrote about how a Catholic high school religious study program established in the 70s and 80s had resulted in frustration, conflict and poor grades. Then in the 90s, when the program no longer assumed a Catholic faith base, students' attitudes changed; marks improved dramatically and the students expressed appreciation for what they were being taught. This new program format was evaluated as being spiritual, rather than religious. This demonstrates some of the benefits of bringing spirituality into the education system and shows the downfalls of teaching religion, without spirituality.

Alexander (1994) points out that a new interest in spiritual education is marking a turn in educational thought away from viewing education primarily as "an agent of economic instrumentalism and epistemology-as it was seen by educational secularists". Spirituality is "a quality of lived experience, rather than a mode of knowing. The experience involves self-transcendence . . . beyond the narrow confines of the ego; and is rooted in . . . a radical openness . . . that is the ground of hope, humility, and growth." Similarity to Alexander's (1994) view on spiritual education, Yob (1994) states spirituality cannot be defined merely as the antonym of materiality for the spiritual education reconnects students with the world, the needs of its peoples, its ecological concerns, its social justice, its distribution of goods, its peace. It does this indirectly by reconnecting students with something other than their material selves: God. Yob's and Alexander's viewpoints demonstrate there is a connection between religion, spirituality and morality which is also supported by Cully. Cully (cited in Yob, 1994) suggests that "the questioning restless heart in search of peace with God is . . . a universal experience . . . . There is no such thing as a person without a God representation, whether one accepts or rejects a belief in God . . . ."

Buddhist, Rizzuto, Tillich and other spiritual leaders, who perceive transcendence in non-personal terms, still speak about a quest for inner peace and spirituality. Additionally, Coles' (1990) research indicates that "children across cultures and ethnic/religious boundaries by their own revelation in conversations and drawings are "soulful, spiritual beings . . . with their own meaning-making representations of God". Coles (1990) findings portray "children as seekers, as young pilgrims". Yob (1994), however, argues that children need further journeying and learning to understand God because they have not, in essence, already arrived. Thus, they should be taught about various religions and how they can be the path towards waking up one's spirituality. Yob (1994) introduces a variety of terms applied to the description of something beyond one's self. "The ultimate is conceived as 'nothingness' in Buddhist thought, as 'psychic necessity' in Rizzuto's . . . 'The Ground of Being . . . or 'Ultimate Concern' in Tillich's . . . . John Hick uses the 'Eternal One' . . . . Cully is insistent on the terms 'the Transcendent' . . . the 'God Within' or the 'near Presence'."

Within the public school classrooms, there may be students who can relate to one of these perspectives while on a personal quest for spirituality and inner peace. "A quest is more than a duty; it is energized by an inner driving force, a search for satisfaction . . . The quest or its repression will be expressed as acts of peace or violence", which is evident in some of the recent school tragedies.. Cooper (1997) takes a different stand on connecting morals, spirituality and religion Children do not have to search for God because the presence of the Divine is evident in all things. One should think of God as "being a verb rather than noun". Renaming

God, 'Goding' to suggests a process, rather than making reference to a noun. "Goding is a mutually interactive verb, one which entails interdependency between two subjects, each being the object for the other". From this perspective, spirituality, morals and religion would be presented as the connecting verbs: "spiriting", "moralling" and "religioning", which could create a narrative integration of them. Cooper (1997) claims people devote themselves to spiritual lives because they "yearn to connect with truth and meaning".

Although he does not refer to people as being on a quest for spirituality, he talks about practices, such as meditation, prayer and mantras and acts of loving kindness as ways to alter one's consciousness. He suggests that spiritual awareness gained from these practices is not intellectual knowledge, but wisdom-a deep knowing-inexplicable, indescribable and exquisite beyond imagination . . . It is what sustains us when we are faced with doubts, nourishes us when the world seems bleak, and comforts us when we face the death of loved ones. This perspective demonstrates the value of learning about the spiritual connection to religion and morals but also demonstrates why there is a resistance to teach about spirituality in the public school system. If spirituality and intellect are viewed as being separate, some educators would argue that teaching spirituality should not be part of the curriculum. However, choosing to introduce spiritual practises could touch the students' hearts, nourish their spirits and educate their conscience. Such practices may also help educators and students to experience spirit in action, God in the Making and a higher awareness of moralistic behaviour.

New Approaches to Educational Leadership

As an educator, Thom (2001) claims his own "spiritual hunger" has motivated him to try to enlighten others about some of the connections between religion, spirituality and morals. "It should be possible for administrators of our schools to be spiritual leaders with a conscience, without apologizing . . .. Spiritual leaders demonstrate sincere caring for an organization, and choose a synergistic, rather than an adversarial approach to leadership. Thus, educators need "to rediscover and renew an old paradigm: one that has the necessary humanistic and spiritual components". Thom's Educational Leadership with Conscience model suggests a leader must rise above an organizational culture that attempts to sway decisions though politics and power. He speculates that his model could be extended to further enrich a balance of both the scientific and spiritual dimensions in shaping leadership and acknowledge the relationship between religion, spirituality and morals. In his model, the educational leader acts with conscience, performing deeds which are characterized by justice and fairness. Justice may be thought of as a universal view of what is right, and fairness as a subjective view of what should be. Justice affirms human worth and dignity and human rights; it means such things as caring, equality, and righteousness. Justice is what is right for our society.

Educators Bolender (1995) and Leung (1997) praise Thom's model for its ability to demonstrate the relationship between morals, spirituality and religion. His model is very close to transformational leadership, which demonstrates high standards of ethical and moral conduct and considers the needs of others over their own. "Thom has added a new dimension to existing leadership models and theories. Defining right and wrong by theological standards takes leadership a step beyond the path prepared by Sergiovanni and others". Bolender states that as an administrator in the public school system, she views Thom's model as reflective of great leaders. "The light shed by Thom's model of leadership may further inform the study and practice of educators struggling amidst a maze of leadership styles and theories". Like Thom, Noddings (1992) notes that schools cannot be all things to all people, but educational systems can encourage spiritual growth and the development of morals, by teaching students to care for themselves and others. She introduces the concept of an educator as the mother of a heterogeneous family, who views students as if they were her own children, in need of care and nurturing. She sets out a model of caring in an educational context.

According to her perspective, caring is the base of all successful education and schooling can be revitalized in its light. Moral education revolves around care and comprises four major components of moral education: modelling, dialogue, practice, and confirmation. Modelling is viewed as vital in moral and spiritual education. In this framework, an educator is not attempting to directly teach students principles and ways of applying them to problems. Instead, educators are demonstrating care and ethics in their relationships with those around them. Noddings (1992) critiques the liberal economic model of education and proposes an alternative vision which encompasses centres of care for: the self, the inner circle, strangers and distant others, animals, plants and the earth, the human-made world and ideas.

Nodding's (1992) and Thom's (1993) models both suggest ways to incorporate spirituality and morals into the educational system. They indicate there is a strong need to reexamine current educational models and initiate some fresh approaches to leadership. They have taken on the task of challenging the cycle of a dysfunctional vision, by introducing leadership models that acknowledge some of the relationships between morals, religion and spirituality. After discussing some of the relationships between the three terms, the paper examined the evolution of various ideologies related to education and legislation, such as the Charter or Rights and Freedoms.

7

Apologetic Challenges of 21st Century

For though we walk in the flesh, we do not war according to the flesh, for the weapons of our warfare are not of the flesh, but divinely powerful for the destruction of fortresses. We are destroying speculations and every lofty thing rose up against the knowledge of God, and we are taking every thought captive to the obedience of Christ. These texts speak to us of the need and obligation of God's people to engage in the discipline of apologetics; to defend the faith once for all delivered to the saints. In connection with this biblical mandate we offer this conference on "Defending the Faith in the 21st Century." And the title of my presentation tonight is "21st Century Apologetic Challenges". That title might sound a bit presumptuous if understood a certain way. I suppose that one could take this to mean that my talk is about all the issues and topics regarding apologetics—the defense of the Christian faith-that the church will face throughout the 21st century, from the present through 2099.

If that were what my talk is about, then I would be very presumptuous indeed and have a pretty high opinion of my prophetic abilities! Of course, there is no way that I can know all the challenges and attacks that Christians will face over the course of the next 91 years. I dare say I can't even tell you all that we will face in the next *ten* years. But what I think I can tell you about are the apologetics challenges that we are *now* facing or are on the verge of facing, some of which I believe will be significant and ongoing challenges for some time to come, perhaps for a decade or two. That is, I can and I will talk to you about what I and other Christian apologists think are the most significant issues in the area of apologetics that we most need to focus our attention on—those things that are or are about to become *most* pressing; those things that the people in our society who we hope to reach with the gospel will use as reasons or excuses to reject Christianity. These are those issues that every Christian who wants to be salt and light in the world and make a difference for the cause of Christ needs to know something about and "be ready to make a defense for the hope that they have".

The Cultural Status of Christianity

Christianity currently occupies in Western and American culture. This is important because it's our cultural status that partly explains why we are facing the apologetic issues that we are. There are basically two expressions that indicate the current cultural status of Christianity. First, we must take note that we in the West and even in America live in a *post-Christian culture*. Most westerners have left Christianity behind. They have "moved on" as it were from what they see as an outmoded, irrelevant religion to other more reasonable and more useful forms of thought and life.

- The church's prestige and influence have given way to the authority of science and government.
- Categories like sin and redemption have given way to the concepts of dysfunction and therapy respectively.
- Self-sacrifice has been replaced with self-indulgence and self-fulfillment.
- Moral law has been overshadowed by moral relativism.

There is no longer any belief in the authority or relevance of the Bible. Indeed, there is even precious little knowledge in our society of the Bible's contents much less any belief in the truth of its contents. Rather than a cultural consensus of real and nominal Christianity, we have today a pluralism of religious beliefs, all seen as equally valid and valuable. There is the firm belief that religious knowledge—real knowledge of religious truths—is unavailable; that all we can truly know is the here and now, the world present to our empirical observations in a word, *secularism*.

There is an obsession with personal autonomy and self-expression. My life is *my* life, and I have the right to do with it as I please without constraint by anyone or anything, least of all by religion and some external system of morality. In the words of Albert Mohler of Southern Seminary, The worldview of most Americans is now thoroughly secularized, revolving around the self and its concerns, and based on relativism as an axiom. We Americans have become our own best friend, our own therapist, our own priest, and our own lawgiver. The old order is shattered; the new order is upon us.

But, not only do we live in a post-Christian culture; we see evidence all around us that we are increasingly living in an *anti-Christian culture*. What I mean is that there are elements in Western (even American) culture that are becoming openly hostile toward Christianity. This should not surprise us since the Christian worldview is diametrically opposed the values of the new culture. This hostility comes out in the open whenever Christians stand up to speak out important social issues. Again, to quote Mohler, to proclaim biblical truth to this culture is to risk social isolation, outright rejection, and, in some cases, potent attacks. . . .The Church which proclaims that adultery, premarital sex, and homosexuality are inherently and unquestionably sinful will quickly discover what it means to be cut off from the cultural mainstream. The preacher who takes on the divorce culture and takes his stand for the enduring covenant of marriage will run into direct confrontation with society's attraction to "open marriage" and what some now describe as "serial monogamy." The Christian who stands in defense of the unborn will be told that her voice is unwanted, unheeded, and unwelcome—and in no uncertain terms.

In some places in the West, strong measures have actually been taken to silence the voice of Christians in the public square. Just a few years ago, a pastor in Sweden was sent to prison for preaching a sermon on Leviticus 18 & 20 condemning homosexuality as sinful. More recently in Canada a Christian was fined $6000 for printing 3 Bible verses against homosexuality, and a pastor was told it is a hate crime to hand out gospel tracts. In Great Britain a couple was denied the opportunity to adopt a child because it was alleged that their Christian faith might prejudice them against a homosexual child placed in their care. Also in Canada, a Christian ministry (MacGregor Ministries) lost its tax-exempt status because they insist that Jehovah's Witnesses are a cult.

Even in the US, some cities and states have passed legislation that has the effect of limiting free speech on religious and moral issues. A Philadelphia law was used recently to indict 11 Christians for a hate crime for staging a legal protest against homosexual activism. Witness also the huge outcry against Pastor Rick Warren's participation in President Obama's inauguration ceremony because of the stance his church takes on moral and social issues. Beyond this, Christianity and Christian believers have become the objects of ridicule and slander. Recall a few years back when a young homosexual man was brutally murdered in Wyoming and Katie Couric on NBC's *Today* show said that it was the fault of all the fundamentalist Christians who preach against homosexuality. Recall the recent "documentary" by Bill Mahr, *Religulous* that makes fun of religious believers and presents them as fools, idiots, and quacks.

And I hope you haven't missed the media blitzes that happen every year around Christmas and Easter in which TV networks and news magazines like *Time* and *Newsweek* broadcast documentaries and publish articles designed to debunk and discredit Christian beliefs (and never give opportunities for contrary presentations from conservative scholars). This is the cultural position of Christianity in our society—we and our churches are seen as vestiges of a bygone era that threatens the health and happiness of the new secular world order. In light of our current status, then, what are the apologetic issues that we will face in the coming years?

Three Crucial Challenges

No doubt there are many questions and issues that we will face in the area of apologetics, but there are three that stand out.

First, we will confront *continued and rigorous attacks on the authority of the Bible*. Challenges to biblical authority and reliability are nothing new, of course, but the natures of the attacks have taken on a different flavor in recent days. There are two specific ways that the Bible is being undermined and dismissed in recent days that many of you may not be familiar with. *The challenge of the so-called pagan roots of Christianity*. This challenge is actually quite old. It was a prominent charge over a century ago, that many central Christian doctrines such as the virgin birth, and the death and resurrection of Jesus, were simply borrowed by early Christians from ancient pagan myths like that involving the Egyptian god Osiris or the Persian deity Mithras. It is alleged that every popular religion in the ancient world had its myths of virgin-born, dying and rising saviors. If Christianity was going to compete in the first-century market-place of ideas, then it too had to come up with its own story of a virgin-born, dying and rising god. So, the early Christians just took these myths from other religions, tweaked them a little bit and imposed them on the biography of this Palestinian Jew named Jesus. Of course, the implication of all this is that Jesus wasn't born of a virgin, he did not die for the sins of the world, and he was not raised from the dead. Such theological beliefs were the invention of the early church.

This theory of the pagan origins of Christianity was laid to rest almost a century ago due to a lack of any concrete evidence for it and the fact that the alleged parallels between the pagan myths and Christian doctrine were superficial at best. Nonetheless, it has come roaring back in recent years. In their recent book, *The Laughing Jesus*, Timothy Freke and Peter Gandy refurbish this old accusation, writing, "The Jesus story has all the hallmarks of a myth. The reason for this is quite simple. It is a myth. Indeed, not only is it a myth, it is a Jewish version of a pagan myth!" This idea has been popularized in Dan Brown's *DaVinci Code* and in a recent issue of *U.S. News and World Report*, and other places.

The challenge of an alleged politicized and canonization process. New Testament scholars Bart Ehrman and Elaine Pagels have made a name for themselves in recent years arguing that the New Testament Canon—that collection of books that the church has considered divinely inspired and authoritative—came about primarily as the result of political motives. They allege that in the earliest days of Christianity (i.e., in the mid-to-late first century) there was no settled Christian orthodoxy, no clear definition of what it means to be a Christian—in particular, there was not just one view about the identity and mission of Jesus.

Some followers of Jesus thought him divine, others did not. Some thought he brought a social message, others a message about divine redemption, others an esoteric Gnostic teaching. And, of course, associated with all these different "Christianities" were different sets of "scriptures," different books purporting to give us the right interpretation of Jesus and his message, and none of them had any claim to more legitimacy than any other. For example, there were numerous gospels that circulated besides those found in the NT such as the Gospel of Thomas and the Gospel of Mary.

So, why did the books we have in the canon made it in and the others did not? Well, according to scholars like Ehrman and Pagels it was all about power and politics. One particular group of Christians gained the upper hand politically and suppressed the teaching and writings of the others, establishing themselves as orthodox Christianity and the others as heretics. But the so-called orthodox school really has no more claims to legitimacy than those now seen as heretical. Bart Ehrman describes what happened this way:

> This one form of Christianity [the party that came to be known as "orthodox"] decided what was the "correct" Christian perspective; it decided who could exercise authority over Christian belief and practice; and it determined what forms of Christianity would be marginalized, set aside, destroyed. It also decided which books to canonize into Scripture and which books to set aside as "heretical," teaching false ideas. . . . And then, as a coup de grace, this victorious party rewrote the history of the controversy, making it appear that there had not been much of a conflict at all, claiming that its own views had always been those of the majority of Christians at all times. . ., had always been "orthodox" (i.e., the "right belief") and that its opponents in the conflict, with their other scriptural texts, had always represented small splinter group invested in deceiving people into "heresy". . .

Both of these challenges to the Bible seek to undermine its authority as a word from God. If key Christian doctrines were borrowed from pagan myths, then the message of the gospel is not unique—it's just one more ancient myth among many. If what we know today as Christianity and its Bible is just one version of a diverse cacophony of Christian voices, one invented by the political machinations of evil men, then again, the message of Scripture is just the message of men and not God. Contemporary Americans may then safely ignore it.

Second, we will confront *an ever-bolder, New Atheism.* You have all heard of them, the unholy trinity: Richard Dawkins with his book *The God Delusion*, Sam Harris and his *Letter to a Christian Nation*, and Christopher Hitchens' *God is not great*. These are the leaders of a new movement of atheists. Of course, atheism has been around for thousands of years, and the US has had a population of atheists hovering around 8 or 9 percent for many decades. But the new atheists are different. They are more vitriolic, more antagonistic toward religion than most of their predecessors. And they are openly evangelistic, seeking to win people to their cause. Why? Because of a couple of twin convictions: (1) religion is dangerous and the source of most of humanity's problems, and (2) atheistic humanism is the key to the success and happiness of the human race. On the danger of religion, Dawkins has this to say:

I am hostile to fundamentalist religion because it actively debauches the scientific enterprise. It teaches us not to change our minds, and not to want to know exciting things that are available to be known. It subverts science and saps the intellect.

More generally . . . what is really pernicious is the practice of teaching children that faith itself is a virtue. Faith is an evil precisely because it requires no justification and brooks no argument. Teaching children that unquestioned faith is a virtue primes them . . . to grow up into potentially lethal weapons for future jihads or crusades. Sam Harris writes, "We have been slow to recognize the degree to which religious faith perpetuates man's inhumanity to man," and that "no real foundation exists within the canons of Christianity, Islam, Judaism, or any of our other faiths for religious tolerance and religious diversity."

Now I should say, along with many critics of the new atheists (which includes both religious and non-religious people), that the arguments they give against the existence of God and the danger of religion are quite simply pathetic. They are simplistic and misleading. For example, the best that Dawkins can say in response to the recent intelligent design arguments is, "Who designed God?"—a question both irrelevant and silly. Moreover, these writers often caricature the arguments of their opponents rather than dealing with them in their strongest forms. Nevertheless, their books are huge best-sellers. They are reaching and influencing a very wide audience. No doubt their influence is partly responsible for the increase in the number of selfprofessed atheists in the nation (from 9 to 11 % in recent years). Where biblical illiteracy abounds and Christians shirk their duty to engage in apologetics, we will only see this movement gain greater ground.

The third most significant apologetic challenge that we will face in the coming years is *the ongoing accommodation of Christians to the culture.* What I mean is that one of the biggest—perhaps the biggest—reason that people in our culture will find to reject Christianity in days ahead is the fact that most people who name the name of Christ have nothing significant to offer our culture by way of an alternative to what they already have. Christianity is losing its saltiness; it has become worldly. There are two specific ways in which this worldliness manifests itself. *Our lifestyles are not really different from those around us*. Christian philosopher and apologist William Lane Craig has said that "the ultimate apologetic is our lives." That is, the most persuasive argument that you can give to an unbeliever as to why he ought to believe that Christianity is true, is a life radically transformed by faith in Jesus Christ. But, that only works if your life-style is noticeably different from that of unbelievers. But consider. . .

- The divorce rate among Christians is almost the same as among the irreligious.
- Christians give only about 3% of their income to charitable causes, including church.

- We spend 7x more on entertainment than on spiritual activities.
- We make most of our important decisions based on self-interest or utilitarian considerations (like unbelievers) rather than biblical principle—b/c most Xns don't really know the Bible that well and so don't have a biblical worldview.

Our lifestyles are not noticeably different from that of the world. Of course, we don't take drugs or watch X-rated movies and the music we listen to has Christian lyrics. But, our lives—how we spend our time and our money, and the kinds of things we seem to care most about—are still mostly about ourselves, our desires, our comforts, our plans and purposes for the here and now. We have also accommodated the world by *our retreat from the objective truth and knowability of the Christian faith*. For many years our culture has taught us that the only things that can be *known*, the only things that rise above the level of mere subjective opinion, are those things that are accessible to the empirical sciences. Through science we can have knowledge of nature and this-worldly matters. But, those things that lie outside the domain of science—religion and ethics—these can only be taken on faith. And Christians have bought into this philosophy and retreated from the intellectual defense of the Christian faith into pragmatism and experientialism. We offer Christianity to people not because we can show that it is true, but because it can offer them practical assistance with their daily lives and lead them into wonderful, warm, fuzzy religious experiences.

And now, in more recent days, some in what's called the emergent church movement have even further accommodated culture by following it into the quagmire of postmodern relativism which does not simply deny that we can know the truth in religion and morality, but denies that there is any such thing as truth at all! Of course, this implies that Christian truth-claims, Christian doctrine like the deity of Christ and the sinfulness of man, are not objectively true, but are just the opinions of our particular subculture. Such cultural accommodations threaten to make it impossible for Christianity to have any real and lasting relevance to the world in which we live. Why should people care about a religion that offers them only a different, cleaned-up version of the same kind of self-centeredness they already have? Why should they take seriously a faith that cannot be known to be true and which is simply one of many equally valid narratives they could adopt? And the reason why I say that this is an apologetics issue is because this kind of cultural accommodation makes apologetics impossible.

It becomes impossible because, on the one hand, no one will take our apologetic arguments seriously when we don't seem to care enough about what we believe to actually live it out; or, on the other hand, by denying that there is any Christian truth to defend, we deny any need for apologetics in the first place. I believe that this cultural accommodation is one of the major reasons why our youth are leaving the church and not coming back. Well, these are the major apologetic challenges we face today in the 21st century. There are others, of course. We continue to face challenges from other world religions like Islam and Buddhism, as well as cultic groups like Jehovah's Witnesses and Mormons. There cultural and ethical issues like samesex marriage and cloning and stem cell research. In light of all of these issues and in light of the biblical mandate to defend the faith once for all delivered to the saints, I believe that we have a calling to fulfill in out time.

These things call us, first, to repent of our cultural accommodations by owning and living out the Christian values we say we believe and by standing steadfast on the conviction that Christianity is true—it's *really* true—and that it can be known to be true. And then we are called to meet the other challenges head-on, *first,* with a robust defense of *natural theology* showing as rigorously and persuasively as we can that God actually exists and that his existence is something that can be *known,* not simply believed; and, *second,* with a thorough rebuttal of those who would undermine the authority of Scripture with groundless speculations about pagan myths and early church conspiracies. This, my brothers and sisters, is what we must do to give a defense in the 21st century.

Non-Reductive Religious Pluralism

There is an overwhelming plurality of varieties of pluralism. In what follows, I will attempt to distinguish among them so that we can understand what is meant by *religious* pluralism. I will argue that even after religious pluralism is distinguished from other sorts of pluralism, a variety of positions could be considered versions of religious pluralism. Among the different sorts of religious pluralism, we may distinguish *reductive* from *non-reductive* varieties. The proponents of reductive forms of religious pluralism attempt to identify a common element among different religions on the basis of which the religions are successful in some specified way.

According to non-reductive religious pluralism, to the contrary, God guides whomever He will, not only by virtue of features common to several religions, but by their unique divine qualities, as well. More specifically, while reductive pluralism is the position that what is good about religions is what is common to a plurality of them; non-reductive pluralism is the view that each of a number of religions has unique features through which God may guide people, even if there is no common essence to all religions. I will argue that there are good reasons for scepticism about reductive religious pluralism, while non-reductive religious pluralism makes more sense, philosophically and theologically, especially given several important features of Islamic theology.

A Plurality of Pluralisms

The term *pluralism* was first used to signify a metaphysical doctrine by Christian Wolff (1679-1754), and later popularized by William James (1842-1910). A different but related sense of pluralism is *moral pluralism.* While metaphysical pluralists hold that there is an irreducible plurality of types of substance, truths, or original principles, *moral pluralists* hold that there is an irreducible plurality of independent moral values. The two sorts of pluralism, metaphysical and moral, are eloquently linked in the work of Isaiah Berlin (1909-1997). Berlin defended moral pluralism throughout his long career. Political theorists use the term for systems in which a variety of ways of life are permitted to coexist or are encouraged. Perhaps the best place to look for a discussion of pluralism in this sense is in the more recent writings of the late John Rawls (1921-2002), particularly in his *Political Liberalism.* Rawls speaks of competing comprehensive systems of thought and value (for example, various religious systems, various theories of socialism, ethical humanism, etc.) whose differences can be expected to persist in democratic societies.

Rawls then attempts to show that reasonable people who hold differing comprehensive views will develop an overlapping consensus with regard to basic procedural principles of justice as fairness. Finally, there is religious pluralism, or rather; there are religious pluralisms, for the label has been used for different and often confused claims. Some writers use the term "religious pluralism" for a theological view that allows salvation for the adherents of different religions and concedes some sort of validity to a plurality of religions. Many other writers, however, use the term in a political sense, for a position that advocates the acceptance of and respect for the followers of different religions. All too often, the different uses of the term are confused. We can give a rather abstract definition of religious pluralism by saying that it is a doctrine according to which some sort of favorable attribution is ascribed to a plurality of religions. This definition has the advantage of making it crystal clear that we can expect to find a wide variety of positions that could be described by the term *religious pluralism*. The variety is so wide that the claim that someone accepts religious pluralism in this sense is almost trivial.

In order to begin to put meat on the bones of this skeletal religious pluralism, two parameters must be specified: (1) the sort of favorable attribution to be ascribed, and (2) the scope of the plurality to which the favorable attribution is ascribed. There are all sorts of positive status that can be claimed for one or more religions. Religions are said to contribute to mental health, to facilitate social arrangements, to lead to salvation, to be true, to be ordained by God, to have a long and rich tradition, and many others. Some of the positive things said about religions make specific reference to their adherents, while other attributions apply to the doctrines, rituals or historical features of religions without making any claims about their followers. For example, with regard to adherents it has been claimed that some religions provide a framework of beliefs and practices within which some their followers have mystical experiences of various kinds. A different sort of example is the claim that the adherents of different religions are entitled to certain rights, e.g., rights of worship. With regard to the content of religions it is said that some religions prescribe beautiful ceremonies, of some it is said that their creeds are true, and of some that the rules they prescribe are morally commendable.

An important way of stopping short of pluralism is to claim that although each of several religions has some particular positive status, they do not have the status *equally*. For example, a Buddhist might hold that all the major religions of the world provide means to obtain peace of mind, but that the means provided by Buddhism is more efficient, or leads to a deeper sense of peace of mind, or brings quicker or longer lasting peace of mind. I don't know of a name that anyone has given for this sort of position, although it has been held by many philosophers and theologians. We might call it *degree pluralism,* but we should keep in mind that many modern defenders (as well as opponents) of religious pluralism would not call this a form of pluralism at all. They define pluralism in terms of a strict *equality* of status. Peter Byrne, for example defines religious pluralism as a three part claim:

1. All major religious traditions are equal in respect of making common reference to a single transcendent, sacred reality.
2. All major traditions are likewise equal in respect of offering some means or other to human salvation.
3. All major traditions are equal in their inability to provide a norm for interpreting the others, and offer limited, revisable accounts of the nature of the sacred.

Byrne's position might be described as a kind of *equality pluralism,* as opposed to *degree pluralism.* Notice also that Byrne does not speak of the equality of religions, but of religious traditions. The difference can be crucial. For Muslims, religion, or *dîn,* is what God has revealed to guide us to Him. Religious traditions, however, include all sorts of things that humans have gathered in their attempts to follow religion. One might be an equality pluralist about religious traditions while taking a more exclusivist view about religions; that is, one could hold that God's guidance for man is to be found in a single religion, but that the religious traditions of mankind fall so far short of what God offers us that none of these manmade traditions can be said to be any better than any of the others. On the other hand, one could take the reverse sort of position and hold that although God has revealed several distinct forms of guidance for human beings, so that there are several true and divinely revealed religions, the followers of all but one of these religions have gone astray by adding and subtracting to and from divine guidance in their cumulative traditions, but that there is one religious tradition that has remained faithful to divine guidance in a manner superior to the other major religious traditions.

Before we decide whether to be in favor of religious pluralism or not, we have to determine exactly what good feature is being attributed to what multiplicity of religions or religious traditions. Although people have said some pretty silly things about religion, no one is an absolute religious pluralist, that is, no one has ever claimed that anything good that can be said of any religion can be said of all of them, with a few important exceptions. Some atheists contend that this is vacuously true of all religions. Some religious believers define *religion* and *religious* in such an exclusive manner that they contend that there is only one religion and only one religious tradition, and so would agree that whatever is good about one is good about all religions, just because they think there are no others. Other people with a much more embracive attitude reach the same conclusion by holding that there is only one religion, which includes all of what are commonly called "religions" and only one religious tradition, which is the religious heritage of all mankind. Most reasonable people, however, will agree that various good things can be said about different religions and about different religious traditions. They will differ about what good things can and cannot be said about them.

This is a point that is also emphasized by Prof. Byrne: "We should be clear from the outset that pluralism is not as such committed to saying that all major religions are equal in every aspect of cognitive endeavour....." Byrne claims that what is required by religious pluralism is the three part equality claim mentioned above, while relative superiority in other respects may be allowed. Other advocates of religious pluralism have defined their versions of pluralism with regard to other features. John Hick, for example, places considerably more emphasis than Byrne on the moral function of religion, while Fritjof Schuon contends that the transcendental unity of religions is to be found in their esoteric dimensions.

Often, when religious pluralism is discussed, the positive status attributed to a variety of religions is left somewhat vague. Worse than this is equivocation that begins by pointing out some common feature among religions and concludes with the claim that the religions are all the same in relation to some other feature. In order to avoid this sort of fallacy, at least the following seven sorts of pluralism should be distinguished. Other dimensions of religious pluralism could also be defined, but the following seem more pertinent to contemporary discussions of religious pluralism.

Soteriological religious pluralism is defined in terms of salvation. According to an equality soteriological pluralism, a plurality of religions is equally effective in guiding people to salvation. A degree pluralist in this regard would hold that people may be guided to salvation through a plurality of religions, although some ways will be more effective than others, either by providing guidance that is easier to follow, or that leads to a higher degree of salvation, or that is more suitable to guide a greater number of people, or by some other criterion could be judged superior in bringing people to salvation.

Normative religious pluralism pertains to how adherents are to treat the followers of religions other than their own. An equality pluralist in this regard would claim that there should be no difference at all in one's behavior toward persons of different religious beliefs. If carried out strictly, this would prevent any sort of participation in a particular religious community, for such participation requires a special sort of cooperation based on religious affiliation. The opposite extreme from equality pluralism would be the view that seems to have been held, unfortunately, by some Muslims as well as Christians, that one has no obligations whatsoever toward those who are not of one's own faith, that their blood is permitted to be shed and their property taken. More reasonable would be the view that we are bound by certain obligations toward all human beings, although we may have additional special obligations to our co-religionists. One might consider Islam to prescribe a sort of normative degree pluralism by issuing duties owed to human beings as such, additional duties owed to the "Peoples of the Book" and further duties owed to other Muslims.

Notice that despite the historical facts linking exclusivist views on salvation with intolerance, soteriological pluralism and normative pluralism are logically independent. Various forms of normative religious pluralism have been the focus of attention of a number of writers, some of whom use the term *religious pluralism* exclusively for various forms of normative religious pluralism. For example, Françoise Champion understands *religious pluralism* to be a political principle, and describes how it has gained currency as such in France over the last fifteen or twenty years among social-science researchers, political analysts and sociologists. She distinguishes two main types of (what I would call) *nor-mative religious pluralism,* which she terms *emancipatory pluralism* and *identity-based pluralism.* Emancipatory pluralism is the claim that the adherents of different religions should be granted equal individual rights. Identity based pluralism is an attempt to go beyond the liberalism of emancipatory pluralism by recognizing an equality of group rights, as has been suggested by some communitarian thinkers.

Often discussions of religious pluralism focus on epistemological issues. *Epistemological religious pluralism* is the view that all the major religious creeds are equally justified according to some proposed criteria of epistemological justification or warrant. This way of putting the matter focuses on the beliefs regardless of who holds them, as though the beliefs themselves have the capacity for being held as justified or warranted beliefs. We could call this *epistemological belief pluralism* and contrast it to *epistemological agent pluralism*, which would be expressed by the claim that the followers of no particular religion have any epistemological advantage in their beliefs over the followers of other religions. Of course, this would be an *equality pluralism*. We should not think that the followers of any of the major religions are a bunch of dummies, but are, generally speaking, epistemic peers. An epistemological *degree pluralist* would hold that the adherents of several religions differ to some degree in being justified or warranted in holding their beliefs, but that these differences are not sufficient for only one group to be justified and the rest unjustified.

Again, this could be defined as belief pluralism or as agent pluralism. It would be reasonable to expect to find differences in degree of average intelligence of the followers of different religions, but these differences do not seem so great that we could reasonably claim that the adherents of one faith alone have justified beliefs while the rest don't know how to think properly. The issue becomes more contentious when we consider *belief pluralism*. Some religious beliefs seem to be intrinsically harder to justify than others. Perhaps every religion has its difficult beliefs and easy beliefs, and perhaps they balance out in the end. But it would not be unreasonable to suspect that there could well be differences on the whole in the justifiability of different creeds.

Alethic religious pluralism is about the truth of beliefs rather than their justification. Unlike epistemological pluralism, there is no division here between belief pluralism and agent pluralism. Equality pluralism here would be the position that all the major religions are equally true. This position could be interpreted in a number of different ways. It would not make much sense to say that all the statements in the creeds of every major religion are equally true, because they contradict one another. Of course, one could adopt a relativist position on truth, but that seems a pretty heavy price to pay. Another way to accept contradictory religious claims would be to adopt what logicians call *dialetheism*, the view that some propositions are both true and false. Although dialetheism accepted by the great Sufi theoretician Ibn Arabi, it does not appear to be an especially promising way to resolve interreligious contradictions. The ordinary way to be an equality pluralist about truth is to claim that the same amount of truth is to be found in the creeds of every religion. The obvious problem here is that we have no way to measure relative amounts of truth. We cannot just add up the beliefs and see how many come out true on each list.

Religions are not theories, nor can they be reduced to their creeds. They also have a practical side. The practical aspect of religion can give rise to two sorts of pluralism. First, one might claim that the major religions counsel equally noble moralities, either with regard to the values they instill, the obligations they place upon their adherents or the virtues they encourage. Let's call this *ethical religious pluralism*. Like epistemological pluralism, ethical pluralism may take the form of agent *pluralism* or precept *pluralism*. Agent ethical pluralism holds that the adherents of no particular religion have any significant moral distinction over the adherents of any other major religion. Precept pluralism is the claim that the moral precepts taught by the major faith traditions are equally right. Once again, this sort of pluralism can be formulated as equality pluralism or degree pluralism.

There are two main approaches to ethical precept equality pluralism. One way is to accept a version of moral relativism. Each religion's morality is excellent by its own lights, and there is no absolute position from which one could be said to be better than any other. The other way, which is more commonly proposed, is to claim that the fundamental moral principles of the entire major religions boil down to some common set of moral principles such as the golden rule, and that the particular differences in moral systems are unimportant. The second sort of pluralism that arises in consideration of the practical aspect of religion pertains to specifically religious obligations instead of moral obligations. Is it possible to fulfill one's religious obligations equally through adherence to any of a plurality of religions?

A negative answer is given by those who reject *deontological religious pluralism*. They hold that God has commanded all of mankind at the present time to accept a specific religion. Choice of religion is not a matter of personal preference, but of obedience to divine prescription. Those who defend religious pluralism usually take religious choice to be a matter of personal preference because of the normative pluralistic claim that no one should impose or force any religion on anyone. However, normative and deontological pluralism should not be confused. One may endorse normative pluralism while denying deontological pluralism, that is, one may affirm that people should make their religious commitments in accord with their own personal consciences, and reject the notion that whatever they decide is in accord with the commands given by God through revelation. Indeed, I will argue that this sort of position is more consistent with a sound Islamic theology than a blanket acceptance of pluralism.

The sort of pluralism advanced by writers such as Ramakrishna (1834-1886), Madame Blavatsky (1831-1891), René Guénon (1886-1951) and Frithjof Schuon (1907-1998) could be called *hermetic religious pluralism.* According to this sort of religious pluralism, although religions are different exoterically, they share a common esoteric core. Although the thesis of hermetic pluralism is characteristically left rather vague, it is often presented as the claim that the major religions lead to the same goal, which is a certain perennial wisdom that comprises various metaphysical principles. A hermetic pluralist could claim that the religions are equally effective means for reaching this knowledge, or merely that the ultimate wisdom is the same, or that some essential portion of it is common to the esoteric traditions of the major religions.

Historically speaking, religious pluralism emerged as a theological position defended as such among Christian thinkers only in the twentieth century. Prior to that it is not difficult to find thinkers of various religious persuasions who advocated something that today we might call religious pluralism, at least in the form of a degree pluralism, but modern religious pluralism arose specifically in reaction to widespread Christian views about salvation. According to the traditional teachings of the Roman Catholic Church, it was held that there is "no salvation outside the Church." Since those outside the Church included unbaptized infants and the Old Testament prophets in addition to those considered damned, the Church taught that at the end of time the souls of such innocents would enter the Church and be saved. In this way it was maintained that there were absolutely no exceptions to the doctrine that only members of the Catholic Church could be saved.

This also explains the severity of excommunication. Excommunication is a form of censure by which the Church announces that a person who has committed a particularly grievous offence, such as heresy or apostasy, is not permitted to take part in the sacraments and is excluded from the Church. The most severe form of excommuni-cation (officially dropped by the Church after Vatican Council II), in which a person was declared anathema, was traditionally announced in a ceremony in which a bishop, wearing violet vestments, would recite a formula concluding with: "We separate him, together with his accomplices and abettors, from the precious body and blood of the Lord and from the society of all Christians; we exclude him from our holy mother the church in heaven and on earth; we declare him excommunicate and anathema; we judge him damned, with the devil and his angels and all the reprobate, to eternal fire until he shall recover himself from the toils of the devil and return to amendment and to penitence."

Excommunication was carried over from Catholicism into many Protestant denominations, although some preferred to speak of "church discipline" instead of excommunication. In any case, the result of Christian sectarianism was the widespread belief that those of all sects other than one's own were destined for hell. Often the belief that a person was destined for eternal punishment was taken as license for this worldly persecution. The Church's Office of the Inquisition would hand over those it found guilty of heresy to the secular authorities who would torture and execute them. The torture and execution stopped before people stopped considering one another damned for being Lutherans or Catholics, and this had more to do with the Enlightenment and the spread of political liberalism than any change in theology.

A major force against the view that Christians not of one's sect are damned came in the form of the ecumenical movement. The ecumenical movement grew out of Protestant missionary activity. In 1910 a number of Protestant missionary societies held a conference in Edinburgh to discuss common goals and overcome sectarian antagonism in the propagation of Christianity.

This eventually led to the formation of the World Council of Churches, in 1948. The Catholic Church took major steps toward ecumenism at Vatican Council II (1962-1965). Not only was there an attempt at reconciliation with Protestants, but a more tolerant attitude toward the adherents of non-Christian faiths was also encouraged. Reconciliation has not been quick. It was only in October of 1999 that in Augsburg, Germany, representatives of the Lutheran World Federation and the Vatican signed a statement lifting the mutual condemnations of the sixteenth century.

Likewise, a respect for non-Christian faiths was advocated among Protestants through the Commission of Appraisal appointed by the Laymen's Foreign Missionary Inquiry in 1932. The report of this commission, chaired by William Ernest Hocking, was seen as unacceptably liberal by conservative Christians, and Hocking defended it from charges of relativism and syncretism. The sort of religious pluralism that emerged from the ecumenical movement has tended to be degree *pluralism*. One religious tradition is generally taken to have an advantage over the others with regard to the truth of its creed, the morality of its precepts, and its efficacy in guiding to salvation. However, the ecumenical thinkers allow that those not of their own sect may attain salvation, lead moral lives, and understand the truth, at least partially.

Sometimes this sort of ecumenical attitude toward other religions is called *inclusivism*. The focus of inclusivism is on salvation. Inclusivism is a form of reductive pluralism as defined above, because it holds that all that are saved through any religion are saved by virtue of an element common to them. Inclusivism is typically degree pluralism because it holds that this common element is found in its best or purest form in a single religion. John Hick, whose entire career has been devoted to a theological defence of religious pluralism, admits that his own pluralistic theology grew out of the ecumenical spirit of inclusivism, as taught by the Jesuit Karl Rahner (1904-1984). Hick moves beyond Rahner's inclusivism by approaching equality pluralism rather than degree pluralism, and by insisting that it is by virtue of moral guidance common to all the major religious traditions that the religions are vehicles of salvation.

Hick's pluralism also shares various features in common with the proponents of hermetic pluralism, since he holds that religious differences are like the masks of an ineffable reality. Hermetic religious pluralism was thrust into the spotlight of theological discussion by the World's Parliament of Religions held in Chicago in 1893, and promoted by Theosophists, Swedenborgians and Transcendentalists. The Theosophist, in particular, advocated a much more radical form of hermetic religious pluralism than that which grew out of the ecumenical movement. The most articulate spokesperson for hermetic religious pluralism today is Seyyed Hossein Nasr.

A Critique of Reductive Religious Pluralism

John Hick attempts to model the rationality of religious belief on that of perceptual belief. While our perceptual beliefs are formed on the basis of sense experience, religious beliefs are formed on the basis of religious experiences. This attempt has given rise to problems that stem from the fact that while there is a great deal of agreement on what perceptual beliefs are supported by our sensory experiences, there is much disagreement about what religious beliefs should be adopted on the basis of religious experience. Aside from this problem, commentators have expressed dissatisfaction with the ineffability of the Ultimate Reality in Hick's theory. "If we are left with nothing to be said about God or the Ultimate as it is in itself," it is argued, "our religious belief more closely approximates unbelief and becomes relatively indistinguishable from atheism."

Another problem with Hick's religious pluralism has to do with the fact that religions are more than collections of doctrines. Religions have important practical dimensions, not only because of the moral codes they promote, but also because of their ritual and aesthetic dimensions. Even if the doctrinal conflicts among religions could be reconciled along the lines suggested by Hick, the practical conflicts would remain. Of course, the practical demands of a religion with a strong juridical element, like Judaism, are integrated with its doctrinal elements. The force of Jewish law derives from its source in God mediated by the prophets. To the extent that the characterization of God presented to Jews through their prophets is considered a merely human product that does not really describe the Supreme Being itself, the force of Jewish law is weakened. The difference between being circumcised and uncircumcised becomes a mere cultural difference.

Ritual and sacrament are able to lift the believer from the mundane world to a confrontation with the Ultimate because they are special; because the Ultimate or the representative of the Ultimate has ordained them. While this is compatible with there being a variety of ritual ways ordained by God, the replacement of particular beliefs about the Ultimate by the notion that particular beliefs and practices are mere cultural products by means of which one approaches an ineffable reality, reduces the specifically religious imperative. If the Jewish law is a cultural expression of God's will that is in no way superior to the absence of such law in Christianity, why bother with it? Hick's religious pluralism is the advocacy of a forced doctrinal synthesis. It will not allow for ultimate differences in religious belief. No matter how strenuously the Hindu or Buddhist denies the personal nature of ultimate reality, and no matter how fervently the Christian asserts it, Hick would claim that there is no real conflict. Each merely expresses features of his or her own avenue to the Ultimate.

This fails to do justice to the lived differences and conflicts among the adherents of the world's religions. While religious pluralism is advertised as a theology of tolerance, it turns out to be intolerant of serious religious differences. According to liberal political theory there is a sharp distinction between the public and private realms. Essentially private individuals posit a public realm through the social contract in order to satisfy mutual interests. Since the society includes those with differing religious ideas, religion is to be excluded from the public realm. Secularism is a corollary of political liberalism. Differences in religious belief are treated as aesthetic differences, or differences in taste. The social dimension of religion is subordinated to the personal. This attitude toward religion is also reflected in the philosophy of religious pluralism advocated by Hick, because he sees differences in religion as cultural differences in the expression of belief. All the religions involve a turning of the individual from self-centeredness to Reality-centeredness, and the differences between the ways in which this is done in the various religions are non-essential, like matters of personal taste.

According to reductive pluralism, preference for the Buddhist, Islamic, or Jewish ways is not to be decided by rational deliberation, for it is simply a matter of feeling, largely determined by one's cultural training. As a result of such a view, reductive pluralists, like liberals, will underrate the social dimensions of religion. The specifically religious is excluded from public discourse by the liberal because of the lack of mutual interest, and by the reductive pluralist because the specifically religious can have no cognitive import, since it is merely an aspect of personal preference. Liberalism and reductive religious pluralism both emphasize faith over practice in religion. The fact that no one should be forced to espouse a given creed is taken by liberals as a definitive statement of religious freedom. The use of the coercive force of the state to impose laws at odds with religious codes, e.g. the illegality of Mormon polygamy, is not considered to impinge on religious freedom, for what is restricted is practice, not belief. Pluralism also emphasizes faith over practice in its very conception of the problem of religious diversity as one to be solved by an ultimate reconciliation of beliefs.

Liberalism and reductive pluralism both present themselves in the guise of neutrality while in fact they both exclude various religious systems of belief and practice. In some cases we may applaud the exclusions. No one should object to the fact that religions in which human sacrifice is a central part are stifled in liberal societies. However, while

Hick is willing to allow for a hidden compatibility among a wide variety of beliefs, exclusivist beliefs themselves are to be rejected rather than reinterpreted. Reductive pluralism dismisses the exclusivist claims of any religion as nonessential, no matter how important in that religion's own tradition.

Neither liberalism nor reductive religious pluralism is religiously neutral. Both discriminate against religious views in which there is a strong emphasis on the practical social dimension of religion. This line of criticism has been levelled against Hick's pluralism by Ninian Smart, who points out those differences among religions in truth-claims are at least matched in importance by differences in practice-claims. A similar critique of the religious pluralism of W. C. Smith has been presented by Ali Quli Qarai, who argues effectively that religion has been understood as law no less than as faith in most of the major religious traditions of the world. Even if an ultimate resolution of truth-claims were a plausible suggestion, this would not resolve the conflict of practice-claims. What is distinctive and important about religions is not only their particular systems of belief, but rituals, ethical ideals, and laws.

If a religion is valuable and worth preserving, much of its value would appears to stem from its practical side. A freedom of religion limited to freedom to believe as one chooses, but not necessarily to practice the ordinances of one's faith, would result in the devaluation of religion. A number of recent critics, whose views are presented and criticized by Peter Donovan (1993: 217-29), have taken note of the similarity between religious pluralism and political liberalism. Both involve compromise, accommodation, and the abandonment of tradition. Some conservative Christian thinkers contend that pluralism must be rejected because it threatens to undermine the doctrines of the Trinity and the Incarnation. As political liberalism undermines the political power of the Church, religious pluralism undermines its dogmas.

Jürgen Moltmann also likens pluralism in religion to the consumerism of Western society, and accuses it of a "repressive tolerance," which allows everything a subjective possibility but is sceptical about any objective reality being adequately mediated by religious symbols. Many of the critics about whom Donovan reports find common cause with post-modernistic critiques of liberalism and the Enlightenment. Donovan finds it ironic "to see the descendants of Calvin and of the Inquisition joining forces with the disciples of Nietzsche to give lessons on tolerance to the children of the Enlightenment" (1993: 219), and he observes that despite their common cause in attacking liberalism, the conservative Christian and the postmodernist are fundamentally opposed on epistemological issues, with the postmodernist rejecting the realism of the conservative, while it is precisely because of his theological realism that the conservative cannot accept liberal religious pluralism.

Donovan himself seeks to defend some form of religious pluralism and liberalism, but only in the sense of respect for differences of belief, which he calls epistemic liberalism in contrast to the ideological liberalism of modernists who seek to bring the beliefs and practices of others into line with a secular, scientific and humanistic world-view to form a uniform global culture. The culture of materialistic consumerism and extreme individualism associated with ideological liberalism threatens to destroy the Christian culture out of which it emerged, a culture that often seems to have been taken for granted by advocates of liberalism themselves, at least prior to the second half of the twentieth century. Although political liberalism arose out of an attempt to protect Christian culture from destroying itself through sectarian strife, the social changes that are justified by contemporary ideological liberalism are no less destructive, particularly the weakening of traditional familial relationships.

The Christian response to the onslaught of ideological liberalism and its attendant social changes has been divided between the resistance and accommodation characteristic of conservative and liberal Christianity respectively. In this conflict, the religious pluralism advocated by John Hick, W. C. Smith and others provides a theological basis for ideological liberalism. Hick claims that on the basis of the common ethical ideals of the great traditions, beliefs may be discredited if they run contrary to the dominant ethical current, e.g. the Jewish doctrine of "the chosen people". Indeed, although Hick is willing to open the gates of heaven to the heathen, this does not mean that he is unwilling to pass moral judgment on religions.

In fact, Hick argues that since reason cannot provide any useful criterion for grading religions, the standard against which they are to be measured is moral, although even here the great religious traditions of the world are so rich and varied that the cannot be judged as totalities:

How do we weigh the savage aspects of life in some Eastern and Middle Eastern countries — the bloody massacres at the time of the partition of India, the cutting off of a thief's hands under Islamic law — against the Christian persecution of the Jews throughout the ages and above all in our own century? (1985: 85)

It is clear from Hick's query that, while religious traditions cannot be easily graded, this does not mean that particular elements and practices are not to be judged. And what are the standards to be used for such judgments? Hick's answer is clear. His preferred moral response to the Ultimate Reality is modern liberalism. He does not mean to claim that Christianity is preferable to other religions because of its liberalism, but rather he invites all to moral approbation under the wide umbrella of religious pluralism to the extent that they are willing to participate in the liberal agenda, about which Hick writes:

These modern liberal ideas have indeed first emerged in the West; but they are essentially secular ideas, which have been and are as much opposed as supported within the Christian churches. Contemporary Marxist, humanist and feminist critiques of economic, racial and sexual oppression have become common currency in Western liberal thinking, and have evoked their echoes in liberation and black and feminist theologies. But it would be erroneous to conclude, from the fact that these ideas have affected Western Christianity first among the religions, that Christianity has a proprietary interest in them. Our contemporary Western liberal-democratic, politically, racially and sexually liberated form of Christianity represents a creative synthesis of the Christian tradition with secular liberalism; and analogous syntheses are beginning to emerge within the other traditions. (1985: 86-87)

Muslims will have no quarrel with the liberal's rejection of racism, but from the standpoint of Islamic morals (and for that matter, traditional Christian morals, as well), "sexual liberation" is a euphemism for licentiousness together with its public acceptance, which has profound social consequences. While the contemporary Western liberal assimilates condemnation of homosexual behaviour to racism, the contemporary Muslim considers any sort of sex out of wedlock, like racism, to be sinful.

Hick's willingness to use his liberal standards to condemn the application of the *shari'ah* is also clearly stated:

But, whilst the enshrining of detailed seventh-century Arabian laws as permanent divine commands for Islamic societies has hindered the development of more humane and sophisticated penal systems, fortunately it has not prevented many modern Islamic states from finding ways to depart in practice from the full rigour of the traditional Shariah. It has made penal advances difficult but happily not impossible. (1989: 336)

We can summarize the criticisms of Hick's religious pluralism as follows. First, it advertises itself as the toleration of different faith traditions while in fact it prescribes the mutilation of these traditions in order to eliminate the ultimate differences among them. Second, it considers the apparent conflicts among religious traditions to be doctrinal rather than practical, thus ignoring the importance of religious law and community. Third, by diminishing the importance of doctrinal differences it weakens the prescriptive force of religious law. Fourth, it dismisses the use of reason as a means to advance religious understanding and settle disputes, despite the fact that such rational argumentation has been prominent in the theological or scholarly traditions of all the major world religions. Fifth, it misconstrues mysticism as a means of obtaining personal religious experiences on the basis of which beliefs may be justified. Sixth, it presupposes the correctness of the modern ethos of political liberalism despite the fact that this, too, is inconsistent with the moral traditions of the world religions as they have been understood for centuries.

On the other hand, it is part of the appeal of Hick's program that it does promise some form of reconciliation, some attenuation of the conflicts among religious believers which cause so much suffering in the world today, even as they have for centuries past. It would seem that an ideal approach to the problem posed by the variety of religious faiths would be one that recognised and allowed for ultimately irreconcilable differences in practice as well as theory, while at the same time providing motivation for tolerance. I believe that valuable suggestions for such an approach to the world's religions can be found within the Islamic tradition, which I shall dub *non-reductive religious pluralism*. Non-reductive pluralism is able to avoid the objections raised against liberal or reductive pluralism while maintaining an attitude of tolerance and rejecting prejudice.

In order to develop a non-reductive pluralism it will be helpful to reflect why the sort of pluralism advocated by Hick might be expected to win little support among Muslims, and why it has won the support of an important, if small, group of Christians. The first difficulty has already been mentioned: Islam, like Judaism, features a legalistic form of piety. Its aspirations are social. No matter how miserably we fail, Muslims aspire to build a society founded on the example of the Prophet's just governance in accordance with Divine law. This aspiration cannot be sustained if the *shari'ah* is nothing more than a by-product of early medieval Arabia's cultural response to its Prophet's confrontation with Reality. In terms of the Christian experience, however, in which legalistic forms of piety are viewed at best with suspicion, if not condemned as outright Pharisaic hypocrisy, the idea that ritual laws and taboos are human constructs rather than Divine ordinances is much more likely to be welcomed.

Another difficulty is that its relationship to other religions is a matter treated fairly extensively within the *shari'ah* itself, and even in the Qur'an. Pre-Islamic paganism cannot be viewed as simply another way in which man relates himself to Ultimate Reality under the pretext that polytheism and monotheism are merely conceptually different approaches to what is inconceivable. This aspect of Hick's pluralism seems to be what is most repugnant to many Christian thinkers, as well as Muslims. Monotheism is inherently iconoclastic, but if monotheism and polytheism are just two ways to the Ultimate, how can we justify Abraham's breaking of the idols? Was his message really nothing more than that the worship of idols had become inappropriate in his time and locale? A non-reductive pluralism should respect the absolute claims of monotheism.

According to traditional Christian thinking, salvation is only possible through belief in Jesus Christ as Lord, and it is through this faith that one participates in the redemptive sacrifice of the Son of God. True belief is a necessary condition for salvation. Christians who are unwilling to go as far as Hick in their acceptance of non-believers, yet who reject the dogmatic assertion of their damnation, have found a third alternative in Karl Rahner's concept of anonymous Christians mentioned above. According to this idea, non-Christians who lead good lives about whom it seems monstrous to claim that they must be damned may be said to be Christians even though they do not recognise this themselves. Rahner goes on to assert that if such people were properly exposed to the true teachings of Christ, they would abandon their former beliefs and become official Christians. Being an anonymous Christian is rather like holding an honorary degree from a university: despite lack of training at the school, one's achievements are recognised by the university and the degree is awarded.

Hick has argued that this view is unsatisfactory for a number of reasons. It is patronizing. It fails to recognise the positive role a non-Christian faith may have in turning one from self-centeredness toward the Ultimate. It also substantially weakens the meaning of salvation through faith in the death and resurrection of Christ. What is needed is a religious pluralism able to fully appreciate the significant differences among religions, able to recognise that different ways toward human perfection and ultimate felicity are offered by the religions, despite their differences, and yet able to grant these points without diluting the strength of the religious claims by any kind of relativism. This is the promise of the non-reductive religious pluralism of Islam proposed below.

The Non-Reductive Religious Pluralism of Islam

When we consider how a non-reductive religious pluralism might be formulated in the context of Islam, we must keep in mind that the issue of religious pluralism emerges in Christianity as a reaction to specifically Christian doctrines about salvation: that it is only through Christianity that one can benefit from the Redemption and gain salvation. A similar exclusivist doctrine can be found in some interpretations of the Jewish claim to be "the chosen people." These doctrines are thoroughly condemned in the Qur'an:

> *And they say none shall enter paradise unless he is a Jew or a Christian, these are their vain wishes. Say, "Bring your proof if your are truthful." Yes! Whosoever submits himself to Allah and he is a doer of good, for him there shall be his reward with his Lord, on such shall be no fear nor shall they grieve.* (Qur'an, 2: 110-11)

Religious pluralism emerges in Christianity as a reaction against the very attitude so eloquently condemned in the verses cited above. According to traditional Christian teaching, there is no way to salvation aside from the redemption offered by Christ, and even the great prophets, peace be with them, must wait in limbo until the resurrection, after which Christ must come to release them! Those Christian theologians who have opposed this line of thought and have sought to allow that non-Christians can achieve salvation have claimed that the saving faith either includes the unconscious acceptance of Christianity or is the common heritage of the world's major religious traditions. Despite their differences, there is a common presumption shared by the various Christian parties to the dispute on pluralism.

For Hick and Rahner, as well as the dogmatist, correct faith is necessary for salvation. In order to widen the opening of the gates of heaven, Rahner extends the notion of correct faith to those who live as if they were Christians and who would accept Christianity if properly exposed to it, while Hick goes further to deny that the apparent differences among the world's faiths are irreconcilable. Hick's ultimate reconciliation is what makes apparently different faiths correct. What Hick does is to loosen the condition of correct belief so that it is reduced to the common factor in all the world's religions, however abstract this may be; nevertheless, it remains as much a part of Hick's doctrine as Luther's that there can be no salvation without correct faith, even if the correct faith according to Hick is something of a least common denominator.

In order to understand how to approach the problem of religious pluralism in the context of Islam, the two issues of correct faith and salvation need to be clearly distinguished. According to Islam, the correct religion ordained by God is that revealed to the last of His chosen prophets, Muhammad (s); this and no other religion is required by Allah of all mankind. In this sense, Islam is exclusivist. However, at various times prior to His final revelation, God ordained other religions by means of His prophets. So, the reason why the religion brought by Moses ('a) is not acceptable today is not that what Moses taught was wrong or incompatible with the teachings brought by Muhammad (s), for they taught basically the same things, but because God has ordained the latter teachings for this era. The previous teachings were not incorrect, and they were sufficient to guide the people for whom they were revealed to salvation.

Although some scholars seek to minimize the importance of this fact by appealing to *riwayat* (narrations) according to which the differences among the revealed religions amount to no more than the details of ritual practice, such as how many prostrations occur in various prayers, the number of days on which fasting is prescribed, and the like, there can be no denying that different paths can lead to God, and in different circumstances have been ordained by Him. All of the divinely revealed religions are called Islam in the general sense of complete submission to the commands of Allah; while Islam is used in a specific sense to refer to the final version of Islam (in the general sense) brought by Muhammad (s). The difference between general and specific Islam gives rise to a number of interesting questions. How much variation can there be in the varieties of general Islam? Could God have ordained a version of general Islam for a people so different from us that we would not recognise it as such? Why did God ordain different versions of general Islam? The exact answers to these questions are with God alone. But in the present age, general Islam implies specific Islam, and this must be understood if one is not to fall into error about the position of Islam with respect to religious diversity.

It is because of the demand that Muhammad (s) be recognised as the Seal of the Prophets (s) that the reductive pluralists' solution to the problem of religious diversity cannot be accepted. To accept only some of the prophets ('a) to the exclusion of others, particularly Muhammad (s), with the excuse that it makes no difference because all the religions are ultimately saying the same thing, is to fail to heed the divine call. Verily those who deny God and His apostles and desire that they differentiate between God and His apostles and say "We believe in some and we deny, some," and intend to take a course between this (and that), these are the infidels, truly and we have prepared for the infidels a disgraceful torment. (Qur'an, 4: 150-151)

According to reductive religious pluralism there can be no better reason for adopting one religion rather than another than cultural affinity. As a result, the importance of the divine law is undermined. In the context of Islam, on the other hand, the *shari'ah* brought by God's final chosen Apostle (s) is understood as the perfection of all previously ordained ways. The divine call to follow the law of Islam is extended to all humanity, not merely to those of a specific cultural setting:

And We did not send you but to all people as a bearer of good tidings and as a Warner, but most people do not know. (Qur'an, 34: 28)

With regard to the question of the correctness of faith, the position of Islam is clear. At various times in human history different faiths and laws were decreed by Allah.

At present, however, there is but one divinely ordained religion, Muhammadan Islam, which requires belief in God's oneness (*tawhid*), prophecy (*nabbuwah*), and the

Resurrection (*ma'ad*). As God says:

> *O you who believe! Believe in Allah and His Apostle and the Book which He has sent down to His Apostle and the Book which He sent down before; and whoever decries Allah and His angels and His books and His apostles and the Last Day has indeed strayed off, far away.* (Qur'an, 4: 136)

In sum, reductive pluralism is incompatible with Islam because according to reductive pluralism there is no requirement to accept all of the prophets ('a) and no requirement to obey the practical laws given through God's last chosen messenger (s), while according to the teachings of Islam, these divine prescriptions are clear. Reductive religious pluralism presents itself as an opening up toward other traditions, while from the standpoint of Islam, it is an attempt to open the way to *kufr*, a covering of one's eyes and ears to the truth of God's final revelation and its practical implications.

The solution proposed by Hick to this conflict is garbed in the euphemism "creative doctrinal development" (1985: 50). The patronizing tone in the following passage is typical of the liberal mentality:

> Islam may be expected to go through essentially the same traumas as Christianity in its encounter both with modern science and with the emerging ecumenical outlook; only whereas the Christian trauma has been spread over a century or more, Islam has to adjust in a single generation to an already formed modern culture. It is to be hoped that the Muslim world will eventually find its own Qur'anic way of combining modern knowledge with its faith in the Transcendent and its commitment to a morality of human community. And we may further hope that this development will also include an increased recognition of the ecumenical point of view that has already been so powerfully expressed within the Sufi strand of Islam.

The final remark about "the Sufi strand of Islam" requires a discussion more detailed than that to be offered here, but if Hick is under the impression that his reductive religious pluralism can find support in true *tasawwuf* or *'irfan*, a fairly powerful argument can be given that he is mistaken, the outlines of which may take the following form. While there may be some degenerate Sufi *tariqat* willing to play the role assigned for them by Hick, and there are orders in the West into which non-Muslims have been initiated, the vast majority of the *'urafa'*, or gnostics, of Islam have required strict observance of the *shari'ah* prior to initiation into spiritual wayfaring (*sayr wa suluk*). Hick is fond of citing the following couplet of Jalal al-Din Rumi: "The lamps are different, but the Light is the same."

But this is what the Qur'an also affirms:

> *Verily We sent down the Torah in which there is guidance and light...* (Qur'an, 5: 44)
>
> *And We caused Jesus son of Mary to follow in their footsteps confirming the Torah which was before him and We gave him the Evangel in which was guidance and light...* (Qur'an, 5: 46)

But the conclusion reached in the Qur'an is not that, because all religions have divine light, it makes no difference which of them we follow, nor that religious choice is a matter of ethnicity. It is not as though we are presented with different lamps from which we are to choose in accordance with our own taste, background and the quality of our personal experiences; rather God presents the lamps to humanity in succession, and it is our responsibility to follow what God has assigned for us at the present age. Rumi was by no means a reductive religious pluralist of the sort Hick makes him out to be. The Sufis have sought to explain the fact that there are differences in the religions that have been divinely ordained with the distinction between the exterior (*zahir*) and the interior (*batin*) of the religions. The differences among them are exterior differences; the interior is the same. However, the vast majority of Sufis have affirmed the duty to follow the prescriptions of the law of Islam with the slogan: no *tariqah* without *shari'ah*. There is no way to the interior except through the exterior, and the exterior required in the current age is that of Islam.

Just as a thing fails if it lacks a kernel so too it fails without a skin. If you sow a seed in the earth without its husk, it fails to germinate, whereas if you bury it in the earth with its husk it does germinate and becomes a great tree. (Rumi 1972: 31)

Nevertheless, a theme commonly found in the Sufi poets such as 'Attar, Rumi and Hafiz is the expression of affinity toward Christianity or Zoroastrianism. This might lead some to the mistaken conclusion that these poets considered the differences between Islam and the other religions to be insignificant. What is really to be found in such expressions is the condemnation of the display of the outward signs of affiliation to Islam without any inward faith. It would be better to have nominal affiliation to an incorrect creed, but to believe sincerely in it and to follow the guidance in it for spiritual advancement than to be a hypocrite who outwardly professes Islam while inwardly he worships idols.

If we are to compare different forms of *kufr*, or unbelief, surely that of the hypocrite is worse than that of the sincere Zoroastrian. The outward denial of orthodoxy found in Hafiz (and even Imam Khomeini), e.g., staining the prayer mat with wine or consulting the Magi (*pir-e moghan*), becomes a means of indicating the interior dimension of religion and denying hypocrisy, but unless the hyperbole is understood in this symbolism, it will appear as apostasy. Hypocrisy occurs with the outward affirmation of Islam and the inward denial. Imam Khomeini, following the example of Hafiz, wishes to emphasize the opposite of hypocrisy, namely sincere belief in Islam, so he exaggerates by invoking the opposite extreme, the outward denial of

Islam with its inward affirmation; in this way *kufr* becomes a symbol for true *iman*!

Kiss the hand of the sheikh who has pronounced me a disbeliever.

Congratulate the guard who has led me away in chains.

I am going into solitary retreat from now on by the door of the Magus.

The great Sufi theoretician, Ibn 'Arabi taught that the fact that God's truth can find expression in different, even apparently conflicting, religions does not mean that people are free to choose whatever religion suits their fancy. Ibn al-'Arabi himself asserts that it is incumbent upon people in the present age to follow the *shari'ah* brought by Muhammad (s), and it is in this sense that all previously revealed religions become invalid (*batil*) with the revelation of the Qur'an. This does not mean that they become false, but that it becomes obligatory to follow the *shari'ah* of specific Islam rather than that of a previous revealed religion. In this sense all previously decreed systems of religious law do become null and void, not because they are worthless, but because whatever is needed from them has been incorporated into the final revelation. He puts it as follows:

All the revealed religions [*shara'i*] are lights. Among these religions, the revealed religion of Muhammad is like the light of the sun among the lights of the stars. When the sun appears, the lights of the stars are hidden, and their lights are included in the light of the sun. Their being hidden is like the abrogation of the other revealed religions: that takes place through Muhammad's revealed religion. Nevertheless, they do in fact exist, just as the existence of the light of the stars is actualized. This explains why we have been required in our all-inclusive religion to have faith in the truth of all the messengers and all the revealed religions. They are not rendered null (*batin*) by abrogation that is the opinion of the ignorant. The difference between the Sufis and the theologians on the diversity of religions is one of emphasis more than explicit doctrine. The Sufis emphasise the inner unity of the revealed religions while the theologians emphasise the outward superiority of Islam, but there is no real difference on either point. The theologians admit that the previous revealed religions contain light and guidance, for this is explicitly stated in the Qur'an.

The fact that in the present age it is only the Islam revealed to Muhammad (s) that is valid and whose law is obligatory is also accepted by the Sufis. Both groups hold that the previously revealed religions, including the Christianity brought by Jesus ('a), do not contain any doctrinal differences from Islam, but the Sufi is more willing than the theologian to look for insights contained in the other religions, despite what is considered by both the theologian and the Sufi to be the accretion of doctrinal error, to the precise extent that the primary concern of the Sufi is spiritual insight rather than doctrine. Because of his attention to the inward dimension, the *'arif* is also willing to allow for greater variance in outward diversity as expressions of a single Truth than those whose major preoccupation is doctrinal and ritual detail. In any case, both groups hold that Islam brings to perfection all that was contained in the previously revealed religions, and is the sole religion prescribed by God for the present age until the end of time. However, the *'arif* is willing to give poetic expression to his faith and to the rejection of hypocrisy through the symbols of the other religions, and even idol worship, as in the following lines from Baba Tahir and Imam Khomeini, respectively:

Synagogue, Ka'abah, idol-temple, monastery,
None are known to be empty of the sweetheart.
At the door of the tavern,
Temple, mosque and monastery,

I have fallen in prostration, as though you had glanced upon me.

Another line of thought about the diversity of religions is to be found in the tradition of Islamic philosophy. After explaining that the common people whom the prophets ('a) sought to guide are not capable of appreciating philosophical wisdom, al-Farabi writes: "These things are thus allegorized for every nation or people in terms familiar to them, and it is possible that what is familiar to one people is foreign to another." In al-Farabi's view, which is to a great extent accepted by Ibn Sina, the religions all express a single philosophical truth in different symbols and through these symbols they serve to organise society and lead humanity to felicity. Furthermore, each great religion contains, in its corpus of revelations, "sufficient glimpses of pure truth to lead the elect seekers of truth to pursue this truth itself and to be able to allegorically interpret the rest of the symbols."

According to al-Farabi, the spiritual content and background of all religion is identical, since this is universal, but it is equally true that the symbols employed by the religions are nor at the same level. Because of this some religions are "nearer to the truth than others, some are more adequate than others in leading humanity to the higher truth, some, again, are more effective than others in gaining the belief of people and becoming the directive force of their lives. Indeed there are religions whose symbolisms are positively harmful." Like the Sufi position on the diversity of religions, nothing in the position of the philosophers contradicts the ideas emphasized by the theologians that in the present age the sole religion prescribed by God for mankind is Islam, that the previously revealed religions have become corrupted, that the beliefs associated with them differ from what was revealed to their prophets, and that Islam is the culmination of all previously revealed religions.

Where the Sufis and the philosophers differ is on how to understand the interior (*batin*) of the revealed religions, through spiritual unveilings or through philosophical argument. What is most notable for its absence is the sort of view advocated by reductive religious pluralism, according to which religions are validated by personal religious experience, that since all the religions express a single interior truth it makes no difference which is followed, and that the common truth of the world's religions in their contemporary forms are sufficient as guides to ultimate felicity. None of these essential elements of reductive religious pluralism would be acceptable within the theological, mystical or philosophical traditions of Islam. The view elaborated may seem to be exclusivist, because of the claim of the sole superiority of Islam among the religions of the world; however, it is pluralistic insofar as it admits that a plurality of religious traditions contain divine light and truth, that it is the responsibility of true believers to treat the followers of other traditions with acceptance and respect, and that the followers of other traditions may find the way to salvation through their own faiths by the grace of God.

One of the major motivations for liberal Christian religious pluralists was to provide the theological groundwork for better relations between Christians and non-Christians. Instead of viewing the non-Christian with contempt as damned, he or she is seen by the Christian pluralist as in essential agreement with Christianity, for all the major religions are held to differ only in their external aspects. Differences in religion are to be understood on the model of ethnic differences, and relations among the participants in different faith traditions are presumed to take shape within the framework of the liberal state, which proclaims complete religious neutrality. In Islamic thought, on the contrary, religious differences are not seen as a matter of personal preference, but as expressions of communal loyalty grounded in spiritual insight and critical evaluation. Those who choose a religion other than Islam are making a mistake, either sinfully or excusably. Since there is no way for us to tell whether or not the mistake is excusable, where good relations with non-Muslims are possible without condoning injustice, the presumption of an honest mistake is morally incumbent upon us.

In Christianity, especially in Protestant Christianity, there is a strong link between salvation and true belief, because it is through faith that one participates in the Redemption, which alone is believed to afford salvation. This link between true belief and salvation survives among Christian proposals for religious pluralism, like those of Wilfred Cantwell Smith and John Hick, in the idea that ultimately the variety of religious beliefs is a matter of surface dif-ferences over a fundamentally single faith, which may not even be expressible in human language. If one denies the doctrine of Redemption, and with it the link between faith and salvation which features so prominently in Christian thought, the obvious alternative, at least obvious in a Christian context, is the idea that faith is to be purchased through good works, an idea emphatically denounced by Luther and by the majority of Christian theologians, including Catholics, after him.

The Islamic tradition appears to offer another approach to the problem. Muslims, like Christians, reject the idea that good works alone are sufficient for salvation. Like Christian writings on the subject, it is not difficult to find Muslim expressions of the idea that there is nothing one can do through one's own efforts to make oneself worthy of salvation without the grace of God. This is a theme which runs throughout Imam Zayn al-'Abidîn's *Sahîfat al-Sajjadîyah*. Good works without faith appear ungrounded, for faith provides the cognitive framework in which the final good is to be understood and intentions to do good works are to be formed, and it is through such orientation and intentions that God draws His servants toward Him by His Mercy. But faith is more than the mere acceptance of a list of doctrines, it is a spiritual readiness to travel the way toward Allah and wholehearted submission to His will.

In Islam, salvation is seen in terms of the movement of the soul toward God, a movement that is explained in terms of the acquirement of the Divine attributes or extinction of the self in God through submission to Him, and whose aim is a beatific encounter with Divinity. To achieve this, God demands faith and good works, and in the present age, this means the acceptance and practice of Islam as revealed to the last of His chosen messengers (s). Ultimately, however, it is neither by faith nor good works that man is saved, but by the grace of God. So, in a sense, there may be a kind of redemption in Islam after all, although not by that name, and not necessarily through anyone's death. It is redemption by the grace of God that can be accomplished in accordance with His will in ways we may never imagine. An Islamic non-reductive pluralism may be contrasted with Hick's pluralism and Rahner's inclusivism in terms of the place of ignorance in the three views. In Hick's view, every major creed, no matter how different, expresses an ultimately single faith. That ultimate faith may not be expressible in human language, so there is a sense in which believers are ignorant of what they really believe. In Rahner's view, Christians know that they are Christians and it is only others who may be ignorant of their latent Christian belief.

According to the non-reductive view, no attempt is made to reinterpret apparently conflicting beliefs to reveal some hidden agreement. Instead of positing ignorance about what we believe, we are to admit our ignorance of how God may guide the sincere, and what beliefs are the results of a sincere quest for the truth. The identities of all the prophets are not known, and in the most famous *hadith* about the number of the prophets, Abu Dharr reports that the Prophet told him there were one hundred twenty-four thousand prophets. Corrupted forms of the teachings of these prophets may survive in any number of the variety of the world's religions and cultural legacies. The admission of ignorance in this matter is an expression of humility before the judgment of Allah; such humility has featured prominently in the Islamic tradition, and it may provide a basis for an Islamic form of a non-reductive religious pluralism. After mentioning some of the good people who will be saved and the hypocrites who will receive a double chastisement, the Qur'an mentions that there are others who must await the command of God. Until then, we cannot say whether they will be rewarded or punished:

> *And others must await the command of Allah, whether we will chastise them or whether He will turn to them. And Allah is all Knowing, all Wise.* (9: 106)

John Hick's religious pluralism is to be lauded as a great improvement over its exclusivist and inclusivist predecessors in Christian theology, and Muslims will be impressed by the fact that the denial of the traditional Christian dogma of the Incarnation brings Hick's theology much closer to Islamic doctrine. Nevertheless, Hick's reductive pluralism hides a set of moral and political values that are at odds with Islam. They are at odds with Islam not only because of the detail of the judgments they inform, but, even more significantly, because of where they set their standards. Islam teaches that we are to look to the Qur'an and the teachings of the Prophet (s) to find guidance in politics and morals, while Hick would have us turn to the worldly currents of modern thought, which are more often than not decidedly opposed to Islam. And although a severe punishment awaits the enemies of Islam, as for those who honestly accept an invalid creed, it must be admitted that this invalid creed itself may be the vehicle through which God extends to them His grace and leads them to salvation.

What is truly of value in Hick's religious pluralism is a tolerance that can be found more completely, in a sense, within the Islamic tradition, and may be formulated along the lines suggested above as a non-reductive religious pluralism. Many of the discussions of religious pluralism bog themselves down is questions of better/worse comparisons that often prompt defensive responses and a breakdown of meaningful dialogue. Through non-reductive religious pluralism, however, we can accept as granted that each person, rightly or wrongly, considers his own faith tradition as the best (in some sense, at least for himself), while admitting that in other traditions there may be genuine religious and moral values to be appreciated. This allows for dialogue without compromise, yet with openness to learning from the other.

Other tendencies that are sometimes found among those who favour interreligious dialogue are relativism and syncretism. Relativism (at least in the common forms one often encounters) is a barrier to meaningful discussion because it deprives one from the ability to criticize others or to seriously consider criticism. Syncretism undermines interreligious dialogue by condoning what is unacceptable by the mainstream of any of the traditions represented in the dialogue. Non-reductive religious pluralism allows one to maintain the absolute validity of one's own religious commitments while admitting that one can learn from and benefit from others.

Non-reductive religious pluralism allows us to maintain a particular religious identity while supporting and encouraging the other in his/her own identity. Identity politics is often one of communal violence and the exclusion of others who are seen as threats to one's identity; but exclusive associations with co-religionists are perfectly compatible with simultaneous interreligious association and cooperation. Perhaps through this sort of view we will be able to find a better way to defend religion in the modern world, to defend religion side by side with others who do not share our own religious views. To defend religion means to support, encourage and defend the dignity of others' faiths and practices to the greatest extent possible. We must confess that this is not unlimited. Each particular relation between faiths has its own specific difficulties and opportunities, and

I do not mean to give the impression that the sort of non-reductive pluralism here advocated means that we must content ourselves with statements and practices in other groups that we consider wrong.

However, it should be possible to defend the dignity of other religious affiliations (at least with regard to the major religious traditions) before our own co-religionists. It is especially appropriate for us to defend the dignity of the religious identity of the other when the other is of a religious faith in the Abrahamic traditions of Judaism, Christianity and Islam. Finally, we should pray together for divine guidance, charity, and understanding, for ourselves and for those of other faiths whom we encounter along the way toward Him.

It may be appropriate to end with a story from the poetry of Jalal al-Din Rumi, who is known in Iran as Mawlavi (my master). The story is told of a shepherd whose prayer is overheard by Moses:

Moses met a shepherd on the road, who kept saying, "O God!" and "O Allah!" "Where are You?— so I can become Your servant, and mend Your sandals and comb Your head. (So) I can wash Your robe, kill Your lice, (and) bring milk in front of You, O Great (Lord). (So) I can kiss Your small hand, massage Your small foot, and sweep Your little (dwelling) place (when) the time for sleep comes. All my goats are a sacrifice for You. (And all) my (shouts of) 'Hey!' and 'Ho!' are in remembrance of You. The shepherd was talking foolishly in this manner, (and) Moses said, "O so-and-so, to whom is this (being said to)?" He replied, "To the One who created us, by Whom the earth and the heavens came into view." Moses said, "Hey! You have become very backwards. You have certainly not become a Muslim. (Rather), you have become an unbeliever. "What is this foolish talk? What is this gibberish and ignorance of (true) belief? Press some cotton into your mouth!"

I do not mean to give the impression that the sort of non-reductive pluralism here advocated means that we must content ourselves with statements and practices in other groups that we consider wrong.

However, it should be possible to defend the dignity of other religious affiliations (at least with regard to the major religious traditions) before our own co-religionists. It is especially appropriate for us to defend the dignity of the religious identity of the other when the other is of a religious faith in the Abrahamic traditions of Judaism, Christianity and Islam. Finally, we should pray together for divine guidance, charity, and understanding for ourselves and for those of other faiths whom we encounter along the way toward Him.

It may be appropriate to end with a story from the poetry of Jalalal-Din Rumi, who is known in Iran as Mawlavi (my master). The story is told of a shepherd whose prayer is overheard by Moses.

Moses met a shepherd on the road, who kept saying, "O God," and "O Allah!" "Where are You?—so I can become Your servant and mend Your sandals and comb Your head. (So) I can wash Your robe, kill Your lice, (and) bring milk in front of You, O Great (Lord). (So) I can kiss Your small hand, massage Your small foot, and sweep Your [illegible] (sleeping place) when the time for sleep comes. All my goats (are) a sacrifice for You. (And) all my laments of 'Hey!' and 'Ho!' are in remembrance of You. The shepherd was talking foolishly in this manner. (and) Moses said, "O sir, addressed, to whom is this (being said to)?" He replied, "To the One who created us, by Whom the earth and the heavens came into view." Moses said, "Hey! You have become very backwards. You have certainly not become a Muslim (believer); you have become an unbeliever." "What is this foolish talk? What is this gibberish and ignorance of (true) belief? Press some cotton into your mouth!"

8

Transitional Justice, Reconciliation and Religion

The quest of international lawyers and human rights activists to have the late Chilean General Pinochet tried for his crimes, Archbishop Desmond Tutu exhorting victims to forgive their perpetrators in South Africa's Truth and Reconciliation Commission, a global breakout of public apologies, including President Bill Clinton's for not intervening in Rwanda, the German government's agreement to pay reparations to victims of forced labour during the Holocaust, scores of seminars, workshops, and forums on dealing with the past in Bosnia, Northern Ireland, Rwanda, Kashmir, South Africa, and many other locales: all are scenes from our age of transitional justice. Each portrays an effort to address the past injustices of a civil war or some form of authoritarianism: communism, military dictator-ship, apartheid. Transitional justice, of course, is nothing new. The punitive reparations imposed on Germany at the end of World War One and the Nuremberg Trials at the end of World War Two are standard chapters in inter-national relations textbooks.

What is novel to the past generation is the frequency, diversity, and innovation of confrontations with the past all over the globe and the accompanying tidal wave of analysis of these confrontations by legal scholars, political scientists, sociologists, anthropologists, historians, theologians, and journalists. In the same period, a separate trend has also risen, this one exemplified by Hindu nationalism in India, the political influence of conservative Christians in the United States, Islamic terrorism, Islamic democratization movements in Turkey and Indonesia, the political influence of Buddhism, both liberal democratic and authoritarian, a wave of democratization in Catholic states, and the remarkable growth of Protestant evangelicalism and Pentecostalism in Latin America and Africa. What these movements manifest is the rise of "public religion in the modern world," to use the phrase of sociologist Jose Casanova. Confounding apostles of the secularization thesis that dominated the social sciences and humanities for decades, public, political religion is global in its impact and diverse in its valences. That these two energetic global trajectories have crossed paths should not be surprising.

All over the world, pastors, prelates, and imams have advocated for truth commissions, trials, and reparations schemes and sometimes have even helped to conduct the commissions, as in Guatelama, where Archbishop Juan Gerardi both formed and led one. The language of faith comes through strongly in performances of apologies and forgiveness. It is often the religious who conduct civil society efforts to deal with the past and repair the body politic. Disproportionately to issues like globalization, climate change, and international trade, the religious are involved in dealing with the past, both as activists and as analysts. Beyond the scenes and anecdotes, though, can anything systematic be said about the nature and impact of religion's role in transitional justice? This essay is an effort to plumb current knowledge about these questions. But what exactly is transitional justice?

Wielders of the term usually have in mind efforts to deal with the injustices of a war or authoritarian regime during the "transitional" period after a peace agreement is signed or the regime has exited power. But this temporal focus is arbitrarily narrow. Activities identical to "transitional" ones often occur long after the actual transition away from war or authoritarianism: Germany's reparations agreement for Holocaust labourers came in the year 2000; the Spanish began digging up mass graves and telling the stories of victims of the Franco dictatorship thirty years after the dictator's death. For some human rights activists, transitional justice is the question of whether war criminals face trial. But this substantive focus is too narrow as well. Political efforts to deal with the past might also involve truth commissions, reparations, apologies, public memorials, forgiveness, as well as measures that civil society actors take to restore citizens and political orders in the wake of massive evil. Indeed, it can be argued that all of these activities constitute "justice." Such a definition of justice is admittedly a leading one, for as I shall explain, it comes from religious traditions.

We can think of transitional justice, then, as the sum total of activities that states and citizens undertake to redress past political injustices in order to restore political orders in the present and in the future. With this widened understanding, I survey present knowledge of religion's impact on transitional justice in two sections, the first on "thinkers," the theologians and other religious scholars who have written about dealing with past political injustices, and the second on accounts of "doers," the religious activists who have involved themselves in dealing with the past. For each section, I ask: All told, how do the religious think about or involve themselves in transitional justice? What, if anything, is distinctive about their approach? How does it differ from secular approaches?

Finally, in what areas might our understanding of religious thought and activity towards transitional justice be deepened? One of the emergent distinctive features of religious involvement in transitional justice is the theme of reconciliation. Although it is not only the religious who talk about reconciliation (secular people do, too), and although the religious do not only talk about reconciliation (as opposed to other approaches like accountability, democratization, and the like), religion and reconciliation still enjoy what Max Weber called an "elective affinity." Reconciliation finds a particularly strong justification in religious texts, traditions, and theologies and is espoused by religious actors disproportionately to secular actors. Religious people are arguably largely responsible for making reconciliation a fixture in today's global political discourse.

The Thinkers

Philosophers, theologians, and legal scholars who reason about transitional justice broadly fall into two sorts of intellectual traditions. The first is what I call the liberal human rights tradition. The second is religious traditions, particularly the Abrahamic traditions, Judaism, Christianity, and Islam, the ones that have said the most about transitional justice. Traditions are not hermetic, alternate universes. Voices in the religious traditions, to greater and lesser degrees, share both assumptions and conclusions with voices in the liberal human rights tradition. In fact, one can discern an increasing convergence in views of transitional justice over the past few years. Each tradition also contains internal disagreements, which indeed drive the tradition's evolution. Still, it is possible to identify distinct centers of gravity in the two traditions, certain commit-ments around which most of their members converge, even if they sometimes debate what these commitments mean. It is from these commitments that they engage with other traditions, sometimes finding common ground, sometimes sharpening their differences.

Broadly speaking, such an understanding is consistent with philosopher Alasdair MacIntyre's classic definition of tradition as "a historically extended, socially embodied argument." The liberal human rights tradition's center of gravity can be found in the arguments of the global community of human rights activists and international lawyers, who place a premium on the punishment of perpetrators and the vindication of victims in response to large scale crimes against humanity, war crimes, and other human rights violations. On what justification? Their arguments usually presuppose the classic retributivist appeal to desert but typically stress even more strongly the value of punishment for bringing about the Rechtstaat – a political order based on the rule of law, human rights, and democracy. Their preferred institution is the trial and their signature accomplishment the international tribunals for Yugoslavia and Rwanda and their subsequent institutionalization in the International Criminal Court.

What they most strongly decry are amnesties, especially blanket amnesties like those that Latin American states yielded to former dictators in the 1980s and early 1990s. They commonly appeal for material reparations for victims. They do not necessarily oppose truth commissions, especially insofar as these reinforce accountability and reparations through exposing political crimes: "All that a truth commission can achieve is to reduce the number of lies that can be circulated unchallenged in public discourse," wrote Michael Ignatieff in an often quoted passage. Indeed, since the days when commissions were typically accompanied by amnesties, as they were in Latin American and South Africa, human rights activists have come to recognize that truth commissions and trials need not be mutually exclusive, either in principle, or, as East Timor and Sierra Leone have proved, in practice. Their bottom line is that accountability should not be sacrificed. The overriding goal of the liberal human rights tradition is to strengthen international institutions and regimes so as to achieve as much accountability for human rights violators and as much compensation for victims as possible – all over the world.

The liberal human rights tradition's approach to past injustices is a close cousin of the "liberal peace building consensus," an approach to the reconstruction of war-torn societies that entails not only lasting peace agreements but also human rights, democracy, and free markets, and economic progress and that has been adopted by the United Nations, by major international institutions like the World Bank, and widely among donor agencies and NGOs since the end of the Cold War. The liberal peace building consensus is much like what sociologists have come to call "world society," "world culture," or the "global polity" namely values that become deeply embedded in global culture and global organizations and that replicate themselves, by pressure and example, widely among more local actors who adopt them.

Both cousins, the liberal human rights tradition and the liberal peace building consensus, share a patrimony in the thought of John Locke, Immanuel Kant, John Stuart Mill, and most recently, John Rawls, who commonly stress equality, liberty, and, in the case of Rawls, distributive economic justice. When it comes to past crimes, liberal thinkers have tended to oscillate between, or to combine complexly, two broad theories of punishment: retribution, which centers upon desert, and consequentialism, which stresses rehabilitation, deterrence, and the improvement of the social order. Some of the most articulate transmittals of these commitments into the politics of transitional justice can be found in a volume of essays written mostly by political philosophers: Truth v. Justice:

The Morality of Truth Commissions, edited by Robert I. Rotberg and Dennis Thompson. Emerging from a conference in South Africa, the essays commonly reflect upon that country's Truth and Reconciliation Commission, easily the most famous and most analyzed truth commission to date, whose prominent features include its offer of amnesty to human rights violators in the apartheid regime in return for their public confession, its dramatic and emotional public hearings, and the leadership of Commission Chairperson Archbishop Desmond Tutu — his charisma and his stress on forgiveness and on the healing of the nation and its citizens. Most strongly embodying a liberal human rights perspective on these proceedings are essays by Amy Gutmann and Dennis Thompson, Rajeev Bhargava, David A. Crocker, and Kent Greenawalt. To their writings might also be added the similarly grounded perspectives of Timothy Garton Ash, whose essays on South Africa and transitional justice elsewhere have appeared in The New York of Review of Books, and of Ignatieff, also a widely read essayist.

Though in some respects all of these writers laud the TRC, in three respects, which they articulate to different degrees, they criticize the TRC, and, by extension, those defenders of the TRC who stress religion and reconciliation. First, several of them express great reluctance towards abrogating punishment, viewing it as a regrettable sacrifice of justice to be pursued only if necessary to achieve some other good like a transition to democracy, not as a measure that reflects some higher or richer conception like restorative justice or reconciliation. Second, they are skeptical that healing and forgiveness belong in politics. In part, they think that in politics these goods are likely to come to grief. When Ignatieff writes, "[a]ll that a truth commission can achieve . . .," he asserts the limits of truth commissions as much as he does their possibilities.

Crocker similarly criticizes Tutu's "ideal of social harmony" as "impractical" and "unrealistic." But liberals' doubts about healing and forgiveness in politics run deeper than pragmatism. "Not only is Tutu's ideal of social harmony impractical," continues Crocker," but it is problematic because of the way it conceives the relation between the individual and the group." Elsewhere he argues that "it is morally objectionable as well as impractical for a truth commission or any other governmental body to force people to agree about the past, forgive the sins committed against them, or love one another." Here, liberal skepticism moves from pragmatic to moral. Political efforts to achieve healing, forgiveness, and harmony violate the autonomy of the individual in pursuing his or her own "conception of the good," to borrow the phrase of philosopher John Rawls. They seek to define the good in areas where the pluralism of values ought to be respected. "As Isaiah Berlin has taught us," Ash writes, "liberalism means living with unresolvable conflicts of values and goals, and South Africa has those in plenty." He concludes that "[t]aken to the extreme, the reconciliation of all with all is a deeply illiberal idea."

Further still, such political pursuits undermine the central democratic virtues of argument and deliberation and promote the democratic vices of settlement and im-position. Third, most of these critics are leery of the role of religion in politics, espousing some version of Rawls' argument that political arguments ought to be expressed in secular, or "public," language.

This, too, they regard as a democratic virtue. Naturally, it is the language of rights and law with which they are most at home. The contrast between the liberal human rights tradition and religious traditions, though, is not equivalent to a contrast between secular and religious traditions. Some of the liberal human rights tradition's critics remain within a secular discourse. A one- dimensional quest for trials of war criminals, argue political scientists Jack Snyder and Leslie Vinjamuri, often undermines peace agreements and the very establishment of the rule of law – a criticism of human rights groups' strategy, but not of the tradition's basic commitments. Other criticisms are more thoroughgoing while still secular.

The Rotberg and Thompson collection also includes

essays by Elizabeth Kiss, whose advocacy of Tutu's restorative justice resonates with religious conceptions, and by Martha Minow, who commends the "restorative power of truth telling" as an independently valuable alternative to trials. Political philosophers Peter Digeser and Trudy Govier and legal scholars Erin Daly and Jeremy Sarkin offer secular arguments for the political practice of forgiveness and link it with the reconciliation of sundered political communities. But if some secular perspectives on transitional justice do not converge neatly with the liberal human rights tradition, religious perspectives reason more typically and consistently from a different center of gravity. Religious traditions, too, of course, have their internal disagreements, evolution, and areas of overlap with outside traditions. Today, for instance, human rights is central to the teachings of the Catholic Churches, major Protestant denominations, and Judaism, while it enjoys more mixed support in Islam, Buddhism, and Hinduism.

In the West, Judeo-Christian commitments have arguably served as vital foundations for human rights. Religiously based approaches to transitional justice often endorse human rights as a goal. But neither human rights nor punishment for human rights violators is their common orienting conception. The idea, around which religious voices most converge, rather, is reconciliation. Not all of them explicitly make reconciliation their central theme, but this idea, or at least a closely resonant logic, runs commonly through their analyses. Indeed, an eruption of religious arguments for reconciliation is one of the unexpected and novel developments of the age of transitional justice. The majority of religious reconciliation promoters have been Christians, but they include Jews and Muslims as well. In all of these centuries-old traditions, reconciliation in the context of the state is a fairly late arrival. Christianity is no exception, despite the prominence of reconciliation in the New Testament.

The reasons for this tardiness are somewhat speculative, but at least three are plausible. The first is the privatization of forgiveness, one of religious reconciliation's most important components, in the medieval Catholic Church and the Protestant Reformation. Whereas in the 11th and 12th centuries, the Holy Roman Emperor would beg for forgiveness from the pope in the snows of Canossa, Italy, and the King of England would do public penance for murdering the Archbishop of Canterbury, three centuries later penance and forgiveness had been relegated to the confessional, to prayer, and to personal relationships. The second is the modern dominance of doctrines for dealing with past sin that tend to negate reconciliation: either legalist notions of the atonement – most prominently, the Calvinist "penal substitution" theory – that privilege a retributive balancing of scales over the restoration of relationships, or their opposite reaction, "exemplarist" theories that view Christ's death as a mere model of love but not as an actual restorative victory over sin and death.

Third, since the Middle Ages, much of Western Christian reasoning about politics, especially in Catholic thought, has been dominated by natural law, which has little to say about forgiveness, repentance, atonement, and reconciliation. But in the nineteenth century, lone voices in Christian theology began to think differently. Theologian John De Gruchy traces the rise of modern theologies who understand atonement to imply the transformation and reconciliation of political orders. In the 1870s, German theologian Albrecht Ritschl sought to escape the confining oscillation between penal substitution and exemplarism in his Christian Doctrine of Justification and Reconciliation, where he argued for Christ's reconciliation as an effective transformation of the world. Reacting to the sulphurous carnage of the First World War and scandalized by the complicity of modern theologians in the cultures of nationalism that bred its battles, theologians like P.T. Forsyth and Karl Barth rejected Ritschl's optimistic liberal theology but adopted the idea that Christ's justification of sinners begets the transformation and reconciliation of political orders. Barth came to believe that the life, death, and resurrection of Christ was a source of analogous principles for politics. He even saw the state as an order of reconciliation.

Out of these very convictions, he became one of the minorities of Christian leaders to speak out against Germany's Nazi government and was forced to resign his academic chair in Germany and return to his native Switzerland because of it. German theologian Dietrich Bonhoeffer reasoned along similar lines about reconciliation; he, too, opposed the Nazi government and was eventually executed for his complicity in the plot to kill Hitler of July 1944. Just after World War II, a small circle of Protestant theologians, including Barth, confessed the complicity of their churches with Nazi crimes in the Stuttgart and Darmstadt Declarations. Other theologians of the midtwentieth century also held that salvation involved political reconciliation, including the Czech scholar Jan Milic Lochman, whose ideas influenced the struggle against apartheid in South Africa. De Gruchy might have added Catholic sources.

Though John Paul II's Dives in Misericordia of 1984 is one of his lesser known encyclicals, its final section includes a call for forgiveness and reconciliation as political principles, a revolutionary idea in Catholic social thought that he would resound in 1997 and then again in January 2002, when, shortly after the attacks of September 11th, 2001, he appended to Pope Paul VI's 1965 maxim "no peace without justice" the corollary "no justice without forgiveness." John Paul II was not entirely original, for Pope Benedict XV had similarly appealed to nations to practice forgiveness and reconciliation at the close of World War I – an appeal that remained largely forgotten until John Paul II's successor, Pope Benedict XVI, named himself partly for Benedict XV and his witness for peace and reconciliation. Prior to the age of transitional justice, however, reconciliation was drowned out by other themes in Christian ethics. More than anyone else, it was Tutu who elicited its meteoric crescendo.

He and other South African religious leaders had long promoted reconciliation in their resistance to the apartheid regime. After the regime fell, inspired by Chile's National Commission for Truth and Reconciliation, the designers of the South African commission made reconciliation its central theme. Tutu's performance as the commission's chairman then delivered the concept its global fame. Reconciliation has subsequently become eponymous for truth commissions in Peru, East Timor, Sierra Leone, Nigeria, Liberia, Morocco, and Chad. It has also made its way into political discourse far more generally. In the United States, the presidentially-appointed Iraq Study Group used it no less than 63 times in its report of November 2006. The Jewish tradition arguably advanced public reconciliation far earlier than Christianity.

Histories of medieval Jewish communities and the writings of the medieval Jewish philosopher Moses Maimonides testify to rich practices of reconciliation known as teshuva, Hebrew for "repentance" or "turning." "I wonder how powerful a teshuva apology process could be on a much larger scale, involving massive injury, murder, or genocide," Rabbi Marc Gopin recently supposed. A professor at George Mason University's Institute for Conflict Analysis and Resolution and an activist for peace in the Middle East, Gopin has made it his life's work to marshal teshuva, as well as other concepts from Jewish scripture and tradition like aveilus – the mourning of loved ones through burial and remembrance followed by healing and recovery –, forbearance towards the enemy, social justice, honour, shame, and dignity, for peace building and reconciliation in the politics of modern states.

The problem, writes Gopin, is that "the post-Holocaust

scholarly Jewish community has not been much in the mood to mine the sources of Judaism for conflict resolution, especially with gentiles." But he believes that in today's Middle East, Jews, as well as Christians and Muslims, cannot afford to ignore the peace building potential of traditional religious concepts. Gopin's Islamic counterpart is Mohammed Abu-Nimer, also an intellectual and an activist, who holds a professorship at American University and has cofounded the Salam Institute for Peace and Justice. Paralleling Gopin, Abu-Nimer has sought to tap concepts and rituals from the Qur'an, the Hadith, and subsequent Islamic tradition for reconciliation and peace building in modern states. He reveals that pre-modern Arab Islam contains rich community rituals of sulh (settlement) and musalaha (reconciliation), similar to Judaism's teshuva.

In modern Islamic politics, as in the other Abrahamic faiths, though, other debates have overshadowed reconciliation, not least the question of the legitimacy of the nation-state itself. But today, both the Middle East conflict and debates over reconciliation in transitional justice proceedings in Muslim majority states like Morocco, Algeria, and Sierra Leone give urgency to the development of an Islamic conception of reconciliation. If reconciliation is the conceptual center of gravity among religious perspectives on transitional justice, what are its common features and how does it differ from the focuses of the liberal human rights tradition? To the degree that reconciliation enjoys a shared meaning, it is "restoration of right relationship." But does not the liberal human rights tradition also advance a form of right relationship in which the members of a political community come to respect one another – as well as members of other states with whom they have been at war – as citizens with full rights?

Though religious conceptions often encompass this dimension of right relationship, they usually also envision something fuller: the confession and repentance of perpetrators, the forgiveness of victims, the empathetic acknowledgment of suffering on the part of other citizens, and the overcoming of enmity. These, of course, are just the sort of transformation whose place in politics makes at least some liberal critics nervous. Another difference between the traditions' outlooks on transitional justice is, obviously, their foundations. The liberal human rights tradition relies upon reason alone, and certain kinds of reason at that: Kantian and utilitarian. Religious arguments for reconciliation in the Abrahamic traditions are typically rooted in the character, purposes and actions of God as these are recounted in scriptures, not primarily in natural law or other modes of philosophical reasoning.

The "vertical" relationship between God and humanity is the source and model for "horizontal" reconciliation within political communities. Perhaps the most sophisticated of the theological reflections on reconciliation of recent years is Yale theologian Miroslav Volf's Exclusion and Embrace: A Theological Exploration of Identity, Otherness, and Reconciliation. A Croat, Volf defended his argument for "the will to embrace" while his own country fought a bloody ethnic war with Serbia and Bosnia in the early 1990's. In the book's preface, Volf recalls the question of his mentor, the prominent German theologian Jürgen Moltmann, following one of Volf's lectures: "But can you embrace a èetnik (Serb fighter)?" Volf's answer was "No, I cannot – but as a follower of Christ I think I should be able to."

Out of this answer flows the argument of his book – an appeal for the practice of a social and political reconciliation that reflects the self-donating love of God, a love that expresses solidarity with victims and wills their liberation, but also, more surprisingly, liberates perpetrators "from the injustice committed through oppression." "But what about truth and justice?" Volf then asks, anticipating readers' natural next question. Does embrace mean foregoing the struggle to overthrow and eventually punish regimes that practice systematic cruelties? Volf and most other recent theologians of reconciliation want to answer no, this aspect of justice is essential. But several of them also answer more ambitiously, redefining the very meaning of justice so as to encompass, but also exceed, human rights and just punishment.

In the Jewish scriptures, the words that translate to the English "justice" – sedeqah and mishpat – also translate into righteousness, meaning comprehensive right relationship as revealed in God's covenants with humanity. The same goes for the various Greek New Testament words for justice that begin with the dikstem, including dikaiosunç, the word that St. Paul uses to denote his central concept of "justification." The Arabic 'adl, is most commonly translated into justice in the Qur'an, similarly means thoroughgoing right relationship. From these scriptural perspectives, reconciliation, which means restoration of right relationship to a state of right relationship, can equally well mean restoration of justice to a state of justice. On this view, we could even say that reconciliation is itself a conception of justice, much as Volf argues towards the end of Exclusion and Embrace that embrace is "part and parcel of the very definition of justice." This way of looking at justice is a further distinctive feature of religious conceptions. It is much like what has come to be known as restorative justice.

Developed first in the context of juvenile criminal justice systems in English speaking countries in the 1970's, then brought into the context of nationwide transitional justice by Tutu in South Africa, restorative justice responds to past evil by seeking to restore relationships among perpetrators, victims, and community members with respect to the distinct ways in which violence has severed these relationships. In transitional settings, restorative justice includes human rights and possibly punishment, though it defends punishment differently than retributivism and consequentialism, but it also includes several other dimensions of restoration like apology, acknowledgment, reparations, and, the dimension of transitional justice that religious perspectives most distinctly advocate, forgiveness.

Forgiveness hovers close to the center of gravity of recent religious perspectives on transitional justice. It is their final distinctive feature. As with justice, these authors define forgiveness more ambitiously than most modern secular authors do. Rather than an act that merely lets perpetrators "off the hook" for deserved crimes, forgiveness is a victim's own exercise of a will towards restoration, an act through which she herself may come to be restored as well. The warrants and ethics of forgiveness differ among the faiths. Jewish and Muslim scholars describe forgiveness as bestowed and commanded by God, and most of them make it conditional upon the prior repentance of perpetrators. In Christianity, forgiveness is a participation in the forgiving act of God in Jesus Christ.

Though Christian theologians are divided on the issue, many argue that victims may forgive unilaterally, absent prior repentance. The practice of forgiveness in public settings is perhaps the most innovate as well as controversial proposal for politics that the recent bevy of religious arguments about transitional justice has put forth. People will differ over the merits of these religious arguments according to their commitments. Anyone, though, can credit these arguments for their creativity. They testify to the riches that traditions can offer. Religious ethicists of reconciliation retrieve from the claims and texts of their faith a way of thinking about justice that differs significantly, but not completely, from the liberal human rights tradition and offers it to the modern politics of societies that are dealing with their past. Their holistic approach of restoration may well enhance such politics — but not without further intellectual labor. It is in their application to politics that theologies of reconciliation require more development. What norms for political action emanate from the religious traditions' center of gravity? How does a theology of reconciliation tackle ethical dilem-mas that arise in the political realm? What is needed is an ethic of reconciliation.

A model for such an ethic is the just war tradition, whose great pioneers, Augustine and Aquinas, and contemporary religious proponents alike typically begin with theological and philosophical premises about God, love, justice, and derive from them concrete guidelines for the statesperson and the soldier: norms of jus ad bellum that govern when war may be undertaken, and ones of jus in bello that prescribe how it may be fought. Today, the tradition has been incorporated into international law, is taught in military academies, and is invoked in political speeches if not always in political actions. An ethic of political reconciliation might not only be patterned on the just war framework but could potentially extend its very scope, offering moral guidance for building peace after hostilities have ended. At the top of ethicists' agenda ought to be the tension between forgiveness and punishment.

Most of the theologians who advocate forgiveness take care not to void punishment. But how are the two practices compatible? It is a question for ethical theory: Can the two practices be justified consistently and complementarily? But also for practice: Reconciliation and retribution, forgiveness and punishment, amnesty and accountability have been pitted against each other in transitional settings all over the world. Can both practices coexist institutionally? If so, how? Good answers will confront the issue of agency. What are the respective roles of the state, of victims, faction leaders and perpetrators in forgiveness and punishment? Questions of agency extend from forgiveness to the practices of reparations and apology. Can groups undertake these practices? Can leaders undertake them on behalf of their members? If so, must they in some way respect the prerogative of their members to participate? Can the living forgive, apologize, or receive reparations on behalf of the dead?

Reparations are particularly tricky: Who are the proper recipients? How much are they to be paid? One of the most difficult dilemmas for transitional justice arises when achieving a peace agreement or regime transition appears possible only at the expense of sacrificing the prosecution of human rights violators. Should peace – or perhaps more accurately, the justice of a Rechtstaat – be preferred to prosecutions? Though many ethicists have by now taken up these questions, few have considered them from the standpoint of a religiously based perspective of reconciliation. This distinct center of gravity portends distinct answers. If they are to be realized in politics, religious perspectives must not only prove their distinctiveness from the liberal human rights tradition but also address its scepticism. One of the trademarks of modern liberal democracy, which most of the religious perspectives endorse as a goal of transitions, is limitations on politics and respect for the freedom of individuals, families, and civil society. But religious perspectives speak of justice as comprehensive right relationship and call for forgiveness, apology, and other practices that involve transformation of the heart.

Do such transformations belong in politics? Or are they illicit soul craft? Recall the scepticism of several liberal political philosophers. The outcome of this debate depends on arguments on the proper place of virtue in politics, the location of the line between the personal and the political, and the competence of state institutions to bring about such transformations. Perhaps governments may justly encourage forgiveness and like measures while also showing great respect for the right of victims to choose them or refuse them. Perhaps it is within civil society that a religious ethic is realized fullest and best. Religious ethicists have far more to tell us about the possibilities and limits of the political. Recall, too, that the very religiosity of the religious evokes liberal scepticism. Are religious advocates of reconciliation obligated to speak secular language in the public realm to accompany religious arguments with public language?

If they have no such obligation, might there still be good reasons for them to develop and deploy secular arguments, say when they are dealing with an international organization or a secular non- governmental organization, when they are operating in a pluralistic population, or when they are dealing with matters of constitutional law? Or do such "translations" only distort, compromise, and neuter their theological rationales? Again, religious commentators on transitional justice have much yet to tell us.

The Doers

In founding the International Center for Religion and Diplomacy (ICRD) in 1999, Douglas Johnston declared that he wanted to created a "do tank" and not another "think tank." Johnston himself is editor of two volumes of essays on the role of the religious in making peace, the first of which, Religion, The Missing Dimension of Statecraft, co-edited with Cynthia Sampson, was one of the seminal efforts to bring the work of religious peacemakers to the world's attention, the second of which, Faith-Based Diplomacy: Trumping Realpolitik, is a sequel to the first. By now, a collection of literature on the subject – mostly edited volumes, but some articles and monographs as well – is in print. These works in fact blur the line between doing and thinking, offering general analyses and conceptual overviews along with a plethora of case studies. Their focus is not on theology, philosophy, or political theory, but rather on the efforts of practitioners. Their work might be called "theory of praxis."

Let us exercise caution, though, against thinking that this literature portrays the sum total of the world's religious peacemaking activities. We do well to remember the story of the man who, when asked why he is searching for his key under a lamppost during the night, responds that here is where the light is. In the past several years, I have witnessed multitudinous religious efforts to build peace, ranging from the diplomacy of bishops and ulema to the exertions of village leaders, both as an observer in the Philippines and Colombia and as a participant in Kashmir. 50 Similar efforts occur on every continent, the vast majority of which are never exposed by the "lamplight" of books published by Oxford or Cambridge University Press. This noted, what has this literature taught us about religious contributions to transitional justice?

Forms of Religious Influence on Transitional Justice

Many of the recorded religious contributions involve transitional justice only in the widest sense: They bring about peace and justice where little existed before. Some occur within civil society and do not engage governments directly; some occur within conflicts rather than after conflicts. Not all of them directly invoke the concept of reconciliation. They involve mediation between government and opposition forces in civil wars and regime transitions, forging cooperation between leaders of different religions, building "zones of peace" in rural villages, training citizens and leaders in conflict resolution, performing rituals of reconciliation, building friendships and communities between members of hostile religious and communal groups, imparting moral vision to civil society leaders, healing victims of trauma and promoting forgiveness at the grassroots, conducting advocacy with national governments and international organizations, and more. Religious leaders and activists, though, also influence transitional justice in the sense that the term is most commonly used: in political efforts to address the injustices of a previous regime or period of civil war.

In those places where they have proved to be influential in shaping these political efforts, religious actors have almost always promoted truth commissions, with prominent exceptions in East Timor and post-communist Germany, where at least some religious leaders have advocated for trials in addition to truth commissions. There are two aspects of transitional justice institutions that religious leaders have shaped: their formation and their conduct. Most dramatic are cases where the religious have organized and carried out the work of a truth commission, unofficially or secretly.

The Catholic Church in Chile and Catholic and Protestant leaders in Brazil investigated the human rights violations of their countries' dictators and later supplied this information to truth commission reports following transitions to democracy. In Guatemala, following a peace agreement that ended three decades of civil war, the Catholic Church, led by Archbishop Juan Gerardi, launched its own Recovery of Historical Memory Project (REMHI), a truth commission that was impressive for the scope of human rights violations that it reported and for the personalist nature of its investigations, which provided psychological and spiritual support for victims. Elsewhere, in South Africa, East Timor, Peru, Sierra Leone, and Germany, religious actors have lobbied their governments for truth commissions, advocated publicly for truth commissions, and, when these actors are lay political leaders, used their power and prerogatives to influence their country's transitional justice institutions.

Once transitional justice institutions have been selected and formed, religious actors sometimes participate in their conduct. Most famously, Tutu led South Africa's Truth and Reconciliation Commission – decked out in full episcopal regalia and frequently invoking religious language and ceremony. In South Africa, religious communities also testified at the country's unique hearings for corporate entities, as did businesses, journalists, parties, and other groups. Not only in South Africa, but also in Guatemala, Peru, East Timor, and Sierra Leone, religious communities contributed logistical support, assisting in organizing and carrying out hearings, finding and encouraging victims and witnesses, and providing counselling once hearings were over. Often they shaped the terms of the public communication and debate surrounding commissions, sometimes bringing the concept of reconciliation into the discourse. In other countries, by contrast, religious communities played little role at all in forming or conducting institutions for transitional justice.

Most starkly, established churches in Rwanda – Catholic, Anglican, and Presbyterian – have exercised little influence on state-level efforts to deal with the past, though they have issued statements of repentance for the role of their own members in the genocide and conducted work for reconciliation in civil society. In Latin America, the Catholic Church had little to do with the work of truth commissions in Argentina or El Salvador. Nor did it wield much sway in the Czech Republic's choice to conduct a "lustration" scheme that disqualified collaborators with the Communist State Security Corps (Stb) from holding office in the new regime. In the former Yugoslavia, too, religious communities did little to bring about the international and national trials that did occur, or, aside from a few exceptions, to lobby strongly for a truth commission that did not occur. Where religious leaders and communities are effective in shaping transitional justice, in whatever form this justice takes, whether on the state or the civil society level, they bring certain assets to bear upon their work.

First, they derive authority from the status that their community enjoys in their society, a status that in turn derives from the principles and beliefs of the community as well as its record of involvement in political matters. Some leaders carry their own charisma as well. Religious actors deploy this authority apart from whether they advocate their cause in religious language. Catholic Bishop Carlos Belo of East Timor, for instance, drew upon his country's Catholicity as well as the Church's history of supporting the country's struggle against Indonesia in championing trials for Indonesian generals who violated the human rights of the East Timorese. Likewise, Iraqi Ayatollah Ali al-Sistani has drawn upon his prestige as a top cleric to urge Shi'ite Iraqis to give their support to a unified national government. Second, religious leaders are motivated and shaped by a set of ideas, doctrines, and beliefs about politics that flows from the divine purposes that are expressed through their scriptures and traditions.

The connection between the vertical and the horizontal that we saw in the work of Miroslav Volf is typical of their thinking, only here it motivates political action rather than a sophisticated theology. Third, religious practitioners of transitional justice retrieve rituals and practices from their traditions for the purpose of political healing. Gopin, for instance, has proposed that the Jewish practice of aveilus could help to heal memories of lost relatives, homes, and land in the Middle East. ICRD's work in Kashmir features a faith-based ritual of reconciliation at the close of a four day seminar on reconciliation, one in which dramatic expressions of healing and forgiveness has taken place. Religious approaches to transitional justice tend also to stress the personal: building relationships and transforming hearts and minds. Though this focus is neither exclusive to nor exhaustive of religious activity, it is a trademark of it – and a fourth asset. The personal pervaded Tutu's conduct of South Africa's TRC, just as it pervades the Mennonites' grassroots, communal approach to peace building. "In my estimation the starting point for understanding and supporting reconciliation processes is a reorientation toward the centrality of relationships. It is in the ebb and flow, the quality interdependence [sic.] of relationships that we find the birthplace and home of reconciliation," writes Mennonite John Paul Lederach, a pioneer in peace building.

Finally, at the center of gravity of religious approaches, in practice as in theory, lies reconciliation, involving forgiveness, apology, healing enmity between estranged groups within and between communities, and all of the other themes embedded in theologies of reconciliation. In their extensive soon-to-be-published survey of faith- based and secular NGOs working in transitional justice, political scientists Leslie Vinjamuri and Aaron P. Boesenecker find that "attention to long-term comprehensive social reconciliation . . . has become a hallmark of religious actors engaged in transitional justice."

The Religious Practice of Transitional Justice

What the literature on the religious practice of transitional justice, and more broadly, peace building, has conveyed to the world is a treasure trove of approaches, episodes, stories, and analyses. Authors, editors, and, most of all, the practitioners that they write about have advanced an important and distinct realm of practice and inquiry. Religion is no longer a missing dimension of statecraft. But if the challenge of theologians and other religious theorists in this area is to take a step towards practice, the challenge of the literature on praxis is now to take another step towards theory. To be sure, many of the works identify common characteristics and "lessons learned" from religious peace building. But systematic analysis of the religious practice of transitional justice has only begun. What can we learn through comparative generalization about such practice justice? Rigorous answers to this question – the logical sequel to the first wave of analyses of religious practice – would serve inestimably the interests of both practitioners and scholars. What follows, then, is an agenda for research. It consists of four broad sets of questions.

1. What sort of actors are religious practitioners of transitional justice, and how do they contrast with other kinds of political and religious organizations and

institutions? Are there existing sociological concepts that can describe them?

2. What distinguishes different religious approaches to transitional justice?
3. What defines effectiveness, and what characterizes those that are most effective?
4. What ethical dilemmas does religious peace building face?

The first question asks where religious practitioners of transitional justice and peace building are located within the global atlas of religious and political organizations. Do they replicate or resemble other sorts of actors? Complement them? Reinforce them? Oppose or speak against them? Overall, there are two kinds of religious actors that seek to help societies deal with pasts of civil war and authoritarianism. The first is the rough equivalent of a non-governmental organization. These are independent, freestanding, and relatively autonomous in their budget and their activities. They are a small manifestation of the global explosion of NGOs in the last century. In some cases, peace building is conducted by an office or subsidiary of a much larger independent faith- based organization like World Vision, which is primarily a relief and development organization. Rare is there a large organization that is solely devoted to religious peace building such as the World Conference on Religion and Peace, which has affiliates in more than 70 countries, or the similarly wide International Fellowship of Reconciliation.

Most of the faith-based NGOs that work in peace building are small, comprising a single office and a handful of people, like ECONI (Evangelical Contribution on Northern Ireland), a Christian organization that works for reconciliation among estranged groups in Northern Ireland in the wake of the Good Friday Agreement of 1998, the International Center for Diplomacy, the Coalition for Peace in Africa (Kenya), and the Salam Institute for Peace and

Justice, a U.S.-based Muslim organization. Some of them are largely the work of a single person, as is the Foundation for Relief and Reconciliation in the Middle East, which supports the faith-based peace building work of Anglican Canon Andrew White, now focused largely in Iraq.

Other initiatives in faith-based peace building are the work of a single person who holds a position in a university or other organization. Examples include Mark Gopin and Mohammed Abu-Nimer, whom I have already mentioned, John Paul Lederach, a Mennonite peace builder who is a professor at the Joan B. Kroc Institute at the University of Notre Dame, and David Steele, who has conducted reconciliation work in the Balkans as a member of the Center for Strategic and International Studies and the Mercy Corps Conflict Management Group. At present, faith-based peace building networks operate fairly independently of one another. Though they know about and often communicate with one another, they do not coordinate their work in the way that "transnational advocacy networks" of environmental, human rights, and women's rights have worked together to bring change on particular issues, as described by political scientists Margaret Keck and Kathryn Sikkink.

By comparison, religious peace builders are diverse and diffuse. A more integrated network of religious peace building organizations might become the brainchild of an entrepreneur. But none yet exists. A second kind of religious actor that plays a part in transitional justice is an organization or person that derives its authority, legitimacy, prestige, and often a good part of its effectiveness from its direct membership in a world religion. The Catholic Church, for instance, hosts the Community of Sant' Egidio, a public lay association that was instrumental in bringing peace to Mozambique between 1990 and 1992, Pax Christi, a peace organization, Catholic Relief Services, a large and prestigious relief and development organization that has adopted peace building as one of its central activities, and individual leaders like Bishop Juan Gerardi in Guatemala and Carlos Belo in East Timor.

Lutheran pastors Joachim Gauck and Rainer Eppelman, both former dissidents in communist East Germany, were important in the politics of reconciliation in post- unification Germany. The Mennonite Central Committee, a widely respected organization in relief, development, and peacemaking, is closely tied to the Mennonite Church. Pastors and imams who forged relationships for peace in the wake of violence in Nigeria each gained authority and prestige by their position in their faith communities.

In present day Iraq, Ayatollah Sistani garnered prestige from his position as a top Shi'ite cleric. Because of these peace builders' vital connection to a larger religious body, the concept of "transnational advocacy networks" does not fit them well, either. The religious bodies themselves are far closer to what Susanne Rudolph has called "transnational civil society" – transnational social actors that comprise hundreds of millions of members and are often a major cultural and political player in the societies where they are found. Their peace builders are not independent agents but something like departments within a huge conglomerate. They derive their authority from the status that their religious body enjoys as an enormous transnational entity, but also, importantly, from the religious body's character in the country where they operate.

The success of Catholic Relief Services in building peace and addressing the injustices of a generation- long civil war in Colombia, for instance, is highly dependent upon the relationship of the Colombian Catholic Church to its national government and the various armed factions. Again, we do well to remember the key searcher and the lamplight. Many religious peace builders will evade even the rays emitted by these two large categories, NGOs and members of transnational religions. In their extensive report, "FaithBased Peace building: Mapping and Analysis of Christian, Muslim, and Multi-Faith Actors," Tsjeard Bouta, S. Ayse Kadayifici-Orellana, and Mohammed Abu-Nimer make the point that Muslims peacebuilders often operate in traditional societies built on "kinship, tribalism, and family ties," in contrast to Western societies, which are "individualistic, professional, and bureaucratized."

As a result, their visibility seems to depend on the personal communication and language skills of the individuals involved in terms of connecting with non-Muslim groups, organizations, academic institutions, and the media, their fund-raising skills and whether they are adopted or supported by non-Muslim, mostly Christian, groups. As many groups lack or do not have the time to develop these skills, it is difficult to identify Muslim peace-building actors without field research that includes interviews with various groups in those communities. The problem points to one of the areas where research can be most fruitful:

Identifying the range of religious actors – individuals, communities, organizations – engage in peace building especially those who take a form that Westerners are not accustomed to.

Anthropologist Rosalind Shaw, for instance, studied the reception of Sierra Leone's Truth and Reconciliation Commission on the village level and found that national level processes often comported ill with local tribal traditions for addressing past injustices. More attention to local and community level faith-based actors who help populations deal with the past would fill an important gap in our knowledge of religion and transitional justice. Accounts of other ways in which religious peace builders organizations vary, according to their local and transnational linkages, their composition of clerical and lay actors, their size, and their structures, can also fill out this terra nullius in our atlas. A thorough atlas, though, would include not just a map of the varieties of religious shapers of transitional justice but a timeline of their trajectory. Although religious peace builders date at least as far back as St. Francis of Assisi, those who shape transitional justice, of course, are far more recent. When exactly did they emerge? Are they growing more numerous? Or have they peaked? Do they have a life cycle?

If so, in what stage of it are they? It may be that religious shapers of transitional justice are on a path somewhat like what political scientists Martha Finnemore and Kathryn Sikkink have described for international norms: first they enter a stage of "emergence" where "entrepreneurs" build organizations and advocate their cause from within them; second, there follows a "norm cascade" in which a swarm of states adopts the norm; and third, the norms are "internalized" into law, bureaucracies, and professions who make them a regular part of political life. Although religious peace builders are actors, not norms, might they nevertheless follow an analogous pathway? It is fair to say, at least within the limits of given knowledge, that religious peace building organizations, whether NGOs or groups within religious bodies, have emerged but have not yet cascaded. The efforts catalogued thus far are too few, insufficiently imitated, and too seldom embraced by governments as normal political actors to be considered widely institutionalized or regularized.

Closer to a cascade is the norm that religious actors (and others) have urged upon truth commissions: reconciliation. Since South Africa followed Chile in making reconciliation the central theme of its truth commission, a wave of other states have followed suit: Sierra Leone, East Timor, Peru, Ghana, and others. Still, it is difficult to argue that reconciliation has become an ensconced norm in the "global polity" or the "normal" approach to which transitional countries default. Other countries have decided against making it their central theme. The concept remains disputed. A final orienting dimension of the conceptual atlas is the contrast between religious and secular organizations that involve themselves in transitional justice. As I already argued, liberal approaches to transitional justice reflect a "global polity" characterized by enlightenment values of individual freedom, market economies, and rights. Two sociologists of the "global polity" school, John Boli and George M. Thomas, corroborate that similar values have characterized the INGO revolution.

Religious actors, at least those who espouse the paradigm of reconciliation, can be viewed as something like what political philosopher Nancy Fraser has called "counter publics" – challengers of the dominant discourse of a society who nevertheless practice "constructive engagement." In his work on reconciliation in South Africa, theorist of rhetoric Erik Doxtader argues further that religious counterparts did not merely challenge apartheid in its own terms but imported an altogether different set of concepts and offered it as a new basis for unity. Might religious actors, perhaps less contentiously, also form a "counter public" to liberal modes of transitional justice?

Further research could investigate this question more deeply. To what degree have religious and liberal paradigms clashed in transitional settings? In what ways do religious actors differ among themselves in their orientation to liberalism? What are the consequences for the politics of reconciliation? These latter questions begin to elide into the second general question for research: How do religious approaches to transitional justice differ among themselves? Two existing works offer insight with maps, typologies, and views of the whole. In his book Ambivalence of the Sacred: Religion, Violence and Reconciliation, historian R. Scott Appleby divides religious approaches to his encompassing category of "conflict transformation" into different roles that religious peace builders play – conflict management, conflict resolution, and post conflict peace building – as well as different modes that they assume, including "crisis mobilization" that often involves opposition to authoritarian regimes, a "saturation mode" in which religious peace builders flood a culture so as to transform it, and an "interventionist" mode that involves mediation and training.

The other work is Vinjamuri and Boesenecker's essay "Religious in Transitional Justice," which charts the work of religious and secular actors – churches and NGOs — in "transitional and post-conflict justice" according to their conception of justice (reconciliation or retributive), the breadth of their language and methodology (communitarian or cosmopolitan), and the domain of their involvement (transnational or local). One of their interesting findings is that religious NGOs are found in virtually all of the same categories in which secular NGOs are found (excepting "cosmopolitan retributivists"), evincing their diversity. Both efforts are rigorous, thorough, and attentive to practitioners' own methodological distinctions. Vinjamuri and Boesenecker's separation of communitarian and cosmopolitan approaches, for instance, captures the differences between religious NGOs that speak explicitly religious language and those that speak a more secular language and strongly resemble secular actors. Other scholars might add new dimensions of comparison. One might be level of operation, distinguishing actors who work primarily in civil society and those who seek to influence the policies of states.

Another might be level of indigenousness, drawing a contrast between those actors who work totally within their own country's borders and those who are headquartered in another state. Researchers might also investigate the operational consequences that flow from whether an organization operates as a free standing entity or whether it is embedded in a much larger religious community. Religious peace builders in the Catholic Church, for instance, benefit from a readymade global "infrastructure" of bishops and parishes. Independent faith-based NGOs, by contrast, carry both the freedom and the burden of cultivating their own networks and contacts. Also, what difference does the religion or theological orientation of a religious actor make? Do Muslim and Christian actors take different approaches to transitional justice? Within these religions, does the denomination or sect make a difference? Typologies in turn lay the groundwork for a third area of inquiry that no one in the field can or should avoid:

Strikingly, the praxis literature is virtually entirely laudatory. One reads in vain for boondoggles or even for unsuccessful religious peace builders. This is understandable insofar as most of the authors and editors are themselves sympathetic practitioners who seek to encourage a field that was little known prior to their efforts. Launching a new vision requires inspiration, not cold detachment. But now that there exists a deposit of knowledge of a large array of efforts, it is high time that analysts began inquiring into the ingredients of success, drawing upon both positive and negative examples. Practitioners themselves will greatly benefit from the inquiry. Of course defining success in itself is an analytical challenge, one that is highly dependent on goals, methodology, values, and the "theory of change" that is embedded in the work of any given religious practitioner.

The criteria for judging a Christian-Muslim zone of peace in the Philippines will look different from those that assess trauma healing work in a Tamil village in Sri Lanka, which differ in turn from those that apply to a national Catholic Church that advocates for a truth commission. Once success is defined, social scientific research can yield knowledge of what fosters it. Comparative analysis can offer a breadth of judgment, analytical leverage, and the isolation of effectual variables. Ethnographic research and case studies can reveal "thick" understandings, culturally contextual knowledge, and precise causal mechanisms. Survey research can measure changes in attitudes and opinions. One area in which parallel experiences provide grist for comparative analysis is the role of religious actors in shaping their countries' choices for institutions of transitional justice: trials, truth commissions, reparations, and the like.

These roles vary from robust and efficacious, as with religious actors in Brazil, Chile, Peru, Guatemala, South Africa, Sierra Leone, East Timor, and the grass-roots of the Protestant Church in East Germany, to weak or impotent, as with religious actors in Rwanda, El Salvador, Argentina, the Czech Republic, Poland, Northern Ireland, and the former Yugoslavia, as well as in the hierarchy of the German Protestant Church. Again, in the preponderance of efficacious cases, religious actors advocated truth commissions; mainly in the East Timorese Catholic Church and among some German Protestant dissidents did powerful calls for trials arise. Close observation of these cases reveals two factors that characterized the influential religious actors. First, they carried a political theology of reconciliation fairly widely within their ranks. Political theology is the set of doctrines that political actors hold about political authority and justice.

Archbishop Tutu is perhaps the paradigmatic example of a religious leader who spoke and thought about politics in terms of reconciliation, but others have done so, too, like Gerardi in Guatemala, and leaders in Chile, Peru, Sierra Leone, East Timor, and the several other sites where religious was influential. Second, during the civil war or authoritarian regime preceding the political transition, efficacious actors practiced what sociologists of religion call "differentiation" from the state, that is, institutional autonomy in their governance and activities. But it was a conflictual differentiation, one that they maintained only through struggle against a regime that wanted to suppress their autonomy. From this island of "moral extraterritoriality," to use the vivid phrase of George Weigel, many of these religious actors opposed the authoritarian regime or prominently mediated the civil war, activities that gave them the prestige and the deepened institutional autonomy with which they later influenced the transition to democracy or peace. By contrast, religious actors like the Catholic Church in Rwanda, Argentina, or the Czech Republic or Protestant hierarchies in Rwanda or East Germany exercised little distance from their regimes and thus had little influence on transitions.

Other actors like the Catholic Church in Poland practiced autonomy (with the exception of some recently collaborator priests) but lacked a widely shared theology of reconciliation and thus had little sway over transitional justice. 75 Orthodox churches of Eastern Europe and Russia were also almost uniformly inefficacious in shaping the politics of the past, and for reasons that corroborate the present argument. A historic pattern of close collaboration with state rulers left them bereft of autonomy from Communist rule, while an accompanying venerable political theology of "caesaro-papism" legitimized this paralyzing symbiosis. If this argument about differentiation and political theology is correct, it ought also to predict where religious actors will influence transitional justice institutions in the future. Thus far, the vast majority of national efforts at transitional justice have occurred in Christian countries.

In part, this is due to an empirical fact: The preponderance of Third Wave democratic transitions, and most of the transitional justice institutions following civil wars, has taken place in majority-Christian countries. But there is some evidence of support for truth commissions among Muslims as well. In South Africa as well as Sierra Leone, whose population is 60% Muslim, prominent Muslim leaders have promoted truth and reconciliation efforts. Morocco is the first country with an almost solely Muslim population to carry out a truth commission. Political leaders and citizens in both Iraq and Afghanistan have expressed strong support for truth commissions or similar institutions. The argument here is that the possibility of truth commissions and national practices of reconciliation depends not solely on what religious is involved – i.e, Christianity, Islam, Judaism, etc., — but on the political theology and differentiation practiced by the local religious actor. In the same way that this analysis argues for the importance of differentiation and political theology, other analyses might make the case for other features of religious actors in other areas of transitional justice.

Perhaps a religious community's degree of unity affects its ability to carry out concerted action and perhaps the size of its population or financial base matters. Another important factor is its rooted ness in a national community. The Polish Catholic Church's ability to identify with the nation and its history, for instance, was a powerful source of its strength in opposing its communist regime. The degree to which a religious actor is able to establish connections among multiple actors, from grass roots to elites, matters too. The Community of Sant'Egidio, for instance, was uniquely efficacious as a mediator for peace because of its ability, through its methodology of personal friendships, to forge ties with disputant party leaders in Mozambique, church officials in both Mozambique and the Vatican, Italian government officials, the Italian Communist party, American diplomats, and United Nations officials alike. A fourth and final area begging for further inquiry is the ethics of religious praxis in transitional justice and peace building. Again, the literature is laudatory. But others are asking tough questions. One concerns religious actors' widely shared emphasis on reconciliation: overcoming enmity, building relationships, trust, friendship, and healing. To be sure, some of the theorists of religious praxis seek to integrate these values with the tougher side of reconciliation: punishment, accountability, ensuring social justice. But some critics will want to press further. Are there some situations in which plain, raw confrontation and coercion are called for? When does reconciliation become a coddling of the evil?

During the apartheid struggle, a group of black theologians in South Africa argued along these very lines in penning the Kairos Document of 1985, upbraiding theologians of reconciliation for opposing apartheid too flaccidly. Today, even as practitioners promote faith-based diplomacy and religious reconciliation as the solution to some of the world's nastiest conflicts, other religiously oriented actors like the U.S. Commission for Religious Freedom argue that oppressive regimes in Saudi Arabia, Sudan, and Burma call for exposure, sanctions, and pressure. In turn, Robert Seiple, the former U.S. Ambassador-at-Large for International Religious Freedom, has criticized the Commission as obtusely confrontational. Seiple himself is the founder of the Institute for Global Engagement, an NGO that promotes religious freedom through building personal relationships with political, religious, and civil society leaders on all sides of the fence in locales where religious freedom is scarce. He cites the example of Laos as a country where IGE's approach succeeded in releasing religious political prisoners – but which the Commission for Religious Freedom decided to sanction anyway.

The questions that beg exploration are: In what circumstances does each approach work best? Are some conflicts prone to one or the other type of approach? Does it matter what stage a conflict is in – say, before or after a peace agreement or transition to democracy? Is it better, as Seiple put it, to "curse the darkness" or to "light a candle"? Other ethical questions are relevant, too. Danish scholar Thomas Brudholm has taken to task the Christian advocacy of forgiveness after mass atrocity for being hasty and uncritical. He does not so much call into question the theology or ethical value of forgiveness as he does the practice of forgiveness by leaders like Tutu, who, he believes, often pressured victims to forgive, denied the potential positive value of anger and resentment, ignored the fact that victims might not share his Christian faith, and generally flouted victims' autonomy. On a practical level, his criticisms are quite similar to those raised by Thompson and Gutmann and Ash as noted in the first half of this essay. Religious "doers" of transitional justice and peace building may well come to the defence of one of their favourite practices, forgiveness, and one of their favourite practitioners, Tutu. Brudholm's challenge, though, points to the need for a set of ethics that governs not only forgiveness, but the entire practice of transitional justice and peace building from a religious perspective.

Advocates of religious approaches to transitional justice, both thinker and doers, have their work cut out for them. This is true not because their thinking or writing contains deep flaws, but rather, quite to the contrary, because their collective efforts have succeeded in showing that the perspectives and methods of a distinct kind of actor have much to offer societies who are facing troubled pasts. Theologies of reconciliation, the role of forgiveness, and responses to past injustices that bring multiple remedies to multiple wounds and religious involvement in peace building both within civil society and at the level of state institutions offer an approach to restoration that is arguably more holistic than, although in many ways compatible with, the approach of the liberal human rights tradition. It is this promise that has led prominent public figures like former United States Ambassador to the United Nations John Danforth to call for the active integration of religion into the politics of peace building.

Theologians can make reconciliation plausible for politics by developing it into practices and tackling ethical dilemmas. Theorists of practice will do well to address some of the analytical and ethical issues that lie beneath the worldwide buzz of religious peace building. Both must answer arguments that the liberal human rights tradition has raised about the religious. If these efforts are successful, then, as Danforth envisions, religious and political leaders might regularly look to one another's abilities and resources as they seek to deal with the past and construct political futures. Whether welcome or not, though, the role of the religious in transitional justice cannot be avoided. Neither the global trend of transitional justice nor the global rise of public religion is likely to peter out soon. Neither then, is the activity that stands at the intersection of these trends.

9

21st Century Religions, Human Rights, and Civil Society

The treatment of religion by civic authorities today is a product of their respective histories and cultures. In almost every country in the industrialized world, however, there is a strong long-term trend from a close association between politics and religion to separation of the two. A series of debates in seventeenth century Britain contributed to this process. In ancient times, religion and the state were closely related. In ancient Greece, Socrates chose to die rather than accept the gods as defined by the state of Athens. Rome required of all its citizens at least a formal acknowledgement of its gods. From the fourth century onwards, with the enthronement of Constantine as emperor, Christianity was elevated to the status of state religion and enjoyed this position in virtually all of the political entities of eastern and western Europe for nearly seventeen hundred years.

The close association of Christianity and the state survived major fractures within the Christian community, including the split between East and West, which became definitive in the eleventh century, as well as the divisions resulting from the Protestant Reformation in the sixteenth century. In both cases, the new dispositions still assured a privileged civic status for the Christian religion, although they introduced diversity in terms of the versions so privileged. Radical change only came with the United States Constitution, which provided for the separation of religion and the state. More radical forms of separation were implemented later in Latin America, as a result of anticlericalism, and in Eastern Europe, under the influence of the atheist tenets of Marxist-Leninism. Today, responding to the growing acceptance of international human rights instruments, the growth of secularist rather than religious beliefs in the West, worldwide population movements that have resulted in religiously diverse societies and the demise of most militantly atheist regimes, many countries are seeking to assure freedom of religion and belief in their societies. In practice, this is resulting in increasing separation of religion and state, although not necessarily following the United States model.

The history of these changes provides some fascinating episodes in the search for ways to accommodate religious diversity. In his 1960 report to the United Nations on religious freedom, the Indian scholar Arcot Krishnaswami reports that twenty-three centuries ago, King Asoka, patron of Buddhism, recommended tolerance to his subjects, on the grounds that [a]cling thus, we contribute to the progress of our creed by serving others. Acting otherwise, we harm our own faith, bringing discredit upon the others. He, who exalts his own belief, discrediting all others, does so surely to obey his religion with the intention of making a display of it. But behaving thus, he gives it the hardest blows. And for this reason concord is good only in so far as all listen to each other's creeds, and love to listen to them. It is the desire of the king, dear to the gods, that all creeds be illumined and they profess pure doctrines.

More recently, in 1998, through the International Religious Freedom Act (the "IRFA"), the United States government adopted another approach to the promotion of religious freedom. The IRFA makes the enforcement of religious freedom through various diplomatic and economic measures a major component of the foreign policy of the United States, the world's most powerful nation. No other nation has yet taken such a position. These two approaches, namely that of Krishnaswami and the United States Government, are very different in time and tone. The first emphasizes the need for the community to examine, debate, and accept common rules, and the full title of the Act reads "An Act to establish an Office of Religious Persecution Monitoring, to provide for the imposition of sanctions against countries engaged in a pattern of religious persecution and for other purposes."

The Church-State Debates

Modern approaches in the West to religious tolerance and eventually separation of church and state grew out of debates that took place in seventeenth century England. It was a time when the country had experienced over one hundred years of tension, if not wars, caused by the religious and social alternatives that had sprung from the Protestant Reformation. At that time, the ideas of John Calvin were especially influential. Like the peoples in other northern European countries, English men and women were responding positively to ideas that emphasized the individual's direct relationship to God rather than through the clergy. This was not only a religious statement; by asserting that the clergy were less important in religious affairs, these ideas implied a diminished role for religion in civil affairs as well. The doctrine put in question the past power and prerogatives of kings. Unhappy with the performance of some of their kings, a large segment of the British population sought a new order of civil government "by the people" on the now accepted premise that civil authorities possessed only as much power as the people gave them.

Many of the groups promoting this principle also affirmed that privileges such as the right to vote belonged not only to landholders but to all people and especially to those ordinary citizens and soldiers who had been fighting for their freedoms against the kings and the system that had thus far denied them those rights. Interestingly, their political arguments were still advanced in religious terms. Many participants in the debates consistently sought to justify their political opinions based on the tenets of their faith and the words of the Gospel. Others argued this was not possible. We have verbatim records of some of these debates that took place in and around London between 1647 and 1649. The 1647 debates were fascinating because they gathered together in different sites around London leaders of the main political factions and commoners, rich and pocr, famous and unknown, to debate some of the options for a new constitutional structure in England.

The topics included the roles of the army and the king, the rights of property holders versus others, and the power of the civil magistrate with regard to a person's religious beliefs. One of the organizers who was personally vocal in the debates was Oliver Cromwell (1599-1658), a very successful military officer who was then in the process of modernizing and professionalizing the British Army. Before he removed the army from politics once and for all, however, he used the units he controlled to force King Charles II into exile in 1646. In the period that followed, before he became Lord Protector of England, he helped organize a series of debates, which led to important consti-tutional changes, but without greater provision for religious freedom.

The debaters represented the mainstreams within Puritanism, which was then the dominant version of the Christian faith in England. Within this tradition, based primarily on Calvin's ideas, there were still many theological factions characterized by names such as Levellers, Diggers,

Ranters, Quakers, and Millenarists. The Putney, or Army, debates, as they were called, lasted for days at a time. Recorded verbatim, they were not transcribed until the beginning of the twentieth century. During this period of massive social change in England, all institutions were questioned with regard to their social function, most notably the universities, the cities, rural life, and Sabbath obser-vance. At issue was the desire to purify the state by imposing higher moral standards on civil or public life in Britain. The problem was agreeing on which standards to impose. The conservatives saw the ideal of individual liberty as the path to moral breakdown, the end of private property, houses, and wives: in a word, the "perdition of souls and bodies."

Their opponents argued the importance of maintaining the Puritan commitment to the supremacy of the individual conscience and to the equality of all men, on the grounds that each person is ultimately answerable to his/her own conscience and to God, no matter what those in authority might say or order. For them, obedience to God took precedence over obedience to civil authority, but there is an interesting perception that God's word comes through the consensus of the many rather than through the opinion of a few. Therein lay another dilemma: how does the civil power prevent anarchy and ensure social order if civil society cannot coerce individual citizens? Out of these debates came a solution to this problem: civil power could rule in public affairs and the individual conscience in private, especially when religious beliefs and worship were at issue. One of the specific political outcomes of these debates was a constitutional order excluding clergy from politics.

Clergy were properly in charge within the church and its activities, especially worship. The net result of this distinction was the definition of two spheres of influence, the one religious and the other civil. While this did not result in what eventually became the Anglican Church being separated from the state, the power of the state and its officers to judge a citizen's religious conviction was circumscribed. There were, however, limitations, as is visible in the following discussion of John Locke's approach to religious tolerance.

The Separation of Church and State

Some thirty to forty years after the Putney or Army Debates, John Locke elaborated a more systematic set of arguments in favor of a separation of religious beliefs from the political process in his treatises (notably his Letter Concerning Toleration). While personally a very religious person, Locke sought to separate religion and politics to prevent an alliance between the civil and religious authorities. In his view, religious freedom and a peaceable civil society required the separation of the two authorities. Tolerance, however, had its limitations, as the late Richard Ashcraft pointed out in one of his studies of Locke:

> Catholics according to Locke (and most of his contemporaries) owed their primary allegiance to a foreign power, the pope. They subscribed to beliefs that were destructive of all human society: that faith was not to be kept with heretics (Protestants) that kings could be deposed for religious reasons, that dominion was founded in grace and other propositions which made Catholics "irreconcilable" enemies to any Protestant government.... Whereas the sphere of religious belief was, in general, governed by persuasion, reason and the individual's own conscience, Locke . . . endorsed the application of force to Catholics as a means by which they might be "converted" to the truth of Protestantism.

This led Ashcraft to note that [t]he political argument for religious toleration while it obviously made use of appeals to individual reason, natural law etc., depended for its practical success upon appeals to prejudices, fears and hatreds shared by the community and directed against Catholics, and to a lesser extent, atheists who were also excluded from membership in political society as defined by Locke's Letter [Concerning Toleration].

While it is easy enough to recognize the historical limitations of Locke's particular definition of religious freedom, Ashcraft uses it to identify a more radical argument, namely, that all such definitions, including that of "rights" itself, are subject to the vagaries of time:

> To see such rights as products of the cultural prejudices of the community, or a fragile political alliance, or a fear of a common enemy etc, may place these rights within a less attractive framework, but at the same time, it reinforces our consciousness that such rights are impermanent, that they are products of political struggle, and that organized human action is necessary to guarantee their preservation. Indeed the very recognition that such rights and the political values of Lockean liberalism generally depended upon shared religious beliefs which are no longer constitutive of our political society ought to make us more, not less concerned with the problematic character of the contemporary rights claims advanced by the individual and against the state.

Twentieth Century Religious Freedom

Moving now to the end of the twentieth century, we are confronted by a very different stage. Religious freedom is now a subject of international debate and foreign, rather than solely domestic, policy. Religious pluralism is no longer a question of accepting differences within Puritanism or even within Christianity, but of the coexistence of all the world's different religions and beliefs. There is an international bill of human rights that defines in basic terms the nature of rights, including freedom of religion and belief, and the obligation of the world's states to enforce them domestically and internationally. In the words of the Universal Declaration of Human Rights (the "UDHR"), today "[e]veryone has the right to freedom of thought, conscience and religion; this right includes freedom to change his religion or belief, and freedom, either alone or in community with others and in public or private, to manifest his religion or belief in teaching, practice, worship and observance."

With the enactment of the IRFA, the United States has radically changed the enforcement scale. Religious freedom is now not only a part of United States foreign policy; it has been incorporated to such an extent that certain actions that publicize the issue are regularly required of the Department of State. Each year, for example, the Department must issue a report on the state of religious freedom around the world. The second such report was published in February 2000. Inevitably, any country portrayed in a pejorative light feels obliged to defend itself in an equally public way. This is aggravated by the fact that the report also groups countries into categories from the worst to least offensive. Thus, the worst category includes countries like Afghanistan, China, Cuba, and Iraq that "control" religious beliefs and practices. Lesser violators are grouped in other categories: those such as Pakistan, Saudi Arabia, and Serbia that are merely "hostile" to some religions, "neglect discrimination" against religions, or still "retain legislation that discriminates," as opposed to those that merely "stigmatize" some religious groups, like France, Belgium, and Germany.

The IRFA also established an ambassador whose task it is to monitor and promote religious freedom around the world. As an ambassador, he now travels the world to represent United States policy to governments that are seen to restrict religious freedom. The Act has thus made religious freedom and the practices of other countries a major component of the diplomacy of the world's most powerful state. In spite of the change in scale, there are still many similarities between the seventeenth and twentieth centuries. The question is still how the civil power should treat the different religious convictions and practices of its citizens. In virtually all countries, some religions are treated differently from others in terms of taxation, property rights, and access to public education, or one's place in the national identity. The problem remains that the diversity of religion and belief results in differences in the way these issues are treated by most states. In addition, religion is still an integral, if not exclusive; factor in civil wars and lesser social tensions. Certain religions are also highly committed to seeking converts, often at the expense of other religions.

The first lesson of history is that we must always be prepared for continuing adjustments and to recognize the imperfections and transitory nature of any given normative synthesis. Locke and the Puritans worked out an ethic for themselves. It took two hundred more years, however, for the political system in Britain to recognize the rights of Catholics. In spite of high ideals, Locke and his contemporaries were willing to use state power for their religious cause, namely to coerce Catholics to convert to Protestantism. Civil power can be misused, and it often takes historical distance to recognize it.

Today, the United States, the world's most powerful nation, has undertaken a very active role in promoting religious freedom, forcing other countries to be reactive. Claiming to rely on the current international definition of religious freedom, the United States is ready to take resolute unilateral action. Importantly, however, the United States Congress passed the IRFA with little or no public debate on the floor. Was that because no elected representative in Washington wanted to appear opposed to religious freedom? The bill was not examined in detail in public debate. In contrast to the British process that relied on weeklong debates among substantial segments of the population, the United States process took place behind close doors, with little national or, given the modern world, international consultation. The second lesson of history is that building consensus is important, even if only in the face of common enemies. Both external sanctions and internal reforms can bring about religious freedom. Both can be effective, but, while sanctions can help, internal reforms within the individual countries are essential.

Governments, notably Cuba and Iraq, have used the imposition of sanctions to strengthen their own authority within the country by portraying themselves as resisting American imperialism. Without a stronger international consensus in the form of a treaty on freedom of religion and belief, even if it appeals to Article 18 of the UDHR, the United States government will be frequently accused of trying to impose its own vision of religious freedom on other countries or of using religious freedom to pursue its political goals. The concept of civil society in seventeenth century England does not correspond to the generally accepted concept in the twentieth century. As opposed to today's definition of the complex of forces and institutions outside the ambit of the state, the seventeenth century model described the realm in which the state could operate without the oversight of the clergy. Certainly, it was not a perfect separation, but it laid the foundation for states to recognize limitations on their powers with regard to the beliefs and personal moralities of their citizens. In other words, states were compelled to become tolerant for a range of, if not for all, religious convictions.

Perhaps the main lesson from the English experience for us today is the degree to which tolerance is often accompanied and conditioned by prejudice and the exclusion of some groups from the consensus. It is not clear which lessons should be learned from the fact that it took two hundred years for Catholics to enjoy religious freedom and full civic emancipation. Ashcraft argues that it shows that any consensus, including human rights, on the part of a given polity is subject to revision. This would seem to underline the importance of each society having institutions that assure continual revision and inclusiveness. It does not indicate whether all those excluded today will or ought to be included tomorrow. While the seventeenth century experience tells us nothing about international diplomacy, reading the verbatim accounts of the often vitriolic debates among highly committed and emotional believers, one cannot help but be struck by the possibilities and benefits of extended verbal exchanges in building consensus among parties. In the field of religion and civil society today, one must, therefore, recommend finding analogous space in both the domestic and international arenas for debate and consensus building among the multiplicity of parties concerned with religion, rights, and civil society around the world.

Broadly speaking religious life may be divided into three periods. These may be described as the periods of 'Faith', 'Thought', and 'Discovery.' In the first period religious life appears as a form of discipline which the individual or a whole people must accept as an unconditional command without any rational understanding of the ultimate meaning and purpose of that command. This attitude may be of great consequence in the social and political history of a people, but is not of much consequence in so far as the individual's inner growth and expansion are concerned. Perfect submission to discipline is followed by a rational understanding of the discipline and the ultimate source of its authority. In this period religious life seeks its foundation in a kind of metaphysics - a logically consistent view of the world with God as a part of that view. In the third period metaphysics is displaced by psychology, and religious life develops the ambition to come into direct contact with the Ultimate Reality. It is here that religion becomes a matter of personal assimilation of life and power; and the individual achieves a free personality, not by releasing himself from the fetters of the law, but by discovering the ultimate source of the law within the depths of his own consciousness.

As in the words of a Muslim Sufi - 'no understanding of the Holy Book is possible until it is actually revealed to the believer just as it was revealed to the Prophet.' It is, then, in the sense of this last phase in the development of religious life that I use the word religion in the question that I now propose to raise. Religion in this sense is known by the unfortunate name of Mysticism, which is supposed to be a life-denying, fact-avoiding attitude of mind directly opposed to the radically empirical outlook of our times. Yet higher religion, which is only a search for a larger life, is essentially experience and recognized the necessity of experience as its foundation long before science learnt to do so. It is a genuine effort to clarify human consciousness, and is, as such, as critical of its level of experience as Naturalism is of its own level. As we all know, it was Kant who first raised the question: 'Is metaphysics possible?' He answered this question in the negative; and his argument applies with equal force to the realities in which religion is especially interested. The manifold of sense, according to him, must fulfill certain formal conditions in order to constitute knowledge. The thing-in-itself is only a limiting idea. Its function is merely regulative. If there is some actuality corresponding to the idea, it falls outside the boundaries of experience, and consequently its existence cannot be rationally demonstrated.

This verdict of Kant cannot be easily accepted. It may fairly be argued that in view of the more recent developments of science, such as the nature of matter as 'bottled-up light waves', the idea of the universe as an act of thought, finiteness of space and time and Heisenberg's principle of indeterminacy in Nature, the case for a system of rational theology is not so bad as Kant was led to think. But for our present purposes it is unnecessary to consider this point in detail. As to the thing-in-itself, which is inaccessible to pure reason because of its falling beyond the boundaries of experience, Kant's verdict can be accepted only if we start with the assumption that all experience other than the normal level of experience is impossible. The only question, therefore, is whether the normal level is the only level of knowledge-yielding experience. Kant's view of the thing-in-itself and the thing as it appears to us very much determined the character of his question regarding the possibility of metaphysics. But what if the position, as understood by him, is reversed?

The great Muslim Sufi philosopher, Muhyaddin Ibn al-'Arabâ of Spain, has made the acute observation that God is a percept; the world is a concept. Another Muslim Sufi thinker and poet, 'Iraq, insists on the plurality of space-orders and time-orders and speaks of a Divine Time and a Divine Space. It may be that what we call the external world is only an intellectual construction, and that there are other levels of human experience capable of being systematized by other orders of space and time - levels in which concept and analysis do not play the same role as they do in the case of our normal experience. It may, however, be said that the level of experience to which concepts are inapplicable cannot yield any knowledge of a universal character, for concepts alone are capable of being socialized. The standpoint of the man who relies on religious experience for capturing Reality must always remain individual and incommunicable.

This objection has some force if it is meant to insinuate that the mystic is wholly ruled by his traditional ways, attitudes, and expectations. Conservatism is as bad in religion as in any other department of human activity. It destroys the ego's creative freedom and closes up the paths of fresh spiritual enterprise. This is the main reason why our medieval mystic techniques can no longer produce original discoveries of ancient Truth. The fact, however, that religious experience is incommunicable does not mean that the religious man's pursuit is futile. Indeed, the incommunicability of religious experience gives us a clue to the ultimate nature of the ego. In our daily social intercourse we live and move in seclusion, as it were. We do not care to reach the inmost individuality of men. We treat them as mere functions, and approach them from those aspects of their identity which are capable of conceptual treatment. The climax of religious life, however, is the discovery of the ego as an individual deeper than his conceptually describable habitual selfhood. It is in contact with the Most Real that the ego discovers its uniqueness, its metaphysical status, and the possibility of improvement in that status. Strictly speaking, the experience which leads to this discovery is not a conceptually manageable intellectual fact; it is a vital fact, an attitude consequent on an inner biological transformation which cannot be captured in the net of logical categories. It can embody itself only in a world-making or world-shaking act; and in this form alone the content of this timeless experience can diffuse itself in the time-movement, and make itself effectively visible to the eye of history.

It seems that the method of dealing with Reality by means of concepts is not at all a serious way of dealing with it. Science does not care whether its electron is a real entity or not. It may be a mere symbol, a mere convention. Religion, which is essentially a mode of actual living, is the only serious way of handing Reality. As a form of higher experience it is corrective of our concepts of philosophical theology or at least makes us suspicious of the purely rational process which forms these concepts. Science can afford to ignore metaphysics altogether, and may even believe it to be 'a justified form of poetry', as Lange defined it, or 'a legitimate play of grown-ups', as Nietzsche described it. But the religious expert who seeks to discover his personal status in the constitution of things cannot, in view of the final aim of his struggle, be satisfied with what science may regard as a vital lie, a mere 'as-if' to regulate thought and conduct. In so far as the ultimate nature of Reality is concerned, nothing is at stake in the venture of science; in the religious venture the whole career of the ego as an assimilative personal centre of life and experience is at stake. Conduct, which involves a decision of the ultimate fate of the agent, cannot be based on illusions. A wrong concept misleads the understanding; a wrong deed degrades the whole man, and may eventually demolish the structure of the human ego.

The mere concept affects life only partially; the deed is dynamically related to Reality and issues from a generally constant attitude of the whole man towards reality. No doubt the deed, i.e. the control of psychological and physiological processes with a view to tune up the ego for an immediate contact with the Ultimate Reality is, and cannot but be, individual in form and content; yet the deed, too, is liable to be socialized when others begin to live though it with a view to discover for themselves its effectiveness as a method of approaching the Real. The evidence of religious experts in all ages and countries is that there are potential types of consciousness lying close to our normal consciousness. If these types of consciousness open up possibilities of life-giving and knowledge-yielding experience, the question of the possibility of religion as a form of higher experience is a perfectly legitimate one and demands our serious attention. But, apart from the legitimacy of the question, there are important reasons why it should be raised at the present moment of the history of modern culture. In the first place, the scientific interest of the question. It seems that every culture has a form of Natura-lism peculiar to its own world-feeling; and it further appears that every form of Naturalism ends in some sort of Atomism. We have Indian Atomism, Greek Atomism, Muslim Atomism, and Modern Atomism.

Modern Atomism is, however, unique. Its amazing mathematics which sees the universe as an elaborate differential equation; and its physics which, following its own methods has been led to smash some of the old gods of its own temple, have already brought us to the point of asking the question whether the casualty-bound aspect of Nature is the whole truth about it? Is not the Ultimate Reality invading our consciousness from some other direction as well? Is the purely intellectual method of overcoming Nature the only method? 'We have acknowledged', says Professor Eddington, 'that the entities of physics can from their very nature form only a partial aspect of the reality. How are we to deal with the other part? It cannot be said that other part concerns us less than the physical entities. Feelings, purpose, values made up our consciousness as much as sense-impressions. We follow up the sense-impressions and find that they lead into an external world discussed by science; we follow up the other elements of our being and find that they lead - not into a world of space and time, but surely somewhere.'

In the second place we have to look to the great practical importance of the question. The modern man with his philosophies of criticism and scientific specialism finds himself in a strange predicament. His Naturalism has given him an unprecedented control over the forces of Nature, but has robbed him of faith in his own future. It is strange how the same idea affects different cultures differently. The formulation of the theory of evolution in the world of Islam brought into being Rëmâ's tremendous enthusiasm for the biological future of man. No cultured Muslim can read such passages as the following without a thrill of joy:

Low in the earth

I lived in realms of ore and stone;

And then I smiled in many-tinted flowers;

Then roving with the wild and wandering hours,

O'er earth and air and ocean's zone,

In a new birth,
I dived and flew,
And crept and ran,
And all the secret of my essence drew
Within a form that brought them all to view –
And lo, a Man!
And then my goal,
Beyond the clouds, beyond the sky,
In realms where none may change or die –
In angel form; and then away
Beyond the bounds of night and day,
And Life and Death, unseen or seen,
Where all that is hath ever been,
As One and Whole.

(Rëmâ: Thadani's Translation)

On the other hand, the formulation of the same view of evolution with far greater precision in Europe has led to the belief that 'there now appears to be no scientific basis for the idea that the present rich complexity of human endowment will ever be materially exceeded.' That is how the modern man's secret despair hides itself behind the screen of scientific terminology. Nietzsche, although he thought that the idea of evolution did not justify the belief that man was unsurpassable, cannot be regarded as an exception in this respect. His enthusiasm for the future of man ended in the doctrine of eternal recurrence - perhaps the most hopeless idea of immortality ever formed by man. This eternal repetition is not eternal 'becoming'; it is the same old idea of 'being' masquerading as 'becoming.' Thus, wholly overshadowed by the results of his intellectual activity, the modern man has ceased to live soulfully, i.e.

from within. In the domain of thought he is living in open conflict with himself; and in the domain of economic and political life he is living in open conflict with others. He finds himself unable to control his ruthless egoism and his infinite gold-hunger which is gradually killing all higher striving in him and bringing him nothing but life-weariness. Absorbed in the 'fact', that is to say, the optically present source of sensation, he is entirely cut off from the unplumbed depths of his own being.

In the wake of his systematic materialism has at last come that paralysis of energy which Huxley apprehended and deplored. The condition of things in the East is no better. The technique of medieval mysticism by which religious life, in its higher manifestations, developed itself both in the East and in the West has now practically failed. And in the Muslim East it has, perhaps, done far greater havoc than anywhere else. Far from reintegrating the forces of the average man's inner life, and thus preparing him for participation in the march of history, it has taught him a false renunciation and made him perfectly contented with his ignorance and spiritual thraldom. No wonder then that the modern Muslim in Turkey, Egypt, and Persia is led to seek fresh sources of energy in the creation of new loyalties, such as patriotism and nationalism which Nietzsche described as 'sickness and unreason', and 'the strongest force against culture'.

Disappointed of a purely religious method of spiritual renewal which alone brings us into touch with the everlasting fountain of life and power by expanding our thought and emotion, the modern Muslim fondly hopes to unlock fresh sources of energy by narrowing down his thought and emotion. Modern atheistic socialism, which possesses all the fervour of a new religion, has a broader outlook; but having received its philosophical basis from the Hegelians of the left wing, it rises in revolt against the very source which could have given it strength and purpose. Both nationalism and atheistic socialism, at least in the present state of human adjustments, must draw upon the psychological forces of hate, suspicion, and resentment which tend to impoverish the soul of man and close up his hidden sources of spiritual energy. Neither the technique of medieval mysticism, nor nationalism, nor atheistic socialism can cure the ills of a despairing humanity. Surely the present moment is one of great crisis in the history of modern culture. The modern world stands in need of biological renewal.

And religion, which in its higher manifestations is neither dogma, nor priesthood, nor ritual, can alone ethically prepare the modern man for the burden of the great responsibility which the advancement of modern science necessarily involves, and restore to him that attitude of faith which makes him capable of winning a personality here and retaining it in hereafter. It is only by rising to a fresh vision of his origin and future, his whence and whither, that man will eventually triumph over a society motivated by an inhuman competition, and a civilization which has lost its spiritual unity by its inner conflict of religious and political values. As I have indicated before, religion as a deliberate enterprise to seize the ultimate principle of value and thereby to reintegrate the forces of one's own personality is a fact which cannot be denied. The whole religious literature of the world, including the records of specialists' personal experiences, though perhaps expressed in the thought-forms of an out-of-date psychology, is a standing testimony to it. These experiences are perfectly natural, like our normal experiences.

The evidence is that they possess a cognitive value for the recipient, and, what is much more important, a capacity to centralize the forces of the ego and thereby to endow him with a new personality. The view that such experiences are neurotic or mystical will not finally settle the question of their meaning or value. If an outlook beyond physics is possible, we must courageously face the possibility, even though it may disturb or tend to modify our normal ways of life and thought. The interests of truth require that we must abandon our present attitude. It does not matter in the least if the religious attitude is originally determined by some kind of physiological disorder. George Fox may be a neurotic; but who can deny his purifying power in England's religious life of his day? Muhammad, we are told, was a psychopath. Well, if a psychopath has the power to give a fresh direction to the course of human history, it is a point of the highest psychological interest to search his original experience which has turned slaves into leaders of men, and has inspired the conduct and shaped the career of whole races of mankind. Judging from the various types of activity that emanated from the movement initiated by the Prophet of Islam, his spiritual tension and the kind of behaviour which issued from it, cannot be regarded as a response to a mere fantasy inside his brain.

It is impossible to understand it except as a response to an objective situation generative of new enthusiasms, new organizations, and new starting-points. If we look at the matter from the standpoint of anthropology it appears that a psychopath is an important factor in the economy of humanity's social organization. His way is not to classify facts and discover causes: he thinks in terms of life and movement with a view to create new patterns of behaviour for mankind. No doubt he has his pitfalls and illusions just as the scientist who relies on sense-experience has his pitfalls and illusions. A careful study of his method, however, shows that he is not less alert than the scientist in the matter of eliminating the alloy of illusion from his experience. The question for us outsiders is to find out an effective method of inquiry into the nature and significance of this extraordinary experience. The Arab historian Ibn Khaldën, who laid the foundations of modern scientific history, was the first to seriously approach this side of human psychology and reached what we now call the idea of the subliminal self.

Later, Sir William Hamilton in England and Leibniz in

Germany interested themselves in some of the more unknown phenomena of the mind. Jung, however, is probably right in thinking that the essential nature of religion is beyond the province of analytic psychology. In his discussion of the relation of analytic psychology to poetic art, he tells us that the process of artistic form alone can be the object of psychology. The essential nature of art, according to him, cannot be the object of a psychological method of approach. 'A distinction', says Jung, 'must also be made in the realm of religion; there also a psychological consideration is permissible only in respect of the emotional and symbolical phenomena of a religion, where the essential nature of religion is in no way involved, as indeed it cannot be. For this possible, not religion alone, but art also could be treated as a mere sub-division of psychology.'

Yet Jung has violated his own principle more than once in his writings. The result of this procedure is that, instead of giving us a real insight into the essential nature of religion and its meaning for human personality, our modern psychology has given us quite a plethora of new theories which proceed on a complete misunderstanding of the nature of religion as revealed in its higher manifestations, and carry us in an entirely hopeless direction. The implication of these theories, on the whole, is that religion does not relate the human ego to any objective reality beyond himself; it is merely a kind of well-meaning biological device calculated to build barriers of an ethical nature round human society in order to protect the social fabric against the otherwise unrestrainable instincts of the ego. That is why, according to this newer psychology, Christianity has already fulfilled its biological mission, and it is impossible for the modern man to understand its original significance. Jung concludes:

'Most certainly we should still understand it, had our customs even a breath of ancient brutality, for we can hardly realize in this day the whirlwinds of the unchained libido which roared through the ancient Rome of the Caesars. The civilized man of the present day seems very far removed from that. He has become merely neurotic. So for us the necessities which brought forth Christianity have actually been lost, since we no longer understand their meaning. We do not know against what it had to protect us. For enlightened people, the so-called religiousness has already approached very close to a neurosis. In the past two thousand years Christianity has done its work and has erected barriers of repression, which protect us from the sight of our own sinfulness.' This is missing the whole point of higher religious life. Sexual self-restraint is only a preliminary stage in the ego's evolution. The ultimate purpose of religious life is to make this evolution move in a direction far more important to the destiny of the ego than the moral health of the social fabric which forms his present environment.

The basic perception from which religious life moves forward is the present slender unity of the ego, his liability to dissolution, his amenability to reformation and the capacity for an ampler freedom to create new situations in known and unknown environments. In view of this fundamental perception higher religious life fixes its gaze on experiences symbolic of those subtle movements of Reality which seriously affect the destiny of the ego as a possibly permanent element in the constitution of Reality. If we look at the matter from this point of view modern psychology has not yet touched even the outer fringe of religious life, and is still far from the richness and variety of what is called religious experience. In order to give you an idea of its richness and variety I quote here the substance of a passage from a great religious genius of the seventeenth century - Shaikh AÁmad of Sirhind - whose fearless analytical criticism of contemporary Sufism resulted in the development of a new technique.

All the various system of Sufi technique in India came from Central Asia and Arabia; his is the only technique which crossed the Indian border and is still a living force in the Punjab, Afghanistan, and Asiatic Russia. I am afraid it is not possible for me to expound the real meaning of this passage in the language of modern psychology; for such language does not yet exist. Since, however, my object is simply to give you an idea of the infinite wealth of experience which the ego in his Divine quest has to sift and pass through, I do hope you will excuse me for the apparently outlandish terminology which possesses a real substance of meaning, but which was formed under the inspiration of a religious psychology developed in the atmosphere of a different culture and coming now to the passage. The experience of one 'Abd al-Mumin was described to the Shaikh as follows:

'Heavens and Earth and God's Throne and Hell and Paradise have all ceased to exist for me. When I look round I find them nowhere. When I stand in the presence of somebody I see nobody before me: nay even my own being is lost to me. God is infinite. Nobody can encompass Him; and this is the extreme limit of spiritual experience. No saint has been able to go beyond this'.

On this the Shaikh replied:-

'The experience which is described has its origin in the ever varying life of the *Qalb*; and it appears to me that the recipient has not yet passed even one-fourth of the innumerable 'Stations' of the *Qalb*. The remaining three-fourths must be passed through in order to finish the experiences of this first 'Station' of spiritual life. Beyond this 'Station' there are other 'Stations' know as *RëÁ, Sirr-i-Khafâ,* and *Sirr-i-Akhf,* each of these 'Stations' which to-gether constitute what is technically called *'ÿlam-i Amr* has its own characteristic states and experiences. After having passed through these 'Stations' the seeker of truth gradually receives the illuminations of 'Divine Names' and 'Divine Attributes' and finally the illuminations of the 'Divine Essence'.'

Whatever may be the psychological ground of the distinctions made in this passage it gives us at least some idea of a whole universe of inner experience as seen by a great reformer of Islamic Sufasm. According to him, *'ÿlam-i Amr,* i.e. 'the world of directive energy', must be passed through before one reaches that unique experience which symbolizes the purely objective. This is the reason why I say that modern psychology has not yet touched even the outer fringe of the subject. Personally, I do not at all feel hopeful of the present state of things in either biology or psychology. Mere analytical criticism with some understanding of the organic conditions of the imagery in which religious life has sometimes manifested itself is not likely to carry us to the living roots of human personality. Assuming that sex-imagery has played a role in the history of religion, or that religion has furnished imaginative means of escape from, or adjustment to, an unpleasant reality these ways of looking at the matter cannot, in the least, affect the ultimate aim of religious life, that is to say, the reconstruction of the finite ego by bringing him into contact with an eternal life-process, and thus giving him a metaphysical status of which we can have only a partial understanding in the half-choking atmosphere of our present environment. If, therefore, the science of psychology is ever likely to possess a real significance for the life of mankind, it must develop an independent method calculated to discover a new technique better suited to the temper of our times. Perhaps a psychopath endowed with a great intellect - the combination is not impossibility - may give us a clue to such a technique.

In modern Europe, Nietzsche, whose life and activity form, at least to us Easterns, an exceedingly interesting problem in religious psychology, was endowed with some sort of constitutional equipment for such an undertaking. His mental history is not without a parallel in the history of Eastern Sufâsm. That a really 'imperative' vision of the Divine in man did come to him cannot be denied. I call his vision 'imperative' because it appears to have given him a kind of prophetic mentality which, by some kind of technique, aims at turning its visions into permanent lifeforces. Yet Nietzsche was a failure; and his failure was mainly due to his intellectual progenitors such as Schopenhauer, Darwin, and Lange whose influence completely blinded him to the real significance of his vision. Instead of looking for a spiritual rule which would develop the Divine even in a plebeian and thus open up before him an infinite future, Nietzsche was driven to seek the realization of his vision in such scheme as aristocratic radicalism. As I have said of him elsewhere:

The 'I am' which he seeketh,

Lieth beyond philosophy, beyond knowledge.

The plant that groweth only from the invisible soil of the heart of man,

Groweth not from a mere heap of clay!

Thus failed a genius whose vision was solely determined by his internal forces, and remained unproductive for want of expert external guidance in his spiritual life, and the irony of fate is that this man, who appeared to his friends 'as if he had come from a country where no man lived', was fully conscious of his great spiritual need. 'I confront alone', he says, 'an immense problem: it is as if I am lost in a forest, a primeval one. I need help. I need disciples: I need a master. It would be so sweet to obey.' And again:

'Why do I not find among the living men who see higher than I do and have to look down on me? Is it only that I have made a poor search? And I have so great a longing for such.'

The truth is that the religious and the scientific processes, though involving different methods, are identical in their final aim. Both aim at reaching the most real. In fact, religion; for reasons which I have mentioned before, is far more anxious to reach the ultimately real than science. And to both the way to pure objectivity lies through what may be called the purification of experience. In order to understand this we must make a distinction between experience as a natural fact, significant of the normally observable behaviour of Reality, and experience as significant of the inner nature of Reality. As a natural fact it is explained in the light of its antecedents, psychological and physiological; as significant of the inner nature of Reality we shall have to apply criteria of a different kind to clarify its meaning. In the domain of science we try to understand its meaning in reference to the external behaviour of Reality; in the domain of religion we take it as representative of some kind of Reality and try to discover its meanings in reference mainly to the inner nature of that Reality.

The scientific and the religious processes are in a sense parallel to each other. Both are really descriptions of the same world with this difference only that in the scientific process the ego's standpoint is necessarily exclusive, whereas in the religious process the ego integrates its competing tendencies and develops a single inclusive attitude resulting in a kind of synthetic transfiguration of his experiences. A careful study of the nature and purpose of these really complementary processes shows that both of them are directed to the purification of experience in their respective spheres. An illustration will make my meaning clear. Hume's criticism of our notion of cause must be considered as a chapter in the history of science rather than that of philosophy. True to the spirit of scientific empiricism we are not entitled to work with any concepts of a subjective nature. The point of Hume's criticism is to emancipate empirical science from the concept of force which, as he urges, has no foundation in sense-experience. This was the first attempt of the modern mind to purify the scientific process.

Einstein's mathematical view of the universe completes the process of purification started by Hume, and, true to the spirit of Hume's criticism, dispenses with the concept of force altogether. The passage I have quoted from the great Indian saint shows that the practical student of religious psychology has a similar purification in view. His sense of objectivity is as keen as that of the scientists in his own sphere of objectivity. He passes from experience to experience, not as a mere spectator, but as a critical sifter of experience, who by the rules of a peculiar technique, suited to his sphere of inquiry, endeavours to eliminate all subjective elements, psychological or physiological, in the content of his experience with a view finally to reach what is absolutely objective. This final experience is the revelation of a new life-process - original, essential, spontaneous.

The eternal secret of the ego is that the moment he reaches this final revelation he recognizes it as the ultimate root of his being without the slightest hesitation. Yet in the experience itself there is no mystery. Nor is there anything emotional in it. Indeed with a view to secure a wholly nonemotional experience the technique of Islamic Sufâsm at least takes good care to forbid the use of music in worship, and to emphasize the necessity of daily congregational prayers in order to counteract the possible anti-social effects of solitary contemplation. Thus the experience reached is a perfectly natural experience and possesses a biological significance of the highest importance to the ego. It is the human ego rising higher than mere reflection, and mending its transiency by appropriating the eternal. The only danger to which the ego is exposed in this Divine quest is the possible relaxation of his activity caused by his enjoyment of and absorption in the experiences that precede the final experience.

The history of Eastern Sufâsm shows that this is a real danger. This was the whole point of the reform movement initiated by the great Indian saint from whose writings I have already quoted a passage. And the reason is obvious. The ultimate aim of the ego is not to see something, but to be something. It is in the ego's effort to be something that he discovers his final opportunity to sharpen his objectivity and acquire a more fundamental 'I am' which finds evidence of its reality not in the Cartesian 'I think' but in the Kantian 'I can.' The end of the ego's quest is not emancipation from the limitations of individuality; it is, on the other hand, a more precise definition of it. The final act is not an intel-lectual act, but a vital act which deepens the whole being of the ego, and sharpens his will with the creative assurance that the world is not something to be merely seen or known through concepts, but something to be made and re-made by continuous action. It is a moment of supreme bliss and also a moment of the greatest trial for the ego:

Art thou in the stage of 'life,' 'death', or 'death-in-life.' Invoke the aid of three witnesses to verify thy 'Station.'

The first witness is thine own consciousness -
See thyself, then, with thine own light.
The second witness is the consciousness of another ego
See thyself, then, with the light of an ego other than thee.
The third witness is God's consciousness -
See thyself, then, with God's light.
If thou standest unshaken in front of this light,
Consider thyself as living and eternal as He!
That man alone is real who dares -
Dares to see God face to face!
What is 'Ascension'? Only a search for a witness
Who may finally confirm thy reality -
A witness whose confirmation alone makes thee eternal.
No one can stand unshaken in His Presence;
And he who can, verily, he is pure gold.
Art thou a mere particle of dust?
Tighten the knot of thy ego;
And hold fast to thy tiny being!
How glorious to burnish one's ego.
And to test its lustre in the presence of the Sun!

Re-chisel, then, thine ancient frame; and build up a new being.

Such being is real being;
Or else thy ego is a mere ring of smoke!

Bibliography

A.H. Armstrong, ed., *Classical Mediterranean Spirituality,* World Spirituality 15, New York: Crossroad, 1989.

Ali, 'Abdullah Yusuf, *The meaning of the Holy Qur'an,* Amana: Beltsville, Maryland, 1989.

Armstrong, Karen, *Muhammad: A Biography of the Prophet,* Victor Gollancz Ltd.: U.K. 1991.

Anderson, H. and E. Foley, *Mighty Stories, Dangerous Rituals,* San Francisco, CA: Jossey-Bass, 1997.

Annemarie Schimmel, *Mystical Dimensions of Islam,* Chapel Hill: University of North Carolina Press, 1975.

Babin, P., *The New Era in Religious Communication,* Minneapolis, MN: Fortress Press, 1991.

Barnstone, Willis (Ed.), *The Other Bible,* HarperSan Francisco, 1984.

Bavinck, J. H., *The Impact of Christianity on the Non-Christian World,* Grand Rapids: Eerdmans, 1948.

Bell, C., *Ritual Thinking, Ritual Practice,* New York: Oxford University Press, 1992.

Buddenbaum, J., *Reporting News about Religion: An Introduction for Journalists,* Ames, IA: Iowa State University Press, 1998.

Burnett, David, *World of the Spirits: A Christian Perspective on traditional and Folk Religions,* London: Monarch, 2000.

Chan, Wing-Tsit, trans. and ed. *A Source Book in Chinese Philosophy.* Princeton: Princeton University Press, 1963.

Chandra, Lokesh, *Iconography of the Thousand Buddhas*, International Academy of Indian Culture: New Delhi, 1996.

Dawood, N.J., (translated with revisions) *The Koran*, Penguin Books: NY, 1997.

De Bary, Wm. Theodore (ed.), *Sources of Indian Tradition*, Columbia University Press: NY, 1958.

Eichhoefer, Gerald W. *Enduring Issues in Philosophy*. San Diego: Greenhaven Press, Inc., 1995.

Gitlin, T., *The Whole World is Watching*, Berkeley, CA: University of California Press, 1980.

Hillary Rodrigues, *Introducing Hinduism*, World Religion Series, New York: Routledge, 2006.

Holm, Jean and John Bowker, eds., *Human Nature and Destiny*, London: Printer Publishing, 1994.

James William Coleman, *The New Buddhism: The Western Transformation of an Ancient Tradition* (New York: Oxford University Press, 2001.

Jeffrey L. Rubenstein, ed., *Rabbinic Stories*, Classics of Western Spirituality, New York: Paulist Press, 2002.

Joseph Dan, *Jewish Mysticism*, 4 vol., Northvale, NJ: Jason Aronson, 1998.

Kurtz, Lester R., *Gods in the Global Village*, Thousand Oaks, CA: Sage, 2007.

Lyden, John. *Enduring Issues in Religion*. San Diego: Greenhaven Press, Inc., 1995.

Malise Ruthven, *Islam: A Very Short Introduction*, New York: Oxford University Press, 2000.

Mark Juergensmeyer, *Global Religions: An Introduction*, New York: Oxford University Press, 2003.

Michael Carrithers, *The Buddha: A Very Short Introduction*, New York: Oxford University Press, 2001.

Ninian Smart, *Dimensions of the Sacred : An Anatomy*

of the World's Beliefs, Berkeley: University of California Press, 1996.

Nouwen, Henri J.M. *The Road to Daybreak: A Spiritual Journey*. New York: Doubleday, 1988.

O'Flaherty, Wendy Doniger (ed. and trans.), *The Rig Veda: An Anthology*. Penguin Books, NY, 1981.

Peter Harvey, *An Introduction to Buddhism*, New York: Cambridge University Press, 1990.

Renou, Louis, ed. *Hinduism*. New York: George Braziller, 1961.

Seyyed Nasr Hossein, ed., *Islamic Spirituality I: Foundations*, World Spirituality 19 (New York: Crossroad, 1987.

Shakir, M. H., (trans.) The Holy Qur'an, Tahrike Tarsile Qur'an, Inc: NY, 1997.

Sushil Mittal & Gene Thursby, eds., *The Hindu World*, New York: Routledge, 2004.

Tu Weiming & Mary Evelyn Tucker, eds., *Confucian Spirituality*, World Spirituality 11, New York: Herder & Herder, 2002.

Warms, Richard, James Garber and Jon McGee, eds., *Sacred Realms: Essays in Religion, Belief & Society*, New York: Oxford University Press, 2004.

William C. Chittick, *The Sufi Path of Love: The Spiritual Teachings of Rumi*, New York: SUNY, 1983.

Wise, Michael, Martin Abegg, Jr., Edward Cook, *The Dead Sea Scrolls: A New Translation*, HarperCollins: NY, 1996.

Xinzhong Yao, *An Introduction to Confucianism*, Cambridge: Cambridge University Press, 2000.

Zaehner, R.C. (translation), *Hindu Scriptures*, J.M. Dent & Sons: London, 1966.

Index

S

T